CW00349048

HARDPRESS.NET
HOME OF HARD-TO-FIND BOOKS

Pictures of German Life in the Xv, Xvi, and Xvii Centuries

by Gustav Freytag

Address:
HardPress
8345 NW 66TH ST #2561
MIAMI FL 33166-2626
USA
Email: info@hardpress.net

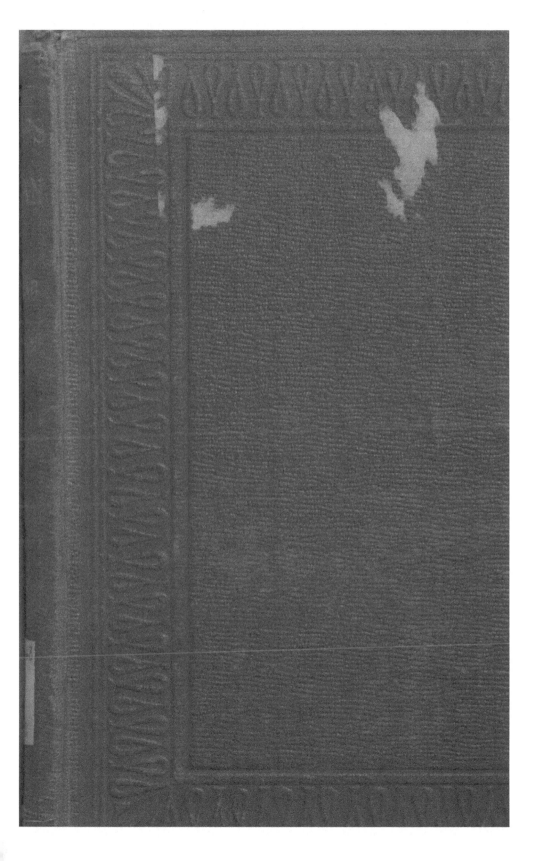

PICTURES OF GERMAN LIFE

IN THE

FIFTEENTH, SIXTEENTH, AND SEVENTEENTH CENTURIES.

VOL. II.

PICTURES

OF

GERMAN LIFE

In the XVth XVIth and XVIIth Centuries.

BY

GUSTAV FREYTAG.

Translated from the Original by

MRS. MALCOLM.

COPYRIGHT EDITION.—IN TWO VOLUMES.

VOL. II.

LONDON:
CHAPMAN AND HALL, 193 PICCADILLY.
1862.

LONDON : PRINTED BY WILLIAM CLOWES AND SONS, STAMFORD STREET.

CONTENTS.

PICTURES OF GERMAN LIFE.

INTRODUCTION TO THE SECOND VOLUME.

THE year 1600 dawned upon a people who had gone through a vast change in the last century. Everywhere we perceive marks of progress. Let us compare any learned book of the year 1499 with one of 1599. The former is written in bad Latin, poor in diction, ponderous in composition, and not easy of comprehension. Of independent spirit and individual conviction we find little trace. There are undoubtedly exceptions, but they are very rare. Even the Latin of the earlier Humanitarians reminds us of the subtle vapidness of monkish language, almost as much as of the artistic phrases of ancient rhetoricians. We are sometimes surprised to find in the theology, an undercurrent of deep-thinking speculations of elevated grandeur; but it is a kind of secret doctrine of souls depressed under the constraint of the cloister. It is certainly philosophy, but deprived of vitality.

A century later we discover, even in mediocre authors, a certain independent individuality. The writers begin to reflect on human life and faith; they understand how to represent their own feelings and the emotions of the soul, and struggles for their own convictions. Yet still they remain too much bound by general prescription, and there is still much that is monotonous, according to our views, in their judgment and learning,

and the cultivation of their minds.   But in their prose we
find a peculiar and often original style, and almost always a
stronger and more active common sense.   Three generations
struggled for their faith, many individuals perished for their
convictions, and thousands were plunged in misery.   Martyrdom
was no longer a monstrous and unheard-of thing, and men
maintained their own judgment on the highest questions.
There were few souls strong enough to do this a century earlier ;
then, among the people, individuals passed their lives without
any community of ideas or activity of mind, seeking in the
narrow circle of their associates no advantage save that of support against insufferable oppression ; that alone was the purport
of their struggles.   But now enthusiasm had been called
forth in the nation, the individual felt himself in close connection with millions, he was carried along the stream by the
unanimous impulse of all who were like-minded ; he acted and
suffered for an idea ; this was especially the case with the
Protestants ; and even Roman Catholics partook of this
blessing : so much nobler had men become.

But every higher development produces new defects ; the
child is free from many complaints which attack the youth.
Protestantism, which had done so much for the people, did
not for a long time achieve its greatest results.   It required the
unceasing inward workings of the minds of individuals ; it
gave an impulse everywhere to self-decision, and yet it could
not raise itself above the worst principles of the old Church.
It wished still to dominate over the faith of its disciples and
to persecute as heresy every deviation from its convictions.
Luther's giant nature had been able to keep zealous spirits
united, but he himself had predicted that after his death they
would not remain so.   He knew his faithful adherents accurately ; their weaknesses, and their eagerness to carry out their
own views.   Melancthon, who though firm in his theology
and in the every-day troubles of life, was embarrassed and un-

certain in matters of great import, could not command the fiery spirits of more determined characters. At that Imperial Diet which was held at Augsburg in 1547, the victorious Emperor had endeavoured, in his way, to compose the disputes of the Churches, and had pressed upon the vanquished Protestants a preliminary formula of faith, called the Interim. From the point of view of the Roman Catholics, it was considered as extreme toleration, which was only bearable because it gradually led back to the Old Church; from the point of view of zealous Protestants, it was held to be insupportable tyranny, which ought to be withstood. The ecclesiastical leaders of the opposition rose everywhere against this tyranny; hundreds of preachers were driven from their benefices and went about with their staffs as miserable pilgrims, and many fell victims to the furious reaction. It was the heroic time of the Protestant faith; simple preachers, fathers with wives and children, manfully suffered for their convictions, and were soon followed by thousands of laity.

But this enthusiasm was fraught with danger. The Interim was the beginning of vehement theological disputes, even among Luther's followers. The struggle of individuals became also the struggle of the Universities. The successors of Frederick the Wise lost the University of Wittenberg as well as the Electoral dignity; Melancthon and the Wittenbergers were under the influence of Maurice and his brothers; while the most zealous Lutherans were assembled at the new University of Jena.

This race of vehement men was followed by another generation of *Epigonen*. At the end of the century German Protestantism appeared in most of the provinces to be secure from outward dangers. Then the ecclesiastics became too self-sufficient and fond of power—the failings of a privileged order. Influential counsellors of weak princes, and rulers of public opinion, they themselves persecuted other believers with

the weapons of the old Church.   They sometimes called down
the civil power upon heretics ; and the populace stormed the
houses of the Reformers in Leipzig ; at Dresden a courtly
ecclesiastic was executed on account of heresy, though perhaps
there may also have been political reasons.   Thus this new
life threw deep shadows over the souls of the people.

In Roman Catholic territories also, a vigorous and extraordinary life was roused.   The Roman Catholic Church gave
birth to a new discipline of the mind, a mode of human culture distinctly opposed to Protestantism.   Even in the old
Church a greater depth of inward life was attained.   A new
system of rapturous excitement and self-denial, with high
duties and an exalted ideal, was offered to satisfy the needs of
the souls of the faithful.   In Spain and Italy this new religious
zeal was aroused, full of resignation and self-sacrifice, full of
great talent, eagerness for combat, and glowing enthusiasm,
and rich in manly vigour.   But it was not a faith for Germans.   It demanded the annihilation of free individuality, a
rending from all the ties of the world, fanatical devotion, and
an unconditional subjection of the individual to a great community.   Each one had to make an offering of his life for a
great aim, without criticism or scruple.   Whilst Protestantism
formed a higher standard, and imposed on each individual, the
duty of seeking independently by an effort of his own mind,
the key to divine and human knowledge, the new Catholicism
grasped his whole being with an iron hand.   Protestantism
was, notwithstanding all the loyalty of the Reformers, essentially democratic ; the new Catholicism concentrated all the
powers of men, of which it demanded the most unhesitating
submission, in a spiritual tyranny, under the dominion of the
head of the Church, and afterwards under that of the State.

The great representatives of this new tendency in Church
and State were the Jesuits.   In the impassioned soul of a
Spanish nobleman smouldered the gloomy fire of the new

Catholic teaching; amidst ascetic penances, in the restricted intercourse of a small brotherhood, the system was formed. In the year 1540 the Pope confirmed the brotherhood, and shortly after, the first members of the order hastened across the Alps and the Rhine into Germany, and began already to rule in the council of Trent. Their unhesitating determination strengthened the weak, and frightened the wavering. With wonderful rapidity the order established itself in Germany, where the old faith still subsisted along with the new; it acquired favour with the higher classes, and a crowd of adherents amongst the people. Some princes gave up to it the spiritual dominion of their countries, above all the Hapsburgers; and besides them, the German princes of the Church, who could not uphold by their own intrinsic strength, the wavering faith of their subjects; and lastly the Dukes of Bavaria, who for more than a century had been in the habit of seeking advantage for their house in a close union with Rome. When the brotherhood first entered Germany the whole nation was on the point of becoming Protestant; even at the beginning of the Thirty years' war, after losses and successes on both sides, three fourths of Germany were Protestant; but in the year 1650, the whole of the new Imperial state, and the largest third of the rest of Germany, had again become Roman Catholic. So well did these foreign priests serve their Church.

The way in which they worked was marvellous; cautiously, step by step, with endless schemes, and firm determination, never wavering, bending to the storm, and indefatigably returning again, never giving up what they had once begun, pursuing the smallest, as well as the greatest plans at any sacrifice, this society presented the only specimen of an unconditional submission of the will, and surrender of everything to one idea, which did not find expression in individuals, but only in the society. The order governed, but no single member of it was free, not even the General of the order.

The society gained honour and favour; it understood well how to make itself beloved, or indispensable wherever it came; but it never found a home in Germany. Its fearful principle of mystery and secrecy was felt, not only by the Protestants, who endeavoured to break its power by their paper weapons, the flying-sheets, and made it answerable for every political misdeed, whether far or near, but also in the Roman Catholic countries. Even there it was only a guest, influential certainly, and much prized, but from time to time ecclesiastics and laity felt that it was a thing apart from them. All the other spiritual societies had become national,—the Jesuits never. It is not unnatural that this feeling was strongest among the Roman Catholic ecclesiastics, for their worldly prospects were often injured by the Jesuits.

Thus from the middle of the sixteenth century two opposite methods of mental cultivation, two different sources of morals and working power have struggled against one another. Devotion and unconditional subjection, against feelings of duty and thoughtful self-assertion; rapid and unhesitating decision, against conscientious doubts; a spirit of energy, working laboriously with much deliberation and scheming after distant aims, against defective discipline; and an urging to unity, against a striving for separation.

These opposing powers appeared everywhere, especially in politics and at the courts of princes. Protestantism in its unfinished shape, though it had elevated the people, was no help to the formation of the character of the German princes; it had raised higher their external power, but it had lessened their inward stability; their youthful training became in general too theological to be practical. However immoral many of them were, they all suffered from conscientious doubts; and there was no ready answer for these doubts, such as the Roman Catholic confessor had always in store for them. The Protestant princes stood isolated; there was no firm bond of union between the Churches of the different states, but much trivial quarrelling and bitter hatred, not only between Lutherans and Reformers, but even amongst the followers of the Augsburg confession; and this diminished the strength of the princes. Whilst the priests of the Roman Catholic Church did their best to unite their rulers, the Protestant ecclesiastics helped to increase the disunion of theirs. So it is not surprising, that the Protestants for a long time stood at a disadvantage in their political struggle with the old faith. The Germans had not yet found, and did not for centuries attain to, the new constitution of State, which transfers the mainspring of government from the accidental will of the ruler, to the conscience of the nation, and which places in a regulated path, citizens of talent and integrity as advisers to the crown; public opinion was still weak, the daily press not yet in existence, and the relation between the political rights of the princes and the people very undefined.

Protestantism had everywhere produced political convulsions, from the peasant war even into the following century. The Reformation had unloosed all tongues, it had given the Germans a freer judgment upon their position as citizens, and had inspired individuals with the courage to fight for their own convictions. The peasant now loudly murmured against exorbitant burdens, the members of guilds against the selfish dominion of the corporations, and the noble members of the provincial estates against the extravagant demands of the sovereign for war expenses. The wild democratic disturbances of 1525 were with Luther's entire approbation easily put down, but democratic tendencies did not therefore cease, and together with them, anabaptist and socialist views spread from city to city. Their teaching, which scarcely forms a system, took a different colouring in different individuals, from the harmless theorist who imagined a community of good citizens without egotism, full of self-abnegation, as did the talented

Eberlin, to the reckless fanatic who tried to establish a new
Zion at Münster, with an illusive community of goods and
wives. These excitements lost their power towards the end
of the century, but still continued to ferment among the
people, especially in those provinces, where the Protestant
opposition of the estates excited the people against the old
faith of the rulers of the country. Thus it was in Bohemia,
Moravia, and Upper Austria. The more zealously the Hapsburgers endeavoured, by means of the Jesuits, to restore the
old faith, the more it was kept in check, even in their own
country, by the demands of the opposition in the estates, and
the commotions among the people. And well did they perceive the threatening connection of this opposition to their
house. Two ways only were therefore open to them, either
they must themselves have become Protestants, which they
found impossible, or they must have resolutely destroyed the
dangerous teaching and pretensions which upset the souls of
men everywhere, especially in their own country. The
Hapsburger appeared who attempted this.

Meanwhile the spirit of the old Church had been raised, by
the great victories which it had gained in other countries.
The Protestant princes combined against the threatened offensive movement of the Roman Catholic party, as before at
Smalkald, and the Roman Catholic party answered by the
formation of the League ; but the object at heart, of the League
was attack, while that of the Protestants was only defence.

This was the political state of Germany before the Thirty
years' war ; a most unsatisfactory state. Discontent was
general, a mournful tendency, a disposition to prophecy evil,
were the significant signs of the times. Every deed of violence which was announced to the people in the flying-sheets,
was accompanied by remarks on the bad times. And yet we
know for certain that immorality had not become strikingly
greater in the country. There was wealth in the cities, and

even in the country increase of prosperity; there was regular government everywhere, better order and greater security of existence, luxury and an inordinate love of enjoyment had undoubtedly increased, together with riches; even among the lower strata of the people greed was awakened, life became more varied and dearer, and much indifference began to be shown concerning the quarrels of ecclesiastics. The best began to be gloomy, and even cheerful natures, like the honest Bartholomäus Ringwald, became prophets of misfortune, and wished for death.

And there was good reason for this gloom. There was something diseased in the life of Germany, an incomprehensible burden weighed it down, which marred its development. Luther's teaching, it is true, produced the greatest spiritual and intellectual progress which Germany had ever made through one man, but the demands of life increased with every expansion of the soul. The new mental culture must be followed by a corresponding advance in earthly condition, a greater independence in faith, demanded imperiously a stronger power of political development. But it was precisely this teaching, which appeared like the early dawn of a better life, that conveyed to the people the consciousness of their own political weakness, and by this weakness they became one-sided and narrow minded. Germany being divided into countless territories under weak princes, its people everywhere involved in and occupied with trifling disputes, were deficient in that which is indispensable-to a genial growth; they needed a general elevation, a great united will, and a sphere of moral duties, which alone makes men pre-eminently cheerful and manly. The fatherland of the Germans extended probably from Lorraine to the Oder, but in no single portion of it did they live like the citizens of Elizabeth or Henry IV.

Thus already inwardly diseased, Germany entered upon a war of thirty years. When the war ended, there was little remaining of the great nation. For yet a century to come, the successors of the survivors were deficient in that most manly of all feelings,—political enthusiasm.

Luther had raised his people out of the epic life of the middle ages. The Thirty years' war had destroyed the popular strength, and forced the Germans into individual life, the mental constitution of which one may truly call lyrical. That which will here be depicted from the accounts of cotemporaries, is a sad joyless time.

CHAPTER I.

THE THIRTY YEARS' WAR.—THE ARMY.

THE opposition between the interests of the house of Haps-burg and of the German nation, and between the old and new faith, led to a bloody catastrophe. If any one should inquire how such a war could rage through a whole gene-ration, and so fearfully exhaust a powerful people, he will receive this striking answer, that the war was so long and terrible, because none of the contending parties were able to carry it out on a great and decisive scale.

The largest armies in the Thirty years' war did not exceed in strength one corps of a modern army. Tilly considered forty thousand men the greatest number of troops that a gene-ral could wish to have. It was only occasionally that an army reached that strength; almost all the great battles were fought by smaller bodies of men. Numerous were the de-tachments, and very great were the losses by skirmishes, illnesses, and desertion. As there was no regular system for maintaining the strength of the army, its effective amount fluctuated in a remarkable way. Once, indeed, Wallenstein united a larger force under his command—according to some accounts a hundred thousand men—but they did not form one army, nay, they were hardly in any military connection, for the undisciplined bands with which, in 1629, he subdued the German territories of the Emperor, were dispersed over half Germany. Such large masses of soldiers appeared to all parties as a terrible venture; they could not, in fact, be kept under control, and after that, no general commanded more than half that number.*

An army in order of battle was considered as a movable fortress, the central point of which was the General himself, who ruled all the details; he had to survey the ground and every position, and every attack was directed by him. Adjutantcies and staff service were hardly established. It was part of the strategy to keep the army together in masses, to defend the ranks by earth works, and not to allow horse or man to be out of observation and control. In marching also, the army was kept close together in narrow quarters, generally within the space of a camp; from this arose commissariat difficulties, the high-roads were bad, often almost impassable, the conveyance of provisions compulsory, and always ill-regulated; and worst of all, the army was attended by an immense baggage-train, which, with the wild-robber system, quickly wasted the most fertile countries.

Great care was therefore taken that no such embarrassment should arise. Neither the Emperor nor the Princes of the Empire were in a condition to maintain forty thousand men out of their income even for three months. The regular revenue of the sovereign was much less than now, and the maintenance of an army far more costly. The greater part of the revenue was derived from tithes in kind, which in time of war was insecure and difficult to realize. The finances of the parties engaged in this war were even at the commencement of it in a most lamentable state.

* Even the great Imperial army that assembled before the battle of Nördlingen, in 1634, was a combination of several armies; that of Wallenstein, an Italian army, Spanish auxiliaries, and troops of Maximilian of Bavaria, altogether perhaps sixty thousand men, they only remained together a short time.

In the winter of 1619 and 1620, half the Bohemian army died of hunger and cold, from the want of pay and a commissariat; in September 1620, more than four and a half million of gulden of pay was owing to the troops, and there were endless mutinies, and the King Palatine Frederick could not aid his Protestant allies with subsidies. The Emperor was then not in much better condition, but he soon afterwards obtained Spanish subsidies. When the Elector of Saxony, whose finances were better regulated, first hired fifteen hundred men in December, 1619, he could not pay them regularly. What was granted by the estates in war taxes, and the so-called voluntary contributions of the opulent, did not go far; loans even in the first year of the war were very difficult to realize ; they were attempted with the banking-houses of southern Germany, and also in Hamburg, but seldom with success. City communities were considered safer debtors than the great princes. There were dealings about the smallest sums even with private individuals. Saxony in 1621, hoped to get from fifty to sixty thousand guldens from the Fuggers, and endeavoured in vain to borrow thirty and seventy thousand gulden from capitalists. Maximilian of Bavaria, and the League, made a great loan for the war of one million two hundred thousand gulden at twelve per cent. from the merchants in Genoa, for this the Fuggers became responsible, and the salt trade of Augsburg was given to them for their security. Just one hundred years before, this said banking-house had taken an important share in the election of the Emperor Charles V., and now it helped to secure the victory of the Roman Catholic party ; for the Bohemian war was decided even more by the want of money than by the battle of the Weissen-Berge. Thus the war began with the governments being in a general state of insolvency ; and therefore the maintenance of great armies became impossible.

It is evident that there was a fatal disproportion between the military strength of the parties and the ultimate object of every war. None of them could entirely subdue their opponents. The armies were too small, and had too little durability, to be able to control by regular strategic operations, the numerous and warlike people of wide-spread districts. Whilst a victorious army was ruling near the Rhine or the Oder, a new enemy was collecting in the north on the shores of the Baltic. The German theatre of war, also, was not so constituted as to be easily productive of lasting results. Almost every city, and many country seats were fortified. The siege guns were still unwieldy and uncertain in their aim, and the defence of fortified places was proportionably stronger than the attack. Thus war became principally a combat of sieges; every captured town weakened the victorious army, from the necessity of leaving garrisons. When a province had been conquered, the conqueror was often not in a position to withstand the conquered in open battle. By new exertion the conqueror was driven from the field; then followed fresh sieges and captures. and again fatal disruption of strength.

It was a war full of bloody battles and glorious victories, and also of excessive alternations of fortune. Numerous were the dark hero forms that loomed out of the chaos of blood and fire; the iron Ernst von Mansfeld, the fantastic Brunswicker, Bernhard of Weimar; and on the other side, Maximilian of Bavaria, and the generals of the League, Tilly, Pappenheim, and the able Mercy; the leaders of the Imperial army, the daring Wallenstein and Altringer; the great French heroes, Condé and Turenne, and amongst the Swedes, Horn, Bauer, Torstenson, Wrangel, and above all the mighty prince of war, Gustavus Adolphus. How much manly energy excited to the highest pitch, and yet how slow and poor were the political results obtained! how quickly was again lost, what appeared to have been obtained by the greatest amount of power ! How often did the parties themselves change the objects after which they were striving, nay even the banner for which they desired victory !

The political events of the war can only be briefly mentioned here; they may be divided into three periods. The first, from 1618 to 1630, is the time of the Imperial triumphs. The Protestant estates of Bohemia, contrary to law and their own word, refused the Bohemian crown to the Archduke Ferdinand, and chose for their ruler the Elector Palatine, a reformer. But by means of the League and the Lutheran Electors of Saxony, Ferdinand became Emperor. His opponent was beaten in the battle of the Weissen-Berge, and left the country as a fugitive. Here and there, the Protestant opposition continued to blaze up, but divided, without plan, and with weak resources. Baden-Durlach, the Mansfelder, the Brunswicker, and lastly the circle of lower Saxony with the Danish King, succumbed to the troops of the League and the Emperor. Ferdinand II., who though Emperor, was still a fugitive in the states belonging to his house, obtained through the assistance of an experienced mercenary commander, Wallenstein, a large body of troops, whom he maintained in the territory of the principality by contribution and pillage. Ever greater did the Emperor's army continue to swell; ever higher rose his claims in Germany and Italy: the old idea of Charles V. after the Smalkaldic war became a living principle in the nephew; he would subdue Germany, as his predecessor had done the peasants and the estates in the Austrian provinces; he would crush all independence, the privileges of cities, the rights of the estates, the pride and family power of princes—he hoped to subjugate all Germany to his faith and his house. But throughout the whole of Germany sounded a cry of grief and indignation, at the horrible marauding war which was conducted by the

merciless general of the Hapsburger. All the allies of the
Imperial house rose threateningly against him. The Princes
of the League, and above all Maximilian of Bavaria, looked
abroad for help; they subdued the high spirit of the
Emperor, and he was obliged to dismiss his faithful General
and to control the barbarous army. Nay, more, even the
Holy Father began to fear the Emperor. The Pope himself
united with France in order to bring Swedish help to the
Protestants. The lion of the north disembarked on the
German coast.

Now began the second period of the war. The swelling
billows of the Roman Catholic power had overflowed Germany
even up to the Northern Sea. From 1630 to 1634 came
the Protestant counter-current, which flowed in a resistless
course from north to south over the third part of Germany.
Even ' after the death of their king, the Swedish Generals
kept their ascendency in the field; Wallenstein himself
abandoned the Emperor, and was secretly murdered. The
Roman Catholic party had begun to lose courage, when, by
a last effort of collected strength, it won the bloody battle of
Nördlingen.

Then followed the third period of fourteen years, from
1634 to 1648, in which victory and reverses were nearly
equal on both sides. The Swedes, driven back to the Northern Sea, girding up their whole strength, again burst forth
into the middle of Germany. Again the tide of fortune ebbed
to and fro, becoming gradually less powerful. The French,
greedy of booty, spread themselves as far as the Rhine; the
land was devastated, and famine and pestilence raged. The
Swedes, though losing one General after another, kept the
field and maintained their claims with unceasing pertinacity.
In opposition to them stood the equally inflexible Maximilian, Prince of the League. Even in the last decade of the
war, the Bavarians fought for three years the most renowned

campaigns which this dynasty has to boast of. The fanatical Ferdinand was dead, his successor, able, moderate, and an experienced soldier, persevered from necessity; he also was firm and tenacious. No party could bring about a decisive result. For years negotiations for peace were carried on; whilst the generals fought, the cities and villages were depopulated and the fields were overgrown with rank weeds. Peace came at last; it was not brought about by great battles, nor by irresistible political combinations, but chiefly by the weariness of the combatants, and Germany celebrated it with festivities though she had lost three fourths of her population.

All this gives to the Thirty years' war the appearance of foredoomed annihilation, ushered in as it was by the most fearful visitations of nature. Above the strife of parties a terrible fate spread its wings; it carried off the leaders and prostrated them in the dust, the greatest human strength became powerless under its hand; at last, satiated with devastation and death, it turned its face slowly from the country which had become a great charnel house.

It is not the intention of this work to characterize the Generals and battles belonging to this period of struggle, but to speak of the condition and circumstances of the German people, both of the destructive and suffering portions of the population, of the army, alike with the citizen and peasant. Since the Burgundian war and the Italian battles of Maximilian and Charles V., the burgher infantry had thrown into the background the knightly cavalry of the middle ages.

The strength of the German army consisted of Landsknechte, freemen, either citizens or peasants, and among them occasionally a few nobles. They were for the most part mercenaries, who bound themselves voluntarily by contract to some banner for a time. They carried on war like a trade, sternly, actively, and enduringly. But the full vigour of their power was of short duration: their decadence may be dated from their revolt against the old Fronsperg; from that hour when they broke the heart of their father, the gray-headed Landsknecht hero. Many things combined to corrupt this new infantry : they were mercenaries, serving only for a time, accustomed to change their banner, and not to fight for an idea, but only for booty or their own advantage. They were not called into existence in consequence of the application of gunpowder to the art of war; but they more especially appropriated this new invention to themselves. The introduction of fire-arms into the army, certainly first showed the weakness of their opponents, the old cavalry of knighthood, but at the same time soon caused the diminution of their own efficiency, for these weapons were too clumsy and slow to insure victory on the battle-field. The final result still depended on the rushing charge of the pikemen and the onslaught of their great masses on the enemy.

To this was added other detrimental circumstances; there were as yet no standing armies : when there was threatening of a feud, troops were assembled by the territorial lords great and small, and by the cities, and at the conclusion of the war they were dismissed. These wars were generally short and local; even the Hungarian wars were only summer campaigns of a few months. The German rulers, always in want of money, endeavoured to help themselves by the depreciation of the coinage, striking a lighter coin expressly for the payment of the soldiers, and also by faithlessly paying them less than had been agreed upon. This unworthy treatment demoralized the men, no less than the shortness of the service. Thus the Landsknechte became deceived deceivers, adventurers, plunderers and robbers.

The infantry at the beginning of the war used either fire-arms or pikes, the former to open the enemy's ranks, the latter to decide the battle by hand-to-hand fighting. At this period we find that the pikemen were the heavy infantry;

they wore breastplates, brassarts, swords, and a pike eighteen feet long with an iron point, the handles of the best were of ash ; the lance-corporals and subaltern officers had halberds and partisans.   The two species of fire-arms which prevailed in the army were the musketoon (which with the Imperialists was a heavy weapon six feet long, with matchlocks and balls, of which there were ten in the pound) and the short hand-gun, a weapon of lighter and smaller calibre, which in the beginning of the war bore amongst the infantry the old name of arquebuss.   The musketeer wore also at his side a hanger, a weapon with a small curved point, and over his shoulder a bandolier with eleven cylindrical cases in which the charges were placed, a match holder, and a musket rest, a staff with a metal point and two metal prongs, on the top of which the musketeer laid his weapon : his head was covered with a helmet or morion ; this last piece of armour was soon discarded.   The foot arquebussier did not carry a rest or a shoulder-belt ; he loaded from his shot-pouch and powder-horn.   There were pikemen and musketeers in the same company, and long even before the great war there were companies in which fire-arms alone were borne.   Out of the light infantry were formed, in the middle of the war, what were called rifle companies, but among whom only a few had rifles.   The grenadiers, who threw hand-grenades, were then formed in small numbers ; for instance, in 1634, by the Swedes at the siege of Ratisbon.

At the beginning of the war the pikemen, as heavy infantry, were considered of importance, and they were put down in the muster-rolls as receiving double pay ; but in the course of it they were found to be too unwieldy for long marches, help-less in attack, in short, almost useless, since the last decision of the battle now devolved upon the cavalry ; thus they gradually sank into contempt, and the clever judgment pronounced by the jovial Springinsfeld, accurately expresses the view that was taken of their utility. "A musketeer is indeed a poor, much harassed creature ; but he lives in splendid happiness compared to a miserable pikeman : it is vexatious to think what hardships the poor simpletons endure ; no one who had not experienced it themselves could believe it, and I think whoever kills a pikeman whom he could save, murders an innocent man, and can never be excused such a barbarous deed : for although these poor draught oxen—they were so called in derision—are formed to defend their brigades in the open field from the onslaught of the cavalry, yet they themselves do no one any injury, and he who throws himself upon their long spears deserves what he gets. In short, I have during my life seen many sharp encounters, but seldom found that a pikeman ever caused the death of any one." Nevertheless the pikemen kept their ground till towards the end of the seventeenth century. The musketeers who were, however, the great mass of the infantry, were rendered more agile by Gustavus Adolphus ; he discarded from the Swedish army the musket rests, lightened their weapons and the calibre of the balls, of which there were thirteen to the pound, and introduced instead of the rattling bandoliers, paper cartridges and pockets ; but the musketeers, without bayonets, slow in firing, unaccustomed to fight in close ranks, were little fitted to decide an engagement.

The influence of the cavalry on the other hand increased. At the beginning of the war there were two contending principles concerning them, the method and arming of old knightly traditions were mixed up with the Landsknechte characteristics, many of whom were also horsemen. The heavy cavalry were still considered an aristocratic corps, the nobleman still placed himself with his charger, his knightly armour, his old knightly lance, and his troop of vassals, for whom he drew pay, under the standard of the cavalry regiments. But the war made an end gradually of this remnant of old customs. It was still, however, an object of ambition to join the army as a soldier of fortune, either with an esquire or alone, and whoever estimated himself highly or had made much booty, thronged to the cavalry standard. In the German army there were four kinds of regular cavalry, the Lancers, in full armour even to the knightly spurs, without shield, with the knightly lance or the spear of the Landsknechte, a sword, and two holster pistols; the Cuirassiers, with similar armour, pistols and sword; the Arquebussiers, called later Carbineers, half armed, with morion, and pistol proof back and breast pieces, with two pistols and an arquebuss on a small bandolier; finally the Dragoons, mounted pikemen, or musketeers, who fought either on foot or on horseback. Besides these there were irregular cavalry Croats, Stradiots, and Hussars, who almost a century before, in 1546, had made a great sensation in Germany when Duke Maurice of Saxony borrowed them from King Ferdinand of Bohemia. Their appearance was not displeasing; they wore Turkish armour, a sabre, and a targe, but they were wild robbers, and in the worst repute. Gustavus Adolphus brought to Germany only Cuirassiers and Dragoons. His Cuirassiers were more lightly armed than the Imperial, but far superior to them in energy of attack. During the whole war the endeavour of the cavalry was to lighten their heavy armour; the more the army separated into military companies the more pressing was the necessity for greater activity.

In the sixteenth century the heavy guns were very varied in calibre and length of barrel, and had divers curious names. The sharp metz, the carronade, culverin and nightingale, the singer, the falcon and the falconet, the field serpent and serpentine, with balls from one hundred pounds down to one pound, besides the organ,* mortars large and small, rifle-bar-

* This machine consisted of a number of short barrels, which, bound in parallel rows, formed a nearly cubic mass, the front of which showed from six to ten rows of as many mouths arranged in a square. This system of

relled guns and rifles.   But in the beginning of the Thirty years'
war the forms were already simplified; they cast forty-eight,
and twenty-four pounders, twelve and six pounders, with forty-
two, twenty-four, twelve and six pound balls;* the first were
fortress and siege guns, the last were field guns; besides these,
disproportionately long culverins and falconets, also chamber
pieces for throwing shells, or bomb mortars which were soon
called howitzers, smaller mortars for throwing fire-balls, stink-
pots, &c.; and in the beginning of the war bombarders, which
fired pieces of iron, lead, small shot, and stones.   Lastly from
forged pieces they fired half-ounce bullets, double, single, and
half-hooks, or grappling irons.   But the length of the barrels
of the guns was too long for balls; the powder was bad, and
the aim consequently uncertain.   Gustavus Adolphus introduced shorter and lighter guns; his leather cannon, made of
copper cylinders with thick hemp and leather coverings † held
together by iron hoops, soon ceased to be used, probably because they were not sufficiently durable, but his short four-
pounders, two of which were given to every regiment, and
which worked best with grape shot, lasted over the war.
These field pieces fired not only from position but were moved
with tolerable rapidity during action, but the bombardes and
petards were unwieldy; the last were twisted round with ropes
more like a sort of cannon than our bombs and grenades, but
were of uncertain effect because the locks were badly prepared

---

barrels rested on a carriage, and was fired in rows.   Every single barrel
was loaded with three or more balls, and could be fired separately or
together.   Fronsperg boasts that after one loading there could be a
thousand shots from the hundred barrels of the gun.
    * Wallhausen, 'Archiley Art of War,' 1617.   For the corresponding
French system of this time, a good description is to be found in the
'Etude sur le passé et l'avenir de l'artillerie par le Prince Napoléon
Louis Bonaparte.'   T. I.
    † In the battle of Breitenfeld the metal guns of Sweden were over-
heated; there the leather cannon did their last great service against the
Croats.

and they did not measure the time for the explosion. The old disposition of the Germans to give life to the inanimate had already in earlier times bestowed especial names on favourite guns, and the custom remained, even after pieces of the same calibre were cast in greater numbers; then particular guns, for example, were called after the planets, months, and signs of the zodiac, like a high sounding alphabet,* and in this case indicated by single letters. There was always a new name given according to the calibre, which in spite of all the simplification was still very varied. The progress of artillery and its influence on the conduct of war was impeded in the last half of the war by the want of experienced master gunners, the greater portion of them were infantry commanders; the loss of an artillery officer of capacity was difficult to replace.

The relative numbers of particular branches of the service were changed during the war. In the beginning the proportion of the cavalry to the infantry was as one to five, but soon they became one to three, and in the latter period they were sometimes the strongest. This striking fact is a proof both of the deterioration of the troops and of the art of war. In the exhausted country, the army could only be maintained by a strong force of cavalry, who could forage further and change their ground with more rapidity. As all who hoped for independence or booty pressed into the cavalry it was in better condition proportionately than the infantry, who at last were reduced to support themselves by reaping the scanty remains left by the horsemen. Undoubtedly the cavalry also became worse, the want of good horses was at last more sensibly felt than that of men, and the heavy cavalry could not be kept up, whilst in the last year the service of the scouts and forag-

---

* Thus generated the ingenious comparison of guns with birds of prey : the thirty-six pounders were called eagles, the twenty-four pounders falcons, twelve pounders vultures, six pounders hawks, three pounders sparrowhawks, and the sixty-pound mortars owls.

ing parties for the commissariat was brought to great perfection. Nevertheless the cavalry were the most effective, for it was their task to decide the battle by their charge. The last army with skilled infantry and Dutch discipline was that of Bavaria under Mercy, from 1643 to 1645.

The tactics of armies had slowly altered in the course of the century. The old Landsknecht army advanced to battle in three great squares,—the advanced guard, the main body, and the rear guard—disregarding roads and corn-fields; before it went pioneers, who filled in ditches and cut down hedges to clear the way for the bulky mass. For battle, the deep square masses of infantry placed themselves side by side, each square mass consisted of many companies, sometimes of many regiments; the cavalry formed in a similar deep position at the wings. There was no regular reserve, only sometimes one of the three masses was kept back for the final decision; a select body of men, the forlorn hope, was formed for dangerous service, such as forcing the passage of a river, covering an important point, or turning the enemy's flank. Since fire-arms had prevailed over pikes, these great battalions were surrounded by files of sharpshooters, and at last special bodies of sharpshooters were formed and attached to them. In the war in the Netherlands, the unwieldiness of these heavy squares led to breaking the order of battle into smaller tactical bodies. But it was only slowly, that formation in line and a system of reserve were organized. Much of the old method continued in the Imperial army in the beginning of the war. Still the companies of infantry were united in deep squares—in battalions. To take firm positions and assume defensive warfare had become too much the custom in inglorious campaigns against the wild storming Turks. The weight and tenacity of deep masses might certainly be effective, but if the enemy succeeded in bringing his guns to bear upon them, they suffered fearfully, and were very unwieldy in all their movements. Gustavus

Adolphus adopted the tactical innovations of the Netherlanders in an enlightened way ; when in battle he placed the infantry six, and the cavalry only three deep ; he distributed the great masses into small divisions, which firmly connected together, formed the unity of the Swedish brigade ; he strengthened the cavalry, placing between them companies of sharp-shooters, and introduced light artillery regiments besides those that were in reserve and position, and accustomed his soldiers to rapid offensive movements and daring advances.   His infantry fired quicker than the Imperial, and at the battle of Breitenfeld the old Walloon regiments of Tilly were routed by their close platoon firing ; he also laid down for his cavalry, those very rules by which a century later Frederick the Great made his, the first in the world ; viz., not to stop in order to fire, but at the quickest pace to rush upon the enemy.

During the battle the soldiers recognized one another by their war-cries and distinguishing marks, the officers by their scarfs.   For example, at Breitenfeld Tilly's army wore white bands on their hats and helmets, and white lace round the arm, and the Swedes had green branches.   The Imperial colour in the field was red, therefore Gustavus Adolphus prohibited his Swedes from wearing that colour,* the scarfs of the Swedish officers at the battle of Lutzen were green, those of Electoral Saxony during the war were black and yellow, and later, after the acquisition of the Polish crown, red and white.

The soldiers were formed in troops or companies, and these were combined in regiments which had administrative unity. The German infantry regiments consisted of three thousand men, in ten companies of three hundred men ; they seldom reached their normal strength, and lost their men in the war with frightful rapidity, so that there were frequently regiments of from a thousand to three hundred, and companies of

* Yet he himself had a brigade which was called red.

seventy to thirty men. Cavalry regiments were required to be from five hundred to a thousand men strong; the numbers of the troops were different, and their effective war strength was still more variable.

The titles and duties of officers had already much similarity to the modern German organization. He who had raised a regiment for his Sovereign, was called the colonel of the regiment, even if he had the rank of General; under him were the Lieutenant-colonel and Major. More important for the object of these pages were the officers of companies; the Captain of infantry or cavalry, with his Lieutenant, an Ensign, and sergeant, or troop sergeant-major, non-commissioned officers and lance-corporals, and finally the provost-marshal.

When an officer at the mustering of his company in a circle, was installed as chief captain and father, he begged his dear soldiers, in a friendly manner, to be true and obedient to him, recounted to them their duties, promised to stand by them in every emergency, and as an honest man, devote himself to them in life or death, and leave them whatever he had. Unfortunately the captain's first duty was to be faithful in money concerns, both towards the colonel and his own soldiers, to procure clever good soldiers for the reviewing officer, not to charge for more mercenaries than was right, and to give the soldiers their full pay; but this seldom happened. The temptation to a system of fraudulent gain was great, and conscientiousness in the uncertain life of war was a virtue which quickly disappeared; even the most honourable fell upon dangerous rocks when the pay had been long in arrear, or not fully given. Besides this, it was necessary for him to be an energetic experienced man, just and kind in disposition, but strict in maintaining rights. During the week, he was, according to the old proverb, to look severe, and not to smile upon the soldiers before Sunday; when

there was preaching in the camp, the soldiers sat on the
ground, but stood up, taking their hats off, before the captain,
but he who wore a morion kept it on.   On the march, the
captain rode, but before the enemy he went on foot, carrying
either the pike or the musket of his company.*

The banner of the infantry, which was held sacred by the
company, had a standard about the size of ours, but the
silken flag, like an enormous sail, reached almost to the end
of the standard; it was of heavy material, according to the
taste of that time, with allegorical pictures painted on it,
and short Latin sentences beautifully illuminated.   The
" cornete " of the cavalry, sometimes vandyked, were smaller,
and fixed to the standard like our banners.   The regiments
were sometimes called after the colours of the banners; for
example, in Electoral Saxony, where the ground of the banners was always of two colours, they were called the black
and yellow, blue and white, red and yellow, regiments; each
of the ten banners of the regiment also had its special em-
blem and motto, and different combinations of the regimental
colours, grained, striped and in squares, yet the chief standard showed the regimental colours only on the border.
The " cornete " of the cavalry had a ground of only one
colour: the corps of cavalry were denoted according to the
colours of their banners, and not by their uniforms, which
they hardly ever wore; for example :—" two corps of orange-
coloured cornet cuirassiers," " five corps of steel-green cornet
arquebussiers."   The Swedes also distinguished their brigades,
which were in Germany frequently called regiments, by the
colour of their banners; thus, besides the yellow (Body Guard)
there were the green, blue, white, and red.   The colours of
regiments were often chosen from the armorial bearings of the
colonel, especially if he had raised the regiment.   Gradually,

---

* The lieutenants carried partisans, the non-commissioned officers
halberds.

however, it became the custom in all the armies to call the
regiments after the names of the officers.

The flag was attached to the standard and erected in the
midst of the circle of enlisted soldiers ; then the Colonel delivered the banner to the Ensign, and thus gave it into his
charge:—" As your bride or your own daughter, from the
right hand to the left ; and if both your arms should be shot
or cut off, you should take it with your mouth ; and if you
cannot preserve it thus, wrap yourself therein, commit yourself to God so to be slain, and die as an honourable man."
As long as the colours were flying, and a piece of the standard left, the soldiers were to follow the Ensign to the death,
till all should lie in a heap on the battle-field, that no evil-
doer or blameworthy person should be sheltered by the flag ;
if any one should transgress against the banner oath, the
Ensign was to furl the banner, and forbid the transgressor to
march under it or mount guard, and he was obliged to go
among the bad women and children with the baggage till the
affair was arranged : the Ensign was not to leave the colours
a single night without permission ; when he slept he was to
have them by him, and never to separate himself from them ;
if they should be torn from the standard by treachery or some
roguish attendant, the Ensign should be delivered over to the
common soldiers to be judged for life or death, according to
their will.   It was necessary for him to be tall, powerful,
manly, and valiant, and a cheerful companion, friendly to
every one, a mediator and peace-maker ; he was not to inflict
punishment on any one, that he might incur no hatred.   In
the open field under the unfurled colours appointments were
declared and the articles of war read.   A trooper was not,
without permission, to be out of sight of the colours when the
army was marching or encamped ; whoever fled from the
colours in battle was to die for it, and whoever killed him
was to be unpunished : if an Ensign should abandon a fort

or redoubt before he had held out against three assaults
without relief, he transgressed the rules of war; a regiment
lost its colours if from cowardice it yielded a fortress before
the time. It was not long since pike-law was given up, the
severe tribunal of the Landsknechte, where, before the circle of
common soldiers, the provost-marshal accused the evil-doer,
and forty chosen men, officers and soldiers, pronounced
judgment: at the beginning of the trial the Ensigns furled
their colours, and reversed them with the iron point in the
ground, and demanded a sentence, because the colours could
not fly over an evil-doer. If the transgressor was condemned
to the spear, or to be shot by the arquebussiers, then the
Ensign thanked them for their judgment on the offender,
unfurled the colours, and caused them to fly towards the
east, comforted the poor sinner, and promised to meet him
halfway, and thereby to deliver him by taking him under the
protection of the colours. When the line of pikes was
formed they went to the end of it with their backs towards
the sun; but the transgressor had to bless the soldiers and
pray for a speedy death, then the provost gave him three
strokes with his staff on the right shoulder and pushed him
into the lane. Whoever had disgraced himself, if the colours
were waved three times over him, was freed from his disgrace. The Ensign received every three years, money for a
new flag or dress (from eighty to a hundred gulden), and for
that he was to make a present to the company of two casks
of beer or wine.

The office of Cornet of cavalry was less responsible. It
was his duty to rush vigorously upon the enemy, and after
the attack to raise his standard on high, that his people
might collect round him. In the Hungarian war the Cornet
passed sometimes into the rank of Lieutenant, and in some
regiments (the Wallenstein army for instance) this custom
was kept up.

The most important man of the company next to the Captain was the Sergeant ; he was the drill-master and spokesman for the soldiers, and had to mark out with flags the position to be taken up by the troops of the Imperial battalions, or Swedish brigades, to arrange the men, placing in the front and rear ranks and at the sides, the best armed and most efficient men, to mingle the halberds and short weapons, to lead and keep with the arquebusiers ; he was the instructor of the company, and knew the proper and warlike use of his weapons.

As the "mob" who came together from far and near under a banner were difficult to keep in order, the greater part of them not to be depended on, and unskilled in the exercise of their weapons, the number of non-commissioned officers was necessarily very great, frequently indeed they formed more than a third of the troop. Any one who had military capacity or could be depended upon, was marked out by the subordinate commander for higher pay and posts of confidence. Amongst the numerous functions and manifold designations of the subalterns, some are particularly characteristic. In the beginning of the war every company had, according to the old *Landsknecht* custom, their "leader," who, in the first instance at least, was chosen by the soldiers. He was the tribune of the company, their spokesman, who had to lay their grievances and wishes before the Captain, and to represent the interests of the soldiery. It may easily be understood that such an arrangement did not strengthen the discipline of the army ; it was done away with in time of war. Even the thankless office of quartermaster was of greater importance than now ; the complaints of the soldiers, who quarrelled about the bad quarters he had provided for them, he met with defiance, and inspired them with fear of his usurious practices. When a company came to a deserted village, the serjeants threw their knives into the hat of the quartermaster; he then went from house to house, sticking the blades as they came to his hand in the door-posts, and every band (of six or eight men) followed their leader's knife. When poor members of the nobility, candidates for commission, of whom the number was often great, presented themselves, their names were inscribed on the list of lance-corporals. Old vagabonds full of pretension were designated in the military kitchen Latin by the title of "*Ambesaten*," and afterwards "*Landspassaten*;" they were orderlies and messengers receiving higher pay, representatives and assistants of the Corporals. There was a general endeavour to add a deputy to every office, as the Lieutenant to the Captain, an under Ensign to the Ensign, to the Serjeant an under Serjeant, and frequently with the infantry a vidette for the sentinels at out-posts; in the same way serjeants were deputies to the officers, and the "*Landspassaten*" to the Corporal, and the provost to the provost-general, &c., &c.

The army consisted, with few exceptions, of enlisted soldiers. The Sovereign empowered an experienced leader by patent to raise for him an army, a regiment, or a company; recruiting places were sought for and a muster place established where the recruits were collected. The recruits were paid their travelling expenses or bounty; at the beginning of the war this was insignificant, and sometimes deducted from their pay, but later the bounty increased, and was given to the soldiers. At the beginning of the war negotiations were carried on with every mercenary, about the pay, at the muster-place. The soldier in quarters received nothing but his pay, which in 1600, for the common foot soldier, amounted to from fifteen to sixteen gulden a month.* With this they had to procure for themselves weapons, clothing, and food. Garrisons were

---

* About 1600 one gulden of the coin of the Empire was equal to forty silver groschen of our money; thus sixteen of these was equal to forty-two of our thalers.

provided with stores by the quarter-master, the cost being reimbursed to him.   During the great war, however, the arrangements about pay were often deviated from, the distribution of it to the soldiers was very irregular.

In the Imperial army the pay, exclusive of food, was nine gulden to the pikeman and six to the musketeer.   In the Swedish army it was still lower, but was in the beginning more regularly paid, and there was more care about the provisions. The whole sustenance of the army was charged upon the province by a hard system of requisition, even on friendly territory.   The maintenance of the upper officers was very high, and yet formed only a small share of their income. During the time of service the troops were entered on the muster-roll by a court of comptrol, the reviewing officer, or commissary of the Prince; in order to prevent the officers and commanders drawing too much pay, when they were assembled round the flag, the names of the deserters were written apart, and beside each name a gallows was painted.   At the time of muster if any one was unserviceable or had served a long time, he was taken off the muster-roll, and declared free, given his discharge, and provided with a pass or certificate.   Whoever wished for leave, obtained a pass from the Ensign.   The soldier had to clothe himself, uniforms were only found exceptionally;   the halberdiers of the life-guards, and the heavily armed cavalry, so far as armour was concerned, were generally furnished by the Sovereign;   but before the war it was only occasionally done, and then pay was deducted for it, or the Colonel took back the armour after the campaign.

The military discipline of the Germans was, in the beginning of the war, in the worst repute.   The German soldiers were considered by other nations as idle, turbulent, refractory bullies;* they had been not a little spoilt by service in half-barbarous countries, as Hungary and Poland then were, and

* Wallhausen 'On the Art of War.'

against the barbarian Turks.   When individuals had to chaffer about their pay, discontent began ; when the Captain would not satisfy the claims of the enlisted mercenary, the malcontent threw his musket angrily at the feet of the former, and went off with the money for his travelling-expenses, there was no means of detaining him.   Though the Ensign was bound by oath, the Captain only too frequently found advantage in favouring plunder and the nightly desertion of the banner, for he had his share of the soldier's booty : the worst thieves were the best bees.

The paymasters were always deeply hated, because they generally gave the regiments short pay and bad coin ; they and other commissaries of the sovereign were exposed to much insult when they came to the camp.   The worst things are related of the Commanders-in-chief, above all, that they received more pay than they distributed to the soldiers ; still worse were the Generals.   Frequently open mutiny broke out, and then the mutineers placed a Colonel or Captain in the middle of them, and chose him for their leader.   The same thing took place in Hungary.   Indeed it happened, during the armistice preceding the Westphalian peace, that in a Bavarian dragoon regiment, a corporal of the garrison of Hilperstein nominated himself Colonel of the regiment, and by the help of his comrades drove away the officers ; the regiment was surrounded by loyal soldiers, the new Colonel with eighteen of the ringleaders were executed, the muskets were taken from the regiment, it was resworn and formed anew as a cavalry regiment.   The arrears of pay were the usual cause of mutiny.   In the year 1620, the regiment of Count Mansfeld mutinied.   He began to pay, but meanwhile leaving his tent, struck down two of the soldiers with his own hands, severely wounding them ; he then mounted his horse, sprang into the midst of the mutineers, and shot many of them.   He alone with three captains subdued the insolence of six hundred men, after having slain eleven, and severely wounded six-and-twenty. If it was difficult to secure obedience to military commands whilst the banner was waving, still greater was the burst of resentment when it was furled and the regiment was disbanded. Then the provost, the prostitutes, and the soldiers' sons hid themselves; the Captain, Lieutenant, and other commanders were obliged to submit to abusive language and challenges, and to hear themselves thus accosted: "Ha, you fellow, you have been my commander, now you are not a jot better than I; a pound of your hair is of no more importance to me than a pound of cotton; out with you, let's have a scuffle!" Whenever punishment was administered, the commanders were in danger from the revenge of the culprit or his friends. The disbanded soldiers quarrelled amongst each other, as they did with their officers, and sometimes there were as many as a hundred parties in one place engaged in duelling. The most wanton death-blows were dealt, and murders perpetrated, such as have never been heard of since the beginning of Christianity. When the banner was unfurled, it was customary for the combatants to join hands and vow to fight out their quarrel when their term of service was ended, and till then to live together in brotherly love. When this disbanding took place, the most disorderly of the soldiers combined together and began an "armour cleaning" of those comrades to whom, during service, the officers had shown favour; that is to say, they robbed them of all, deprived them of their clothes, beat and almost killed them. All these crimes were tolerated, and the powerless commander-in-chief looked passively on these proceedings as a mere custom of war.

During the Hungarian campaigns the soldiers adopted the habit of only remaining by their banners during the summer months; they found their reckoning in serving a short time, and mutinying if more was desired of them; for during the autumn and winter they went with two, three, or more boys as "*Gartbrüder*"* through the country, a fearful plague to the farmers in eastern Germany. In the frontier countries, Silesia, Austria, Bohemia, and Styria, it was even commanded by the sovereigns to pay a farthing to every soldier who was roving about as "*Gartbrüder*." Thus by their refractory conduct they daily obtained a gulden or more; their boys pilfered where they could, and were notorious poachers. Wallhausen, whilst making other energetic complaints, reckons that the support of a standing army would cost less to the princes and states, and secure greater success against the enemy, than this old bad system.

More than once during the long war, these wild armies were brought under the constraint of strict discipline by the powerful will of individuals, and each time great military successes were obtained; but this was not of any duration. The discipline of the Wallenstein army was excellent in a military point of view; but what the commander permitted with regard to citizens and peasants was horrible. Even Gustavus Adolphus could not preserve for more than a year, the strict discipline which on his landing in Pomerania was so triumphantly lauded by the Protestant ecclesiastics. It is true that the military law and articles of war contained a number of legal rules for all soldiers, concerning the forbearance to be observed even in an enemy's land towards the people and their property. The women, invalids, and aged were under all circumstances to be spared, and mills and ploughs were not to be injured. But it is not by the laws themselves, but by the administration of them, that we can judge of the peculiar characteristics of a period.

The punishments were in themselves severe. With the

. * A name given to bands that went about pillaging the fields, orchards, and gardens.

Swedes,—for the embezzlement of money intended for the hospitals or invalid soldiers, the wooden horse with its iron fittings was awarded, or running the gauntlet (for this hardy fellows were hired to take upon them the punishment), or loss of the hand, shooting, or hanging. For whole divisions,— the loss of their banners, cleaning the camp and lying outside it, and decimation. In the beginning of the war many of the old Landsknecht customs were maintained, for instance, their criminal court of justice, in which the law was decided by the people through select jurymen. And before the war, together with this, court-martials had been introduced. During the war a military tribunal was organized according to the modern German method, under the presidency of the advocate-general, and the provost-marshal superintended the execution. But even in punishments there was a difference between the army and the citizens and peasants. The soldier was put in irons, but not in the stocks or in prison ; no soldier was ever hanged on a common gallows, or in a common place of execution, but on a tree or on a special gallows, which was erected in the city for the soldiers in the market-place; the old form by which the delinquent was given over to the hangman was thus expressed: "He shall take him to a green tree and tie him up by the neck, so that the wind may blow under and over him, and the sun shine on him for three days ; then shall he be cut down and buried according to the custom of war." But the perjured deserter was hanged to a withered tree. Whoever was sentenced to death by the sword, was taken by the executioner to a public place, where he was cut in two, the body being the largest and the head the smallest portion. The provost and his assistant also were in nowise dishonoured by their office ; even the avoided executioner's assistant, the "*Klauditchen*" of the army, who was generally taken from among the convicts, and who was allowed to choose between

punishment and this dishonourable office, could, if he fulfilled his office faithfully, become respectable when the banner was unfurled; he could then receive his certificate like
any other gallant soldier, and no one could speak evil of
him.

There was one circumstance which distinguished the armies
of the Thirty years' war from those of modern days, and
which made their entrance into a province like an eruption of
a heterogeneous race of strangers: each soldier, in spite of his
short term of service in the field, was accompanied by his
household. Not only the higher officers, but also the troopers
and foot-soldiers, took their wives, and still more frequently
their mistresses with them in a campaign. Women from all
countries, adorned to the utmost of their power, followed the
army, and sought entrance into the camp, because they had a
husband, friend, or cousin there. At the mustering or disbanding of a regiment, even respectable maidens were, through
the most cruel artifices, carried off by disorderly bands, and
when the money was all spent, left sometimes without clothes,
or at some carousal sold from one to another. The women
who accompanied the soldiers cooked and washed for them,
nursed the sick, provided them with drink, bore their blows,
and on the march carried the children and any of the plunder
or household implements which could not be conveyed by the
baggage waggons. It is known that the King of Sweden on
his first arrival in Germany would not suffer any such women
in the camp; but after his return from Franconia, this strict
discipline seems to have ceased. Whoever peruses the old
church records of the village parishes will find sometimes the
names of maidens, who, having been carried off, returned at
the end of a year to their village home, and submitted themselves to the severest Church penances in order to die amongst
the ruined population of their birthplace. The women of the
camp were also under martial law. For great offences they

were flogged, and driven out of the camp; the soldiers too were hard masters, and little of what had been promised them in the beginning was kept.

The children accompanied the women. In the Swedish army military schools were established by Gustavus Adolphus, in which the children were instructed even in the camp. In these migratory schools strict military discipline prevailed, and a story, which cannot be warranted, is told of a cannon-ball having passed through a school in the Swedish camp, and having killed many of the children, but the survivors continued their sum in arithmetic.

Some soldiers maintained one or more lads, a crafty, stubborn set of good-for-nothings, who waited upon their masters, cleaned their horses, sometimes bore their armour, and fed their shaggy dogs; nimble spies who prowled about far and near on the traces of opulent people, and on the look-out for concealed money.

The plundering by the baggage-train was almost worse in a friendly country. When the soldiers with the women and children came to a farmhouse, they pounced like hawks upon the poultry in the yard, then broke open the doors, seized upon the trunks and chests, and with abusive language, threatened, importuned and destroyed, what they could not consume or take away. On decamping they compelled the owner to horse his waggons and take them to their next quarters. Then they filled the waggons with the clothes, beds, and household goods of the farmers, binding round their bodies what could not otherwise be carried away.

"Frequently," says the indignant narrator Wallhausen, "the women did not choose to be drawn by oxen, and it was necessary to procure horses, sometimes from a distance of six miles, to the great cost of the country people, and when they came with the waggons to the nearest quarters, they would not allow the poor people to return home; but dragged them with them to another territory, and at last stole the horses and made off."

In the beginning of the war, a German infantry regiment had to march for some days through the country of their own sovereign ; there were as many women and children with the baggage-train, as soldiers, and they stole in eight days from the subjects of their sovereign almost sufficient horses for each soldier to ride. The colonel, a just and determined man, frequently dragged the soldiers himself from the horses, and at last enforced their restoration by extreme severity. But it was impossible to prevent the women from riding ; there was not one who had not a stolen horse, and if they did not ride them they harnessed them three or four together to the peasants' carts.

Only a few of the otherwise copious writers of that time make mention of this despised portion of the army ; yet there are sufficient accounts, from which we may conclude that great influence was produced by the baggage-train on the fate of the army and the country. Especially by the enormous extent of it. At the end of the sixteenth century Adam Junghans reckons, that in a besieged fortress where the camp-followers were reduced to the smallest possible number, to three hundred infantry soldiers, there were fifty women and forty children, besides sutlers, horseboys, &c., &c., somewhat more than a third of the soldiers. But in the field the proportion was quite different even in the beginning of the war. Wallhausen reckons as indispensable to a German regiment of infantry, four thousand women, children, and other followers. A regiment of three thousand men had at least three hundred waggons, and every waggon was full to repletion of women, children, and plundered goods ; when a company broke up from its quarters, it was considered an act of self-denial if it did not carry away with it thirty or more waggons. At the beginning of the war a regiment of north

leave wives and children, abandon their duties, and follow the army; all that will not follow the pursuits of their fathers and mothers, must follow the calf-skin which is spread over the drum, till they come to a battle or assault, where thousands lie on the field of battle, shot or cut to pieces; for a Landsknecht's life hangs by a hair, and his soul flutters on his cap or his sleeve. Besides, three kinds of herbs always grow with war; these are, sharp rule, fifty forbidden articles, and severe judgment with speedy sentence, which fits many a neck with a hempen collar.

"It is not enough that a soldier should be strong, straight, manly, tyrannical, bloody-minded, in his actions like a grim lion, and behave like a bully, as if he himself would catch and eat the devil alone, so that none of his comrades should partake of him; but these trigger-pullers wantonly bring themselves to destruction by their stupidity, and other good fellows with them. Another is a snorer, and a kicker, and stamps like a wild horse on the straw, and when he goes into battle, and the balls whistle about his head, he is a martyr and poor sinner, who would for very fear soil his hosen, and allow his weapon to fall from his hand. But when they sit at the tap, or in the cantinières' stalls, or in public-houses, then they have seen much and can do nothing but fight, then a fly on the wall irritates them, there is no peace with them, then they are ready to fight the enemy with great curses. Such 'bear-prickers' are generally found out; one seldom finds one who is not maimed in the hands or arms, or has a scar on the cheek, and they have never really all their lives long, faced the enemy. The captain may well keep clear of such fellows, for they are generally seditious mutineers. A wise soldier avoids quarrels and public-house brawls whenever he can, that he may have his skin whole and uninjured to bring in front of the enemy. To be wounded by the enemy is an honour, but he who injures himself wantonly

must expect scorn and derision, and is of no use to any army.
Such a fellow must remain all his life a paltry beggar; he
roves about the country, begs bread and sells it again, feeds
like a wolf, and when the rats and mice are drowned in the
countrywoman's milk, he maintains himself on the cheese
made from it, and must submit to the rough words of the
peasants, and herd with other poor beggars to the end of his
life.   Besides these, there are many who wish to be soldiers,
mothers' sons, beardless boys, like young calves, who know
nothing of suffering, who have sat beside the stove and
roasted apples, and lain in warm beds.   When they are
brought to a foreign country, and meet with all kind of
strange arrangements, food, drink, and other things, they
are like soft eggs that flow through the fingers, or like paper
when it lies in the water.   It is thus not only with foot
Landsknechte, but also with young nobles.   When they are
led to the field in devastated countries, where all is consumed
and laid waste, and they can no longer carry their well-filled
bread wallets and drinking-flasks on their necks, they first
pine away, hunger and thirst, then eat and drink unusual
things, from which result all kinds of maladies.   These
delicate vagabonds ought to remain at home, attend to the
tillage, or sit in the shop by the pepper-bags, and shift for
themselves, as their fathers and mothers have done, fill their
stomachs at eventide, and go to bed; thus they would not be
slain in war.   It is truly said that soldiers must be hardy
and enduring people, like unto steel and iron, and like the wild
beasts that can eat all kinds of food.   According to the
jocose saying, the Landsknechte must be able to digest the
points of their wheel-nails; nothing must come amiss to
them, even if necessity required that they should eat dogs'
or cats' flesh, and the flesh of horses from the meadow must be
like good venison to them, with herbs unseasoned by salt or
butter.   Hunger teaches to eat, if one has not seen bread for

three weeks.   Drink one may have gratis, for if one can get
no water from the brook, one can drink with the geese out of
the pond or the puddle.   One must sleep under a tree, or in
the field ; there is plenty of earth to lie on, and of sky for a
canopy ; such must often be the Landsknecht's sleeping-room,
and from such a bed no feathers will stick to his hair.
Hence arises the old quarrel between the fowls and geese and
the Landsknechte, because the former can always sleep in
feathers, whilst the latter must often lie in straw.   There is
another animal that clashes with the Landsknechte, that is
the cat ;   as the soldiers know well how to pilfer, they are
enemies to the cats, and friendly to the dogs.   According to
the old doggerel, a Landsknecht should always have with
him a beautiful woman, a dog, and a young boy, a long
spear, and a short sword ; he is free to seek any master who
will give him service.   A Landsknecht must make three
campaigns before he can become an honourable man.   After
the first campaign, he must return home wearing torn clothes ;
after the second, he should return with a scar on one cheek,
and be able to tell much of alarms, battles, skirmishes and
storming parties, and to show by his scars that he has got
the marks of a Landsknecht ; after the third, he should
return well appointed, on a fine charger, bringing with him
a purse full of gold, so that he may be able to distribute
whole dollars as he would booty-pence.

" It is truly said, that a soldier must have to eat and drink,
whether it is paid for by the sacristan or the priest ; for a
Landsknecht has neither house nor farm, cows nor calves, and
no one to bring him food ; therefore he must procure it himself wherever it is to be found, and buy without money
whether the peasants look sweet or sour.   Sometimes they
must suffer hunger and evil days, at others they have abundance, and indeed such superfluity, that they might clean
their shoes with wine or beer.   Then their dogs eat roast ;

the women and children get good appointments, they become stewards and cellarers of other people's property. When the householder is driven away with his wife and children, the fowls, geese, fat cows, oxen, pigs, and sheep have a bad time of it. The money is portioned out in their caps, velvet and silk stuffs and cloth are measured out by long spears; a cow is slaughtered for the sake of the hide; chests and trunks are broken open, and when all has been plundered and nothing more remains, the house is set on fire. That is the true Landsknecht's fire, when fifty villages and country towns are in flames. Then they go to other quarters and do the like again; this makes soldiers jolly, and is a desirable life for those who do not pay for it. This entices to the field many a mother's child, who does not return home, and forgets his friends. For the proverb says: 'The Landsknechte have crooked fingers and maimed hands for work, but for pilfering and plundering all the maimed hands become sound.' That has been so before our days, and will remain so truly after us. The longer the Landsknechte learn this handiwork the better they do it, and become circumspect, like the three maidens who had four cradles made, the fourth as a provision in case one of them had two children. Wherever the soldiers come, they bring with them the keys of all the rooms, their axes and hatchets, and if there are not enough stalls in a place for their horses, it does not signify, they stall them in the churches, monasteries, chapels, and best rooms. If there is no dry wood for fire, it matters not, they burn chairs, benches, ploughs, and everything that is in the house; if they want green wood, no one need go far, they cut down the fruit trees in the nearest orchard; for they say, whilst we live here we keep house, to-morrow we go off again into the country, therefore, Mr. Host, be comforted; you have a few guests you would gladly be free from, therefore give freely and write it on the slate. When the house is burnt the account is burnt also. This is the Landsknechts' custom ; to make a reckoning and ride off, and pay when we return.

" The French, Italians, and Walloons are as adverse to the Germans as to dogs, but the Spaniards are friendly to them ; they however have an unheard-of weakness for women, and are disposed to profligate and godless conduct. Altogether, the Germans are but little thought of by these nations, who call them nothing but drunkards, proud featherpates, mighty braggadocios, blasphemers of God, '*Hans Muffmaff*' with the beggar's wallet, who would willingly play the great man. And if one comes to look at it, it is not far from the truth. For there is a new custom amongst the North Germans when they go to war, or collect together under a master, they spend all their goods and possessions on ostentatious splendour, as if they were going to a bride, or riding to a banquet. Thus the Germans who were formerly called the Blackriders, come riding along with silver daggers, seven pound in weight, in velvet clothes, and shining boots, with short holster pistols inlaid with ivory, and large wide padded sleeves ; they are ashamed of carrying cuirass or armour, or indeed a spear, or any other murderous weapons, as in the olden time. Hence it arises, that they never hold together. Then when Hans Spaniard comes with his tilting spear and proof armour, these chaw-bacons, with their short holster pistols, must run away or yield their money and blood.

" Further, it is a misfortune to the Germans, that they take to imitating, like monkeys and fools. As soon as they come amongst other soldiers, they must have Spanish or other outlandish clothes. If they could babble foreign languages a little, they would associate themselves with Spaniards and Italians. The Germans would like to mingle with foreign nations, and take pleasure in outlandish dress and manners, ' but one should not place the vermin in the fur, it comes there without.' It is clear that foreign people have become our neighbours, and it is to be feared that they will in a few years come nearer.   The frontier lords, who still rest in tranquillity, fight against the wind, speak quite wisely thereupon, comfort themselves, and have in talk, all their cities and villages full of soldiers to defend the country and withstand all enemies.   But I fear that they prefer sitting by the stove in winter, and in the shade in summer, playing draughts, or striking the guitar, or dancing with *Jungfrau* Greta, to providing their houses with good weapons or armour.

"On this account, and because all foreign nations cry out all over Germany, '*Cruci, cruci, mordio, mordio !*' and grind their teeth like ravenous wolves, and desire and hope to bathe in German blood, one must earnestly pray God not to withdraw his hand, but to take under his protection this little vessel, tossed on the wild sea, cover it with his wings, and preserve it from all storms ; for we see how the Roman Empire has declined from day to day, and still continues to do so.   These sufferings come from nothing but the proceedings of the ecclesiastics, whereof the whole world complains.   If one finds one right-minded preacher there are ten to the contrary ; every tradesman praises his own wares, everyone will feed his own flock, and lead them the right way to heaven, yet no one knows, save the devil and our Lord, where the false shepherds go to themselves.   Every one abuses, slanders, and condemns the other ; when they stand in the pulpit, the devil is their preceptor, who helps them to manage so that one kingdom is at variance with another, one country rebellious against the other ; neighbour can no longer agree with neighbour ; nay one finds even at one table four or five different faiths, one will worship on this mountain and another on yonder.   May the eternal Almighty God strengthen the hearts of the dear North Germans, give them an upright spirit, and raise them up again, that they may one day rise from the ashes, and renew their ancient repute, and their good name.   God help the righteous."

Thus writes an honourable officer before the year 1600.

CHAPTER II.

THE THIRTY YEARS' WAR.—LIFE AND MANNERS OF THE SOLDIERS.

ALMOST all the people of Europe sent their least promising sons to the long war. Not only did foreign mercenaries follow the recruiting drum like crows to the battle-field, but the whole of Christian Europe was drawn into the struggle; foreigners trampled on the German soil in companies and regiments : English and Scotch, Danes, Fins and Swedes, besides the Netherlanders (whom the people considered as countrymen), fought on the side of the Protestants. Even the Laplanders came with their reindeer to the German coast; in the winter months of 1630 they brought upon their sledges over the ice, furs for the Swedish army. But still more chequered did the Imperial army look. The Roumaun Walloons, Irish adventurers, Spaniards, Italians, and almost every Sclavonic race broke into the country; worst of all the light cavalry,—Cossacks, Polish auxiliaries (who were for the most part slaughtered by the country people in 1620), Stradiots (among them undoubtedly some Mahomedans), and, most hated of all, the Croats. The position of the Emperor in the beginning of the war was striking in this respect, that he had almost nothing but Sclavonic and Roumaun soldiers, and only Roumaun money to oppose the Germans. By them the national rising was crushed, and it is probable that half the troops of the League consisted of foreigners.

Each army was a sample of the different nationalities; in each there was an intermixture of many languages; and the hatred of nations seldom ceased even when fighting under the same colours. It was especially necessary in the camp to arrange the regiments according to the good understanding between them. Germans and Italians were always kept apart.

The Field-marshal or Quartermaster-general chose the site of the camp; if possible by running water, and in a position which was favourable for defence. First of all was measured out the place for the General and his staff; large ornamented tents were raised on the ground thus set apart, which was divided from the rest of the camp by barriers and by planting spears, frequently even by fortifications. An open place was left close to it for the main-guard; if the army remained long encamped, a gallows was erected there as a warning. The position of each regiment and company was marked out with branches; the troops were marched in, the ranks were opened, the colours of each regiment were planted in the ground in rows side by side; behind in parallel lines lay the encampment of the company, always fifty men in a row; near the colours was the Ensign, in the middle the Lieutenant, at the rear the Captain, and behind all the tents of the superior officers and officials; the surgeon next to the Ensign, and the chaplain near the Captain. The officers lived in tents, often in conical forms fastened with cords to the ground. The soldiers built themselves little huts of planks and straw. The pikemen planted their pikes in the ground near the huts; the pikes, short spears, halberds, partisans, and standards showed from afar the rank and weapons of the inhabitant of the tent. Two or four soldiers were generally housed in a hut, with their wives, children, and dogs. Thus they lay encamped, company by company, regiment by regiment, in great squares or circles, the whole camp surrounded by a large space which served as an alarm post.   Before the Thirty years' war it was customary to set up a barricade round the camp; then the train or baggage-waggons were pushed together in double or more rows, and bound by chains or fastenings to the great square or circle, leaving free the necessary openings.   Then also the cavalry had their camp next the inner side of the waggons; the necessary partitions were erected for the horses near the huts and tents of the horsemen.   This custom had become obsolete, and it was only occasionally that the waggons surrounded the camp, but it was protected by trenches, mounds, and field-pieces.   At the openings sentinels were posted, outside the camp, troops of horse and a chain of outposts of musketeers or arquebusiers were stationed. Each Ensign planted the colours before his tent; near it was the drummer of the company, and a musketeer kept watch with a burning match in his hand and his musket supported horizontally on its rest.

In such a camp it was that the wild soldiery dwelt in unbridled licence, insupportable to the neighbourhood even in a friendly country.   The provinces, cities, and villages were obliged to supply wood, straw, fodder, and provisions, the waggons rolled along every road, and droves of fat cattle were collected.   The neighbouring villages quickly disappeared; as all the wood-work and thatching was torn away by the soldiers and employed in building their huts, only the shattered clay walls remained.   The soldiers and their boys roved about the neighbourhood, plundering and stealing, and the cantineers drove about with their carts.   In the camp the soldiers congregated in front of their huts; meanwhile the women cooked, washed, mended the clothes and squabbled together; there was constant tumult and uproar and bloody crimes, fighting with bare weapons, and combats between the different services or nations.   Every morning

the crier and the trumpet called to prayer, even among the
Imperialists; early on the Sunday the regimental chaplain
performed service in the camp, then the soldiers and their
households seated themselves devoutly on the ground, and it
was forbidden for any one during service to loiter and drink
in the canteens. It is known how much Gustavus Adolphus
inculcated pious habits and prayers; after his arrival in
Pomerania he caused prayers to be read twice a day in his
camp, but even in his army, it was necessary in the articles of
war to admonish the chaplains against drunkenness.

In the open space in front of the main guard was the
gambling ground, covered with cloaks and set with tables,
round which all the gamesters crowded. There the card-
playing of the old Landsknechte gave place to the quicker
games of the dice. The use of dice was frequently forbidden
in the camp, and stopped by the captain of the guard and the
provost; then the gamblers assembled privately behind the
fence, and played away their ammunition, bread, horses,
weapons, and clothes, so that it was found necessary to place
them under the supervision of the main-guard. Three
square dice were rolled on each cloak or table, called in camp
language "Schelmbeine;" each set had its croupier; to him
belonged the cloak, table, and dice; he had the office of judge
in cases of dispute, and his share of the winnings, but also
frequently of blows. There was much cheating and cogging;
many dice had two fives or sixes, many, two aces or deuces,
others were filled with quicksilver and lead, split hair, sponge,
chaff, and charcoal; there were dice made of stags-horn,
heavy below and light above, "Niederländer,"* which must be
slid along, and "Oberländer,"† which must be thrown "from
Bavarian Heights" for them to fall right; often the noise-
less work was interrupted by curses, quarrels, and flashing

* Because they slide and skate.
† A mocking allusion to the mountainous country of Bavaria.

rapiers. Lurking tradespeople, frequently Jews, slipped in, ready to value and buy up the rings, chains, and booty staked.

Behind the tents of the upper officers and the regimental provost, separated from them by a wide street, stood the shops of the cantineers in parallel cross rows. Cantineers, butchers, and common victuallers formed an important community. The price of their goods was decided by the provost, who received a perquisite in money or in kind ; for example, he received a tongue for every beast that was killed. On every cask which was to be tapped, he wrote the retail price with chalk. By these compacts, and the favour of the powerful, which was to be bought by time-serving, the purveyors of the army maintained a proportionably secure position, and insured themselves the payment, though irregular, of their long tallies, which were scored equally for the officers and soldiers. In good times traders came from afar to the camp with expensive stuffs, jewels, gold and silver workmanship, and delicacies. In the beginning of the war especially, the officers set a bad example to the army by their extreme luxury ; every captain would have a French cook, and consumed the dearest wine in great quantities.

The military signals of the camp were, for the infantry the beat of the drum, for the cavalry the trumpet : the drum was very large, the drummer often a half-grown boy, sometimes the fool of the company. In the beginning of the war, the German army had in many cases a uniform beat. Every command from the General to the camp, had to be proclaimed by a herald riding through it with a trumpeter. On such occasions the herald wore over his dress a "tabard" of coloured silk, embroidered before and behind with the arms of the sovereign. This proclamation, which announced to the camp in the evening the work of the following day, was very destructive to secret and rapid operations ; it was also very injurious to discipline, for it announced to the loiterers and robbers of the camp, the night when they might steal out for booty.

When times were prosperous, a battle won, a rich city plundered, or an opulent district laid under contribution, everything was plentiful, food and drink cheap; and it once happened, in the last year of the war, that in the Bavarian camp a cow was bought for a pipe of tobacco. The Croats of the Imperial army in Pomerania, in the winter of 1630 and 1631, had their girdles overlaid with gold, and whole plates of gold and silver on the breast. Paul Stockmann, a pastor at Lützen, relates, that in the Imperial army, before the battle of Lützen, one horseman had his horse decorated with a quantity of golden stars, and another with three hundred silver moons ; and the soldiers' women wore the most beautiful church dresses and mass vestments, and that some Stradiots rode in plundered priests' dresses, to the great mirth of their comrades. In these times also carousers drank to one another in costly wine from the chalices, and caused long chains to be made of the plundered gold, from which, according to the old knightly custom, they severed links to pay for a carousal. But the longer the war lasted the more rare were these golden times. The devastation of the country revenged itself fearfully on the army itself; the pale spectre of hunger, the forerunner of pestilence, glided through the lines of the camp, and raised its bony hand against every straw hut. Then supplies from the surrounding districts ceasèd, the price of provisions was raised so as to be almost unattainable ; a loaf of bread, for example, in the Swedish army in 1640, at Gotha, cost a ducat. Hollow-eyed pale faces, sick and dying men, were to be seen in every row of huts ; the vicinity of the camp was pestilential from the decaying bodies of dead animals. All around was a wilderness of uncultivated fields, blackened with the ruins of villages, and the camp itself a dismal city of death.

A broad stream of superstition had flowed through the souls of the people from ancient times up to the present day, and the soldier's life of the Thirty years' war revived an abundance of peculiar superstitions, of which a portion continues even now; it is worth while to dwell a little upon these characteristic phenomena.

The belief that it is possible to make the body proof by magic against the weapons of the enemy, and on the other hand to make your own arms fatal to them, is older than the historical life of the German people. In the earliest times, however, something gloomy was attached to this art; it might easily become pregnant with fatality, even to its votaries. The invulnerability was not unconditional, and succumbed to the stronger counter-magic of the offensive weapon : Achilles had a heel which was not invulnerable; no weapon could wound the Norse god Baldur, but the waving of a branch of misletoe by a blind man killed him; Siegfried had a weak spot between the shoulders, the same which the soldiers of the Thirty years' war considered also as vulnerable. Among the numerous Norse traditions are many accounts of charmed weapons : the sword, the noblest weapon of heroes, was considered as a living being, also as a slaying serpent or a destroying fire; when it was shattered, it was spoken of by the Norse poets as dying. It was unnecessary to charm swords forged by dwarfs, as there was a destroying magic concealed in them; thus the sword of Hagens, the father of Hilda, was death to any man when it was drawn from the sheath, magic Runic character being scratched on the hilt and blade of it.

The introduction of fire-arms gave a new aspect and a wider scope to this superstition; the flash and report of the weapon, and the distant striking of the ball, imposed the more on the fancy, the less the imperfect weapon was certain of hitting : the course of the deadly shot was con-

sidered malicious and incalculable.   Undoubtedly the literature of the Reformation seldom touched upon this kind of
magic; it first made itself heard in the middle of the
century, when it served to portray the condition of the
people.   But in armies, the belief in magic was general and
widely spread, travelling scholars and gipsies were the most
zealous vendors of its secrets, one generation of Landsknechte
imparted it to the next: in Italy and in the armies of
Charles V., Italian and German superstitions were mixed,
and in the time of Fronsperg and Schärtlin almost every
detail of the art of rendering invulnerable is to be found.
Luther, in 1527, inveighs against the superstition of the
soldiery: "One commits himself to St. George, another to
St. Christopher, some to one saint, some to another; some
can charm iron and gun-flints, others can bless the horse and
his rider, and some carry the gospel of St. John,* or somewhat else with them, in which they confide."   He himself
had known a Landsknecht, who, though made invulnerable
by the devil, was killed, and announced beforehand the day
and place of his death.   Bernhard von Milo, Seneschal at
Wittenberg, sent to Luther for his opinion on a written
charm for wounds; it was a long roll of paper written in
wonderful characters.

When the Augsburg gunner, Samuel Zimmermann the
elder, wrote the experiences of his life up to 1591, in a folio
volume, under the title of 'Charms against all Stabs,
Strokes, and Shots, full of great secrets,' he mentions
only the defensive incantations, which he did not consider as
the works of Belial; but it is apparent from his manuscript
that many devilish arts were known to him, which he intended

* It was especially John the Baptist, who, according to the third
chapter of St. Luke, was the merciful protector of soldiers; but at the
beginning of the Reformation the difference between the Baptist and
Evangelist was little understood by Landsknechte, nor indeed by all
ecclesiastics.

to conceal.   Another well-known Zimmermann, who was
hardened, received a fearful blow from a dagger ; there was
no wound to be seen, but he died shortly after from the
internal effect of the blow.   In 1558 there was an invulnerable soldier in the regiment of Count Lichtenstein, who,
after every skirmish, shook the enemy's balls off his dress and
his bare body ; he often showed them, and the holes burnt
through his clothes ; he was at last slain by some foreign
peasants.

   When the Italians and Spaniards entered the Netherlands
in 1568, they carried along with them, with little success,
whole packets and books full of magic formulas of conjurations
and charms.   The French found talismans and magic cards
fastened round the necks of the prisoners and the dead, of the
Brandenburg troops who had been led by Burgrave Fabian
von Dohna, in 1587, as auxiliaries to the Huguenots.   When
the Jesuit George Scheerer preached at the Court Chapel at
Vienna in 1594, before the Archduke Matthias and his
Generals, he found it necessary to exhort them earnestly
against the use of superstitious charms for cuts, stabs, shots,
and burns.

   It is therefore unjust in later writers to state, that the art
of rendering invulnerable was introduced at Passau by a
travelling scholar in the seventeenth century, as Grimmelshausen informs us, or as others will have it, that it was
brought into the German army by Kaspar Reithardt von
Hersbruck, the executioner ; for when Archduke Leopold, the
Bishop of Passau, raised the reckless and ill-disciplined bands
which spread terror through Alsace and Bohemia by their
barbarities, his soldiers only adopted the old traditions which
were rooted in German heathenism, and had lingered on
through the whole of the middle ages ; nay, even the name,
" *Passau art*," which has been customary since then, may
rest on a misunderstanding of the people, for in the sixteenth

century all who bore charms about them to render them invulnerable were called by the learned soldier, "*Pessulanten*," or "*Charakteristiker*," and whoever understood the art of dissolving a charm was a "*Solvent*." It is possible that the first of these popular designations was changed into "*Passauer*."

Even in the first year of the Thirty years' war, the art of rendering invulnerable was eagerly discussed. A good account of it can be found in 'The true narrative of the siege and capture by storm of the city of Pilsen in Bohemia, 1619.' The passage according to our dialect is as follows :

"An adventurer under Mansfeld, called Hans Fabel, once took a tumbler of beer up to the city trenches and drank it to the besieged. They saluted him with powder and shot; but he drank up his tumbler of beer, thanked them, entered the trenches and took five balls from his bosom. This '*Pilmis-kind*,' * although he was so invulnerable, was taken very sick, and died before the capture of the town. This magical art, 'Passau art,' has become quite common ; one would sooner have shot at a rock than at such a charmed fellow. I believe that the devil hides in their skin. One good fellow indeed often charms another, even when the person so charmed does not know it, and still less desires it. A small boy from fourteen to fifteen years of age was shot in the arm when he was beating the drum, but the ball rebounded from the arm to the left breast, and did not penetrate ; this was seen by many. But those who use this magic come to a bad end ; I have known many such lose their lives in a terrible way, for one delusion struggles against another. Their devilish sorcery is expressly against the first and other commandments of God. Assiduous prayer and faith in God gives other means of support. If any one in presence of the enemy perishes not, it is

* Bilwiz-kind, same as child of the devil. Bilwiz is an old name for magician or hobgoblin.

God's will. If he is struck, the angels take him to heaven,
but those who are charmed are taken by Black Kaspar."[*]

Numerous were the means employed by men to make themselves and others invulnerable. Even this superstition was
governed tyrannically by fashion. Of very ancient date are
the charmed shirts, and the Victory and St. George's shirts;
they were prepared in different ways for the Landsknechte.
On Christmas night, according to ancient tradition, certain
virgins used to spin linen thread in the name of the devil,
weave and stitch it; on the breast two heads were embroidered, the one on the right side with a beard, and the left
like that of king Beelzebub, with a crown, dark reminiscences
of the holy heads of Donar and Wuotan. According to later
custom the charmed shirt must be spun by maidens under the
age of seven; it was to be sewed with particular cross stitches,
laid secretly on the altar till three masses had been read over
it. On the day of battle such a charmed shirt was worn under
the dress, and if the wearer received a wound, it was owing
to other thread having been mixed with that which was
charmed.

Superstition gladly availed itself of the miraculous power
of the Christian Church, even when in opposition to law.
The gospel of St. John was written elaborately on thin paper
and placed secretly under the altar cover in a Roman Catholic
church, and left there till the priest had thrice read the mass
over it; then it was placed in a quill or the shell of a hazel nut,
and the opening was cemented with Spanish lac or wax, or
this capsule was framed in gold or silver and hung round the
neck. Others received the host at the Lord's supper, accompanying it with a silent invocation to the devil; taking the

* One is tempted to change this passage to an old heathenish form:
"Whoever falls by honourable weapons on the field of battle, will be
carried to Walhalla by the virgins of battle; those who contend with the
sorcery of the gods of death, Helja takes to herself." We find the name
of Black Kaspar for the devil even in the sixteenth century.

wafer out of their mouths again, they separated the skin from the flesh in some part of the body, placed the wafer there, and let the wound heal over it. The most reckless gave themselves up entirely to the devil; such people could not only make other men invulnerable, but even eatables, such as butter, cheese, and fruit, so that the sharpest knife could not penetrate them.*

There was a change of form and name in the written parchments also which contained charms.

" *Pope Leo's blessing* " originated in the early Lands-knecht times ; it contained good Christian words and pro-mises. Besides this there was the " *Blessing of the Knight of Flanders*," so called because a knight who had once worn it could not be beheaded ; it was written in strange characters and types interspersed with signs of the cross. Then there was " *The benediction*," or charm in time of need, which in a moment of danger arrested the sword or gun of the enemy.†

Similar were the " *Passau charms* " of the seventeenth century, written on post paper, virgin parchment, or the host, with a peculiar pen in bat's blood ; the superstition was in strange characters, wizard feet, circles, crosses, and the letters of foreign languages ; according to Grimmelshausen ‡ the rhyme runs thus : Devil help me, body and soul give I thee. When fastened under the left arm they expelled the shot and closed the guns of the enemy. Sometimes even the charms were eaten. But opinions concerning their efficacy were fluctuating. Some thought them safeguards only for four-and-twenty hours ; but according to others their magic did not begin to work till

---

* Königl. schwedischer Victorischlüssel a. a. O.

† Zimmermann, Goth. Msc. a. a. O.

‡ Grimmelshausen speaks of the art of rendering invulnerable as credible, but as a thing long known. He was more interested in the superstition which was prevalent in 1660—the art of becoming invisible and of witch-craft. At the end of the century magic rods were common, and familiar spirits powerful. Wunderbares Vogelnest. ii. Th. Satyrischer Pilgram ii. Th.

after the first four-and-twenty hours, and whoever was shot before that time belonged to the devil.   Other charms were also used for protection, everything odious and dismal was collected together, and what had been fearful in the ancient mythology continued to retain its old power.   A piece of the cord or chain by which a man had been hung, or the beard of a goat, the eyes of a wolf, the head of a bat and the like, worn round the body in a purse of black cat's skin, rendered a person invulnerable.   Hair balls (a mass of hair from the stomach of the chamois), and the caul in which children are born, gave invulnerability ; he who had never eaten kidneys was secure from shot or pestilence, and it was believed at Augsburg, that a famous knight and experienced General, Sebastian Schärtlin, had thus protected himself before the enemy.

Old magic herbs, as endive, verbena, St. John's wort, chickweed, vervain, mallow, and garlick were used as charms, and the most powerful of all, the deadly nightshade.   It was necessary to dig them up with the best new sharpened steel, and never to touch them with the bare hand, least of all with the left, and they were carried like an *Agnus Dei*.   They were circular, and only found on the battle-fields of great battles, and were, as Zimmermann says, sacred for the sake of the dead.   Besides these there was a fire-coloured flower which Cabalists called " Efdamanila ;" it not only protected the wearer from shot, stabs, and fire, but when it was hung over the wall in a besieged town near the enemy's cannon, they were spell-bound for a whole month.

Amulet medals also were early in use : in 1555, at the battle of Marienburg, between the Princes of Orange and Nevers, a little child was struck on the neck by a shot, a silver medal was doubled up, and the child remained unhurt ; this great effect was then ascribed to an amulet parchment which the child wore round his neck near the medal.   But

about the same time the " Sideristen," who were experienced
in astronomical science, poured out heavenly influence in invulnerable medals of silver and fine gold, which were worn
round the neck. Thurneisser spread also these kinds of
amulets in Northern Germany. An accidental circumstance
brought the Mansfeld St. George's thaler into repute in the
Thirty years' war, especially those of 1611 and 1613, bearing
the inscription, " With God is counsel and action."

Not only the common soldiers, but many great commanders
also had the repute of being invulnerable : not Pappenheim,
indeed, who was wounded in almost every action, but Holk,
who was supposed at last to have been carried away to hell
by the devil in person ; Tilly, for whom, after the battle of
Breitenfeld, the affrighted surgeon found he had only bruises
to dress ; Wallenstein and his kinsman Terzka ; even the
sword of Gustavus Adolphus was considered to be enchanted.
Ahaz Willenger also, leader after the death of Fardinger, of
the revolted Austrian peasants, was rendered so hard that a
cannon-ball at seven paces rebounded from his skin without
penetrating it ; he was at last killed by an officer of Pappenheim. All the Princes of the house of Savoy were considered
invulnerable, even after the Thirty years' war. Field-Marshal Schauenburg tried it with Prince Thomas when he besieged him in an Italian fortress ; the bullets of the best
marksmen missed their aim. No one knew whether the
members of that noble house had especial grace, because they
were of the race of the royal prophet David, or whether the
art of rendering themselves invulnerable was hereditary.

There were hardly any who did not believe in the mystic
art. The renowned French General Messire Jacques de
Puysegur, in the French civil war in 1622, was obliged to
compass the death of an opponent, *qui avait un caractère*, by
blows of a strong pole on his neck, because he had no weapon
that could kill him ; he recounts this circumstance to his King.

At the blockade of Magdeburg in 1629, the complaint against these practices became so general, that the parties engaged in this war entered into negotiations concerning it. Gustavus Adolphus, in his first article of war, earnestly forbade idolatry, witchcraft, or the charming of weapons as sins against God.

But the dark powers which the soldier invoked to his aid were treacherous. They did not protect against everything ; it was, to say the least, very unsatisfactory that they did not preserve from the hand of the executioner : Zimmermann relates many cases in which the far-reaching hopes of an invulnerable person and his adherents were disappointed at the place of execution. Certain portions of the body, the neck, and the back between the shoulders, the armpits, and the under part of the knee, were considered not hard or invulnerable. The body also was only charmed against the common metals of lead or iron. The simplest weapons of peasants, a wooden club, bullets of more precious metals, and sometimes inherited silver could kill the invulnerable. Thus an Austrian governor of Greifswald, on whom the Swedes had fired more than twenty balls, could only be shot by the inherited silver button that a soldier carried in his pocket. Thus too a witch in Schleswig was changed into a were-wolf, and shot by inherited silver.* The magic also could be broken by other mixtures, by cast balls, and by magically consecrated weapons. Rye bread which had been leavened and baked on Easter night, was rubbed crosswise over the edge of the steel, and signs were indelibly impressed on blades and barrels : it was known how to cast balls which killed without injuring the skin, others which must draw blood, and some which broke every invulnerability ; these were prepared by mixtures of pulverized grains of corn, antimony, and thunder-stones, and cooled in poison. But these arts were considered supernatural and dangerous. Besides these they

---

* Müllenhof, Sagen. S. 281.—Femme, Pommesache Sagen. Nr. 244.

tried "natural" devices which might be resorted to with advantage, even by an honourable soldier. They imagined they could prepare gunpowder with a mixture of pounded dogs' bones, which would make no report. Powder was also prepared by which the person shot was only stunned for hours; other powder that did not explode, even when glowing steel was inserted. By a mixture of borax and quicksilver they produced a mining powder by which the enemy's pieces were blown up, in case there was not time to spike them. They sought after the secret of giving a man double strength without magic.

There was a peculiar and also very old kind of magic, which spell-bound the enemy by mystic sentences, which were recited in moments of danger. The adept could fix whole troops of horsemen and infantry: in the same way, by other sentences, they could dissolve the spell. There was still another kind of sorcery; horsemen were made to appear on the field of battle, that is to say, when support was required in imminent danger, deceptive appearance was produced, as if soldiers were approaching in the distance. Both these conjurations are relics of the heathen occult sciences, the echoes of which may still be discovered in manifold tales and traditions, even up to the present day.

The gloomy provost was the man in the regiment who was held in the most awe; he was naturally considered as pre-eminently an adept. In 1618, it was supposed that the executioner of Pilsen could, with the help of an assistant, fire daily three fatal balls against the camp of Mansfeld; after the capture of the city, he was hanged on a special gallows. The provost of the Hatzfeld army of 1636 was still more versed in sorcery: he was killed by the Swedes with an axe, because he was magically hardened. It was very much in the interest of these authorities to keep up amongst the revengeful soldiery the belief in their invulnerability.

We may add to these delusions, the endeavours of individuals to read from the course of the stars the events and issue of the war, and their own fate. Prognostics accumulated, the terrors of the approaching year were unweariedly prophesied from constellations, shooting-stars, comets, and other atmospheric phenomena; the casting of horoscopes was general. Some individuals also possessed second sight, they foresaw to whom the approaching future would be fatal. When in 1636 the Imperial Saxon army was lying before Magdeburg, there was an invalid mathematician in the camp who foretold to his friends that the 26th of June would be fatal to him. He was lying in a closed tent when a lieutenant rode up, and unloosening the tent cords, forced himself in and begged the sick man to draw his nativity. After refusing a long time, the invalid prophesied to him that he would be hanged that very hour. The lieutenant, very indignant that any one should dare to say such a thing to a cavalier, drew his sword and killed the sick man. There immediately arose a great tumult, the murderer then threw himself upon his horse and tried to escape; it happened however, accidentally, that the Elector of Saxony was riding through the camp with General Hatzfeld and a great retinue. The Elector exclaimed, that there would be bad discipline in the Imperial camp if the life of a sick man in bed could not be secured from murderers. The lieutenant was hanged.

Whoever was considered the possessor of such secrets was feared by his comrades, but not esteemed. "For if they were not cowardly, dastardly ninnies, they would not use such charms." Certain officers in the sixteenth century caused every prisoner to be hanged upon whom were found jagged or iron-coated balls, "which were consecrated for the sake of a soul." In the Thirty years' war, a coward begged of his comrade a Passau parchment, who wrote on a strip of paper three times: "Defend yourself, scoundrel," folded it up and made the dastard sew it in his clothes. From that day every one imagined that he was invulnerable, and he went about on all occasions amongst the enemies' weapons, as hard as horn, like a *Siegfried*, and always came out unwounded.

But the soldier had not only to win the favour of the Fates, but still more the approbation of his comrades. Whoever carefully examines this period, without ceasing to view with horror the numerous and refined atrocities which were prac- tised, will at the same time perceive that this scene of bar- barity was occasionally brightened by milder virtues, and sometimes healthy integrity comes to light. A peculiar code of soldier's honour was soon formed, which preserved a kind of morality, though a lax one. We have but few records of the good humour which arose from consciousness of having the mastery over citizen and peasant. But the proverbial modes of speech often bear sufficiently the impress of the same disposition which is idealized in Schiller's "*Reiterlied.*" "The sharp sabre is my field, and booty making is my plough." "The earth is my bed, heaven my canopy, my cloak is my house, and wine my eternal life."[*] "As soon as a soldier is born, three peasants are selected for him; the first provides for him, the second finds him a beautiful wife, and the third goes to hell for him."[†]

We have reason to suppose that sensuality was in general unbridled and shameless; the old German vice, drunkenness, prevailed as much amongst the officers as soldiers. The smoking and chewing tobacco, or as it was then called, "tobacco drinking"—"eating and snuffing," spread rapidly through all the armies, and the guard-room was a disagreeable abode for those who did not smoke. This custom, which at the beginning of the war was introduced into the army by

---

[*] Philander von Sittewald, "Gesicht von Soldatenleben."

[†] Grimmelshausen, "Seltsamer Springensfeld."

the Dutch and English auxiliaries, was at the end of it so common, that a pipe was to be found in every peasant's house, and nine out of ten of the day labourers and apprentices smoked during their work.

The German language also was jargonized in the army; it soon became the fashion among the soldiers to intermix Italian and French words, and the language was enriched even by Hungarian, Croat, and Czech : they have left us besides their "*karbatsche*" and similar words, and also sonorous curses. Not only was their discourse garnished with these strong expressions, but gipsy cant became the common property of the army. It did not indeed begin in the great war, for long before, the Landsknechte, as " Gartbrüder " and members of the beggars' guild, had learned their arts and language. But now the camp language was not only a convenient help to secret intercourse with the bad rabble who followed the army, with guild robbers, Jewish dealers and gipsies, but it also gave a certain degree of consideration round the camp fire to be able to bandy mysterious words. Some expressions from the camp language passed among the people, others were carried by runaway students into the drinking-rooms of the universities.*

The daily quarrels gave rise amongst the common soldiers also to the cartel, or duels regulated by many points of honour. Duels were strictly forbidden ; Gustavus Adolphus punished them with death even among the higher officers ; but no law could suppress them. The duellists fought alone, or with two or three seconds, or an umpire was selected : before the combat the seconds vowed to one another and gave their hands upon it, not to help the combatants, either before, in, or after the encounter, nor to revenge them ; the duellists shook hands and exchanged forgiveness beforehand, in case of the death of either. They fought on horseback or on foot,

* *Dionys Klein. Kriegsinstitution*, 1598, 8. *S*. 288.

with carbines, pistols, or swords; in the fight, a throw in wrestling or unhorsing was sufficient; stabbing was considered un-German, above all a thrust in the back was of doubtful propriety.*

As it was so usual to change parties, a corporation feeling was formed amongst the soldiers which also embraced the enemy. The armies had a tolerably accurate knowledge of each other, and not only the character of the upper officers, but of old soldiers was known; any day an old comrade might be seen in the enemy's ranks, or installed as a tent companion to a former adversary. Indeed, quarter was often proffered; but any one who had fought against the customs of war, or was suspected of using devilish acts, was to be killed even if he sued for pardon. Cartels were concluded between the courteous conquerors and the vanquished, the conquerors promised to protect, and the prisoners not to escape; the weapons, scarfs, and plumes were taken away from the vanquished; all that he concealed in his clothes belonged to the conqueror, but he who got Dutch quarter, kept what was enclosed in his girdle; a courteous prisoner himself presented what he had in his pockets. If a desperate man did not stand by his conditions of quarter, he was killed, if he did not rapidly escape. During the transport they were coupled by the arm, and the string taken from their hose, so that they were obliged to hold their small-clothes with the hand that was free. The prisoners could be ransomed, and this ransom was fixed by tariff in each army. Towards the conclusion of the war, when soldiers became scarce, the common prisoners were summarily placed in the regiments without giving them a choice. Such soldiers were naturally not to be depended on; they gladly took the first opportunity to desert to their former colours, where they had left their women, children, booty, and arrears of pay. Distinguished prisoners were

* Simplicissimus i. 3, 9, and Philander von Sittenwald, 'Soldatenleben.'

sometimes bought from the common soldiers by the colonels of their regiments ; they were treated with great consideration in the enemy's quarters, and almost every one found there either an acquaintance or a relative.

Booty was the uncertain gain for which the soldier staked his life, and the hope of it kept him steadfast in the most desperate situations. The pay was moderate, the payment insecure ; plunder promised them wine, play, a smart mistress, a gold-laced dress with a plume of feathers, one or two horses, and the prospect of greater importance in the company and of advancement. Vanity, love of pleasure, and ambition, developed this longing to a dangerous extent in the army.

The success of a battle was more than once defeated, by the soldiers too soon abandoning themselves to plundering. It often happened that individuals made great booty, but it was almost always dissipated in wild revelry ; according to the soldier's adage : " What is won with the drum will be lost with the fifes." The fame of such lucky hits spread through all armies. Sometimes these great gains brought evil results on the fortunate finders.* A common soldier of Tilly's army had won great booty at the capture of Magdeburg, it was said to be thirty thousand ducats, and was immediately lost in gambling. Tilly caused him to be hanged after thus accosting him : " With this money you might have lived all your life like a gentleman, but as you have not understood how to make use of it, I cannot see of what use you can be to my Emperor." At the end of the war a man in Königs- mark's troop had obtained a similar sum in the suburbs of Prague, and played it away at one sitting. Königsmark wished in like manner to despatch him, but the soldier saved himself by this undaunted answer : " It would be unfair for your Excellence to hang me on account of this loss, as I have hopes of acquiring still greater booty in the city itself." This

* Grimmelshausen, ' Springenfeld.'

answer was considered a good omen.   In the Bavarian army
a soldier in the Holtz infantry was famed for a similar lucky
hit.   He had been for a long time musketeer, but shortly before the peace had sunk to be a pikeman, and was ill-clad ; his
shirt hung behind and before out of his hose.   This fellow
had obtained at the taking of Herbsthausen a barrel filled with
French doubloons, so large that he could hardly carry it off.
He thereupon absconded secretly from the regiment, dressed
himself up like a prince, bought a coach and six beautiful
horses, kept many coachmen, lackeys, pages, and *valets de
chambre* in fine liveries, and called himself with dull humour
Colonel Lumpus.*   Then he travelled to Munich, and lived
in an inn there splendidly.   General Holtz accidentally put
up at the same inn, heard much from the landlord of the
opulence and qualities of Colonel Lumpus, and could not remember ever having heard this name among the cavaliers of
the Roman empire, or among the soldiers of fortune.   He
therefore commissioned the landlord to invite the stranger to
supper.   Colonel Lumpus accepted the invitation, and caused
to be served up at dessert, in a dish, five hundred new French
pistoles and a chain worth a hundred ducats, and said at the
same time to the General : " May your Excellence be content
with this entertainment and think thereby favourably of me."
The General made some resistance, but the liberal colonel
pressed it upon him with these words : " The time will soon
come when your Excellence will acknowledge that I am wise
in making this gift.   The donation is not ill applied, for I
hope then to receive from your Excellence a favour which will
not cost a penny."   On this, Holtz, according to the custom
of that time, accepted the chain and money with courteous
promises to repay it under such circumstances.   The General
departed, and the fictitious colonel lived on there ; when he
passed by the guard, and the soldiers presented arms to do

* Lump, German for ragamuffin.

him honour, he threw to them a dozen thalers. Six weeks after, his money came to an end. Then he sold his coaches and horses, afterwards his clothes and linen, and spent all in drinking. His servants ran away from him, and at last nothing remained to him but a bad dress and a few pence. Then the landlord, who had made much by him, presented him with fifty thalers for travelling, but the colonel tarried till he had spent it all; again the host gave him ten thalers for travelling expenses, but the persevering reveller answered that if it was money to be spent, he would rather spend it with him than another. When that also was dissipated, the landlord offered him another five thalers, but forbade his servants to let the spendthrift have anything. At last he quitted the inn and went to the next one, where he spent his five thalers in beer. After that he wandered away to his regiment at Heilbronn. There he was immediately confined in irons, and threatened with the gallows, because he had been away so many weeks. He insisted on being taken before his General, presented himself to him, and reminded him of the evening at the inn. To the sharp rebuke of the General he answered that he had all his life wished for nothing so much as to know what were the feelings of a great lord, and for that he had used his booty.

In the Hungarian war it was made a law, that the booty should be equally distributed, but that soon ceased. Still those who were fortunate enough to make great gains, found it advisable to give a share to the officers of their company. This common interest in the booty, as well as the necessity of maintaining themselves by requisition, in remote countries, developed in great perfection partisan service. There were not only whole divisions of troops, which performed in the armies the service of marauding corps, as for example those of Holk and Isolani in the Imperial, but there were also individual leaders of companies, who selected the most expert people for this lucrative employment. A marauding party, departing on a secret expedition, must consist of an uneven number to bring good luck. These parties stole far into the country to plunder a rich man, to fall upon a small city, or intercept transports of goods or money, and to bring away with them cattle and provisions. There was often an agreement made with the enemy's garrisons in the neighbourhood, as to what was to be spared in the districts common to them. Every kind of cunning was practised in such expeditions; they knew now to imitate the report of heavy artillery, by firing a hand-gun, doubly loaded, through an empty barrel; they used shoes with reversed soles, and caused the horses to be shod in the same manner, the feet of stolen cattle were covered with shoes, and a sponge was put in the pigs' food to which a packthread was fastened. The soldiers disguised themselves as peasants or women, and paid spies amongst the citizens and country people of the neighbourhood. Their messengers ran hither and thither with despatches, and were called in camp language "*feldtauben*" (field doves); they carried these despatches in their ears rolled up as small balls, fastened them in the hair of shaggy dogs, enclosed them in a clod of earth, or sewed them with green silk between the leaves of a branch of oak, that they might be able to throw them away, without suspicion, in time of danger.* These despatches were written in gipsy language or gibberish, in foreign characters, and if there were runaway students in the companies, they were written perhaps in French with Greek letters; they employed, for these purpose, a simple kind of short-hand writing, displacing the letters of the words, or agreeing that only the middle letter of the words should have signification.† The transition from such partisan service to becoming dishonourable marauders and freebooters was

* Philander von Sittewald, 'Soldatenleben.'
† Moscherosch und Grimmelshausen, a. v. O.

easy.   In the beginning of the war, the newly raised regiment of Count Merode was so reduced by long marches and
bad nourishment, that it could hardly set its guard ; it
dissolved almost entirely, on the march, into stragglers, who
lay under the hedges and in the byways, or sneaking about
the army with defective weapons, and without order.   After
that time, the stragglers, whom the soldier wits had before
called " *sausänger*," and " *immenschneider* " (drones), were
now denoted as " Merode-ing brothers."   After a lost battle
their numbers increased enormously.   Horsemen who were
slightly wounded, and had lost their horses, associated themselves with them, and it was impossible, from the then state
of military discipline, to get rid of them.

The most undisciplined, abandoned the route of the army,
and lived as highwaymen, footpads, and poachers.   Vain
were the endeavours of the sovereigns, at the end of the war,
to annihilate the great robber bands ; they lasted, to a certain
extent, up to the beginning of the present century.

Such was the character of the war which raged in Germany
for thirty years.   An age of blood, murder, and fire, of utter
destruction to all property which was movable, and ruin to
that which was not ; and an age of spiritual and material
decay in the nation.   The Generals imposed exorbitant contributions, and kept part in their own pockets.   The colonels
and captains levied charges on the cities and towns in which
their troops were quartered, and merciless were the demands
on all sides.   The princes sent their plate and stud horses
as presents to the Generals, and the cities sent sums of
money and casks of wine to the captains, and the villages,
riding horses and gold lace to the cornets and sergeant-
majors, as long as such bribery was possible.   When an
army was encamped in a district, any landed proprietors of
importance, monasteries, and villages, endeavoured to obtain
the protection of a " *salva guardia*."   They had to pay dear

for this guard, yet had to bear with much unseemly conduct from them.   If a place lay between two armies, both parties had to be asked for *salva guardia*, and both guards lived by agreement in peaceful intercourse at the expense of their host. But it was seldom that either individuals or communities were so fortunate as to be able to preserve even this unsatisfactory protection; for it was necessary for the army to live.   When a troop of soldiers entered a village or country town, the soldiers rushed like devils into the houses; wherever the dung-heaps* were the largest, there the greatest wealth was to be expected.   The object of the tortures to which the inhabitants were subjected, was generally to extort from them their hidden property; they were distinguished by especial names, as the "Swedish fleece," and the "wheel."   The plunderers took the flints from the pistols and forced the peasants' thumbs in their place; they rubbed the soles of their feet with salt, and caused goats to lick them; they tied their hands behind their backs; they passed a bodkin threaded with horse-hair through their tongues, and moved it gently up and down; they bound a knotted cord round the forehead and twisted it together behind with a stick; they bound two fingers together, and rubbed a ramrod up and down till the skin and flesh were burnt to the bone; they forced the victims into the oven, lit the straw behind them, and so they were obliged to creep through the flames.   Ragamuffins were everywhere to be found who bargained with the soldiers, to betray their own neighbours.   And these were not the most horrible torments.   What was done to the women and maidens, to the old women and children, must be passed over in silence.

Thus did the army misbehave amongst the people, dishonouring every bed, robbing every house, devastating every field, till they were themselves involved in the general ruin.

* At the beginning of the war it was customary for people to conceal their treasures in the dung-heaps.

And the destruction of these thirty years increased progressively. It was the years from 1635 to 1641 which annihilated the last powers of the nation ; from that period to the peace, a death-like lassitude pervaded the country ; it communicated itself to the armies, and one can easily understand that the bitter misery of the soldiers called for some consideration for the citizens and peasants. The remaining population were once more reduced to despair, as they had to pay the cost, maintenance, and peace subsidies for the standing army. And the army dispersed itself amongst the population.

CHAPTER III.

THE THIRTY YEARS' WAR.—THE VILLAGES AND THEIR PASTORS.

Oft have the soldier's sword
And jeering Croat horde,
With usage rude and fierce,
Threaten'd my heart to pierce.
Yet I drew unhurt my breath,
No mishap could bring me death.

In water, 'gainst my will,
Plunged deep, I far'd but ill ;
Closed in a wat'ry grave,
God deign'd my life to save ;
Wond'rous 'tis I was not drown'd ;
Brought to land all safe and sound.

Into my mouth once or more,
As 'twere a tub, they did pour
A mess of liquid dung ;
Four churls, cords round me strung :
Yet I drew unhurt my breath,
No mishap could bring me death.

One of an exile band,
There in Thuringia's land,
At Notleben, I dwelt,
Till I God's blessing felt,
And to Heubach's parsonage pass'd
Where kind Heaven sent peace at last.

God's servant, here have I
The church kept orderly,
Have preach'd the word therein,
The bad expell'd, of sin
Absolv'd the penitent heart,
And labour'd truth to impart.

From 'Four Christian Hymns of Martin Bötzinger.'   (1663.)

WHOEVER could portray the desolation of the German people, would be able to explain to us the striking peculiarities of the modern German character ; the remarkable mixture of fresh youth and hoary wisdom, aspiring enthusiasm, and vacillating caution ; but above all, why we, among all the nations of Europe, still strive in vain after much which our neighbours, not more noble by nature, not more strongly organized, not more highly gifted, have long secured to themselves.

The following documents will only furnish an unimportant contribution to such an explanation. Individual examples will render the ruin of the village and city communities comprehensible, and what counteracting power there was, together with the destroying power which supported the remaining vitality, and prevented the final annihilation of the nation.

From these we shall see thoroughly the condition of one particular province, which suffered severely from the miseries of war, but not more than most other parts of Germany, not indeed so much as the Margravate of Brandenburg and many territories of Lower Saxony and Suabia. It is the Thuringian and Franconian side of the " Waldgebirge," which formed, in the middle of Germany, the boundary between the north and south ; more especially the present Dukedoms of Gotha and Meiningen. The following details are taken from the church documents and parish records, and many, from the voluminous church and school stories which were published by clerical collectors in the former century.

Germany was supposed to be a rich country in the year 1618. Even the peasants had acquired during the long peace a certain degree of opulence. The number of villages in Franconia and Thuringia was somewhat greater than now ; they were not entirely without defences, and were often surrounded by broad ditches and palisades, or clay and stone walls ; it was forbidden to form entrances in them, but at the end of the main streets were gates which were closed at night. The churchyard was usually defended by particularly strong walls, and more than once it was used as the citadel and last refuge of the inhabitants. There were night and day patroles through the villages and fields. The houses were indeed ill formed and only of wood and clay, often crowded together in narrow village streets, but they were not deficient in comfort and household furniture. The villages were surrounded by orchards, and many fountains poured their clear waters into stone basins. Small poultry fluttered about the dung-heaps in the enclosed courtyards, immense troops of geese fed in the stubble fields, teams of horses stood in the stables, far more numerous than now, probably of a larger and stronger stamp ; they were rustic descendants of the old knightly chargers, the pride and joy of their owners ; and besides these were the " Kleppers," the small and ancient race of the country. The large parish herds of sheep and cattle grazed on the stony heights and on the rich grass marshes. The wool fetched a high price, and in many places much value was attached to a fine breed ; the German cloths were famed, and these were the best articles of export. This national wool, the result of a thousand years of cultivation, was entirely lost to Germany during the war. The district round the village (where the old Franconian divisions of long strips were not maintained) was divided into three fields, which were much subdivided, and each division carefully stoned off. The fields were highly cultivated, and fine grained white wheat was sown in the winter fields. Woad was still zealously cultivated with great advantage in the north of the Rennstiegs. Although even before the war the foreign indigo competed with the indigenous dye, the yearly gain from the woad in Thuringia could be computed at three tons of gold ; this was principally in the territory of Erfurt and the Dukedom of Gotha ; besides this, anise and saffron produced much money ; the cultivation of the teazel also was formerly indigenous, and the wild turnips, and (by the Rhine) the rape seed were sowed in the fallows. Flax was carefully prepared by steeping it in water, and the coloured flowers of the poppies, and the waving panicle of the millet, raised themselves in the corn-fields.

But on the declivities of warmer situations in Thuringia and Franconia there were everywhere vineyards, and this old cultivation, which has now almost disappeared in those countries, must in favourable years have produced a very drinkable wine, as now on the lower range of the Waldgebirge ; for the wine of particular years is noted in the chronicles as most excellent. Hops also were assiduously cultivated and made good beer. Everywhere they grew fodder, and spurry and horse-beans. The meadows, highly prized, and generally fenced in, were more carefully handled than two hundred years later ; the mole-heaps were scattered, and the introduction and maintenance of drains and watercourses was general.   Erfurt was already the centre of the great seed traffic, of garden cultivation, also of flowers and fine orchards.   On the whole, when we compare one time with the other, the agriculture of 1618 was not inferior to that of 1818.   It must be confessed in other respects also, our century has but restored what was lost in 1618.

The burdens which the peasants had to bear both in service and taxes, were not small, and greatest of all on the properties of the nobles ; but there were many free villages in that country, and the government of the rulers was less strict than in Southern Franconia or in Hesse. Many ecclesiastical properties had been broken up ; many domains, and not a few of the nobles' estates, were farmed by tenants ; leases were a favourite method of raising the rent of the ground.   All this was for the advantage of the peasant.   The damage done by game indeed occasioned great suffering, and there still continued much of the old bond-service on the property of the impoverished nobles.   But the greater part of the country people were pronounced by lawyers, newly educated in the Roman law, to be possessors of their property ; it was the greatest blessing bestowed by Roman law on the Germans in the sixteenth century. It is an error to suppose that the bureaucratic rule is a production of modern days ; it already prevailed in those times, and the villages had often to pay the small travelling expenses of the ducal messenger who brought them their letters. It was already decided by superintending officials how many fire buckets every one was to procure, and how many doves were to be kept ; they saw to the clearing of the fruit trees from caterpillars, the cleansing of the ditches, and the annual planting of young trees. The parish accounts had for nearly a hundred years been kept in an orderly manner, and inspected by the government of the country, as also the district certificates and registers of birth. There was also a good deal of commercial inter-course. A large commercial road passed through Thuringia, in a line almost parallel with the mountains, from the Elbe to the Rhine and Maine ; and from the descent of the mountains near to the Werra, lay the military road which united the north of Germany with the south. The traffic on these unconstructed roads demanded numerous relays of horses, and brought to the villages gain, and news from the distant world, and many opportunities of spending money.

After the Reformation there were schools, at least in all the villages where there was a church ; the teachers were often divines, and sometimes there were schoolmistresses for the girls. Small sums were paid for the schooling, and a portion of the inhabitants of the village were initiated into the secrets of reading and writing. The difference between the countryman and the citizen was then still greater than now. The "stupid peasant" was the favourite object of ridicule in the rooms of the artisans, who attributed to him, as characteristic qualities, roughness, simplicity, disingenuous cunning, drunkenness, and love of fighting. But however retired his life then was, and poor in varied impressions, we should do him great injustice if we considered him essentially weaker or less worthy than he is now ; on the contrary, his independence was not less, and was frequently better established. His ignorance of foreign states was undoubtedly greater, for there were as yet no regular gazettes or local papers for him, and he himself generally did not wander farther than to the nearest town, where he sold his products, or occasionally over the mountain when he had to drive cows ; or if a Thuringian, to go to the woad market at Erfurt, if a Franconian, perhaps to Bamberg with his hops. Also in dress, language, and songs, he was not fashionable like the citizens ; he preferred using old strong words, which they considered coarse ; he swore and cursed after the ancient style, and his ceremonial of greeting was different from theirs, though not less precise. But his life was not on that account deficient in spirit, morals, or even in poetry. The German popular songs were still vigorous, and the countryman was the most zealous preserver of them ; the peasant's feasts, his domestic life, his lawsuits, his purchases and sales, were rich in old picturesque customs and proverbs. The genuine German pleasure also in beautiful specimens of handicraft, in clean and artistic heir-looms, was then shared alike by the countryman and citizen. His household gear was superior to what it is now. Ornamental spinning-wheels, which still pass for a new invention, neatly carved tables, carved chairs and cupboards, have in some instances been preserved to our times, with the earthenware apostle jugs, and similar drinking-vessels, which may be bought by art collectors. Great were the treasures of the country-women in beds, linen, clothes, chains, medals, and other ornaments, and not less worthy of note were the numerous sausages and hams in the chimneys. A great deal of ready money lay concealed in the corners of chests, or carefully buried in pots or other vessels, for the collection of bright coins was an old pleasure to the peasantry ; there had been peace as long as they could remember, and woad and hops brought a high price.   The peasant had abundance, and was without many wants ; he bought lace in the city for his clothes, and silver ornaments for his wife and daughters, spices for his sour wine, and whatever metal utensils and implements were necessary for his farm and kitchen.   All the woollen and linen clothes were wove and made up by the women of the house, or the neighbour in the village.

Thus did the peasant live in middle Germany, even after the year 1618.   He heard in the ale-houses on Sunday of the war alarms in Bohemia, about which he cared little ; he bought indeed a flying-sheet of a crafty dealer, or a satirical song on the outcast King of Bohemia ; he gave some of his bread and cheese to a fugitive from Prague or Budweis, who came begging to his door, and shook his head as he listened to his tale of horror.   An official messenger brought into the village an order from the sovereign, from which he found it was expected of him to deliver into the city, money and provision for the newly raised soldiers; he was indignant, and hastened to bury his treasures still deeper.   It soon, however, became clear that bad times were approaching him also, for the money which he received in the town was very red, and all goods were dear; thus he was involved in the wretched confusion which after 1620 was brought upon the country by the coinage of bad gold.   He went no longer to the city, but kept his corn and meat at home : he had constant disputes however with the townsmen and his neighbours, because he wished to rid himself of the new gold in his own payments, whilst he would receive only the good old money : his heart was full of ominous forebodings.   Thus it went on till the year 1623.

He then saw evil coming in another quarter; theft and burglary increased, foreign vagabonds were often seen on the high-roads, trumpeters rushed into the towns with bad news, hired soldiers, insolent and bragging, drew up before his farm demanding entertainment, stole sausages, and carried off his poultry in their knapsacks. *Defensioners*, the newly raised country militia, galloped into the village, quartered themselves upon him, demanded provisions, and molested him more than the rogues whom they were to drive away from the cattle-sheds.

At last began—in Thuringia not till after 1623—the passage of foreign troops through his country, and the great sufferings of the war fell upon him; foreign soldiers of strange appearance, reckless from blood and battle, marched into his village, occupied his house and bed, ill treated him and his, demanded provisions and other contributions besides gifts, and broke, destroyed, or plundered whatever came before their eyes. Thus it went on after 1626, worse and worse every year, troop followed upon troop, more than one army settled itself round him in winter quarters, the requisitions and vexations appeared endless. The yeoman saw with dismay that the foreign soldier had the power of tracing—which he ascribed to sorcery—the treasures which he had concealed deep in the earth; but if he had been too sly for them, his fate was still worse, for he himself was seized, and by torments which it would be painful to describe, compelled to make known the place where his treasure was concealed. On the fate of his wife and daughter we must remain silent; the most horrible was so common, that an exception was extraordinary. Other sufferings also followed; his daughters, maid-servant, and his little children were not only maltreated, but were in imminent danger of being carried off by persuasion or force, for every army was followed by the coarse, worthless baggage-train of women

and children.   But the yeoman's homestead was devastated in still other ways ; his farming-man had perhaps
borne for some years the blows of the foreign soldiers, at last
he himself was exposed to them ; the team was dragged from
the plough, the cattle were fetched from the meadow, and
the tillage of the fields thus often rendered impossible.   Yet
pitiful and helpless as was his position in the beginning of
the war, up to the death of Gustavus Adolphus, its horrors
were comparatively bearable; for there was as yet a certain
system even in plundering and destruction, some degree of
discipline kept together the regular armies, and an occasional
year passed without any great passage of troops.   It is
possible for us to discover at this time how many exactions
were made on particular parishes, for there were already
country authorities who sat in their offices, and after the
passage of troops through a parish, demanded the usual
liquidation of their loans, the amount of which was indeed
seldom returned to them.   Whoever will glance over the
liquidations in the parish archives, will find the names of ill-
famed commanders, whom he may know from history or
Schiller's Wallenstein, in very near connection with the
history of a Thuringian village.

The effect produced by such a life of insecurity and
torment on the souls of the country people, was very sad.
Fear, trembling, and dread pervaded and enervated all
hearts : their minds had always been full of superstition, now
everything was sought for, with impulsive credulity, which
could be significant of the attacks of supernatural powers.
The most horrible countenances were seen in the heavens,
the signs of fearful wickedness were discovered in numerous
abortions, ghosts appeared, mysterious sounds were heard on
earth and in the heavens.   In Ummerstadt for example, in
the dukedom of Hildburghausen, white crosses illuminated
the heavens when the enemy entered ; when they forced their

way into the court of chancery, a spirit clothed in white met them and motioned them back, and no one could advance; after their departure, a violent breathing and sighing was heard for eight days in the choir of the church which had been burnt.   At Gumpershausen a maid-servant made a great sensation through the whole country; she rejoiced in the visits of a little angel, who appeared, sometimes in a blue, sometimes in a red shirt sitting on the bed or by the table, cried out "Woe," warned against cursing and blasphemy, and predicted horrible bloodshed if men would not give up their vices, their pride, and their stiff blue ruffs,—then a new fashion.   When we look at the zealous protocols which were drawn up by the ecclesiastics concerning the half-witted maiden, we find that the only circumstance which was matter of surprise to them, was that the angel did not visit themselves instead of a simple maiden.

Not only terror, but a spirit of defiance and wild despair possessed all souls.   A moral recklessness prevailed fearfully among the country people.   Wives abandoned their husbands, children their parents; the customs, vices, and maladies of the passing armies left lasting traces, even when the pillagers had quitted the desolated and half-ruined villages.   The brandy drinking, which had been introduced among the people since the Peasant war, became a general vice; respect for the property of others disappeared.   In the beginning of the war the neighbouring villages were disposed to help one another; if the soldiers had driven away the cattle from one village, and disposed of them again at their next night-quarters, the buyers often returned their new purchase to the former proprietors at the purchase price.   This was done in Franconia, by both Catholic and Protestant communities, out of pure kindness.   Gradually, however, the country people began to rob and plunder like the soldiers; armed bands combined together, passed the frontiers into other villages, and carried off whatever they needed. They waylaid the stragglers of the regiments in dense woods or mountain passes, and often after a severe struggle took a bloody revenge on the vanquished; indeed, they far surpassed the skill of the soldiers in the contrivance of barbarities; and there were wooded hills, in whose shades the most horrible crimes were now committed by those who had formerly frequented them as peaceful wood-cutters and stone-breakers, singing their simple songs. There arose gradually a terrible hatred betwixt the soldiery and peasantry, which lasted till the end of the war, and caused more than anything else the ruin of the villages of Germany. There were feuds also between the provinces and individual towns; that which is related here was only a harmless one of that gloomy time.

A violent enmity subsisted for many years after the war between the citizens of Eisfeld and the monastery of Banz, on account of the two fine-toned bells of their parish church, the "*Banzer*" and the "*Messe*." A Swedish officer had carried off both bells from Banz and sold them to the town. Twice, when the Catholic army was stationed at Eisfeld, the monks had come with waggons and ropes to fetch back their bells, but the first time they fell into a quarrel with a certain Croat who was quartered there, because they wished to take away with them the steeple clock. The Croat rushed upon the pious men with his sword, and he and his comrades ran up the tower and vehemently pulled the bell, so that the monks of ·Banz could not fetch it down, and were only able to take away the clock with them. The second time they did not succeed better; at last, after the peace, another bell was offered to them as compensation. But when they dis-covered this sentence upon it: "Preserve us, Lord, by thy word," they returned to their house shaking their heads. At last the pious Duke Ernest arranged the affair; he took for himself as a thank-offering the small bell, and hung it on the Friedenstein in Gotha.

The villages did all in their power to defend themselves from the rapacity of the soldiers. As long as they had money, they endeavoured to buy off the officers who were sent forward to seek for quarters, and many rogues took advantage of their fears, and appearing under the disguise of quartermasters, levied heavy contributions on the deluded villagers. Watchmen were placed on the church towers and elevations of the plain, who gave signals if troops were visible in the distance. Then the countryman brought whatever he could save, and the women and children their movable chattels, hasting to some distant place of concealment. These hiding-places were selected with great sagacity; by a little additional labour they were made still more inaccessible, and for weeks, indeed months, the fugitives passed their anxious existence there. On the dark moor, midst ditches, rushes and elders, in the deep shade of woody glens, in old clay-pits, and amid the ruins of decaying walls, did they seek their last refuge. The countryman in many places still shows with emotion such spots. There is a large vault with an iron door in an old tower at Aspach, whither the Aspachers fled whenever small bands of soldiers approached the village; for a more distant refuge they had a field of many acres, overgrown with thick hornbeam, and there they planted thorns which from the fertility of the soil grew into large trees and became like a thick wall. Within this barricade, which could only be attained by creeping on the belly, the villagers often concealed themselves. After the war the thorns were rooted up, and the land changed into hop, and afterwards cabbage grounds. But a portion of this land is still called the "Schutzdorn," "thorn-defence." When the soldiers had withdrawn, the fugitives returned and repaired with their scanty means what had been laid waste. Often, indeed, they found only a smoking pile.

All however who fled did not return.   The more wealthy
sought a refuge for themselves and their property in the
cities, where martial discipline was a little more rigorous, and
the danger less.   Many also fled into another country, and if
they were threatened by enemies there, again into another ;
and most of them assuredly had not less misery to suffer there.
Those who remained in the country did not all return to their
own fields.   The wild life in hiding-places and woods, the
rough pleasure in deeds of violence and pillage, turned the
boldest of them into robbers ; provided with rusty weapons,
which they had perhaps taken from some dead marauder, they
carried on a lawless life under the mountain pines, as companions of wolves and crows, as poachers and highwaymen.

Thus did the population of the plains decrease with frightful rapidity.   Even in the time of the King of Sweden many
villages were entirely abandoned, the beasts of the woods
roamed about among the blackened rafters, and perhaps the
tattered figure of some old beldame or cripple might be seen.
From that time ruin increased to such an extent, that nothing
like it can be found in modern history.   To the destructive
demons of the sword were added others, not less fearful and
still more voracious.   The land was little cultivated and the
harvest was bad.   An unheard-of rise in prices ensued, famine
followed, and in the years 1635 and 1636 a pestilence attacked
the enfeebled population, more terrible than had raged for
more than a century in Germany.   It spread its pall slowly
over the whole of Germany, over the soldier as well as over
the peasant, armies were dissipated under its parching breath,
many places lost half their inhabitants, and in some villages
in Franconia and Thuringia there remained only a few individuals.   The little strength which had remained in one
corner of the land was now broken.   The war raged on still
twelve long years after this time of horror, but it had become weaker, the armies were smaller, the operations without

plan or stability, from the want of provisions and animals, but where the fury of war still blazed, it devoured mercilessly what remained of life. The people reached the lowest depths of misfortune; a dull apathetic brooding became general. Of the country people of this last period there is little to be told; they vegetated, reckless and hopeless, but few accounts of them are to be found in village records, parish books, and small chronicles. They had forgotten in the villages the art of writing, nay even their crying grievances. Where an army had carried devastation and famine raged, men and dogs ate of the same corpse, and children were caught and slaughtered. A time had now come when those who had held out during twenty years of suffering, laid violent hands on themselves; we read this in the accounts of ambassadors, who for years worked in vain for peace.

It may be asked how, after such sufferings and utter ruin, the survivors could still form a German nation, who at the conclusion of peace could again cultivate the country, pay taxes, and after vegetating in poverty for a century, again engender energy, enthusiasm, and a new life in art and science. It is certainly probable that the country people would have entirely scattered themselves in roving bands, and that the cities would never have been in a condition to produce a new national life, if three powerful causes had not contributed to preserve the German countryman from being altogether lost; —his love of his paternal acres; the endeavours of the magistracy; and above all, the zeal of those who had the care of his soul, the village pastors. The love of the peasant for his own field, which works inimically against the most benevolent agrarian laws, is even now a strong feeling, but in the seventeenth century was still more powerful. For the peasant knew very little of the world beyond his own village, and it was difficult for him to pass the boundaries which separated him from other vocations, or from establishing himself on the property of other lords. He ever returned with tenacity from his hiding-place to his devastated farm, and endeavoured to collect together the trampled corn, or to sow the few seeds he had been able to preserve. When his last beast had been stolen, he harnessed himself to the plough. He took care not to give his house a habitable appearance ; he accustomed himself to dwell amidst dirt and ruins, and concealed the flickering fire of his hearth from the gaze of marauders, who might perhaps be seeking in the night for some warm resting-place. He hid his scanty meal in a place which would disgust even a reckless enemy, in ditches and coffins, and under skulls. Thus he lived under the powerful pressure of habit, however little hope there might be that his labour would prove advantageous to him. If a landed proprietor stood valiantly by his village, even in times of comparative tranquillity, he accompanied his beasts to the fields, armed to the teeth, ready to fight against any robbers who might pounce down on him.

It was no less the interest of the landed proprietor and his officials, than of the peasant himself, to preserve the villages. The smaller the number of tax-payers became, the higher was the tax on the few who remained. The rulers, from the cities in which they resided occupied themselves during the whole war through their officials, bailiffs, and receivers, with the fate of the villages, nay even of individuals. The keeping of the parish records was only interrupted during the most troubled time, and was always recommenced. Certificates, reports, memorials, and rescripts passed hither and thither amidst all the misery.* Petitions for remission of rents and liquidation of costs were incessantly demanded, and many a poor school-

---

* The parish receiver, Johann Martin at Heldburg, writes, for example, on the 13th September, 1640, on behalf of the helpless pastor, and proposes his removal, because in this village there remained only a widow and another woman, and he himself could not obtain a groschen from the annual fees of his district, which formerly amounted to some hundred thalers.

master obediently gave his service as parish writer whilst the snow floated into his schoolroom through the shattered windows, the parish chests lay broken in the streets, and the parishioners, whose accounts he was writing, went armed into the woods with dark illegal projects, which were never reported to the government.   Useless as this system of writing in many cases was, it formed numerous links which bound individuals more closely to their states ; and in the pauses of the war, and at the conclusion of it, was of the greatest importance, for it had preserved the mechanism of the administration.

It was however to the country clergy and their holy office that the maintenance of the German people is chiefly owing. Their influence was undoubtedly not less in the . Catholic than in the Protestant provinces, though there remain few accounts of it ; for the Catholic village pastors were then as averse to writing as the evangelical were fond of it.   But the Protestant pastors had a far greater share in the mental cultivation of their time.   The Reformers had made the German learned education essentially theological, and the village clergy were, in the estimation of the noble proprietors and peasantry, the representatives of this intelligence.   They were generally well skilled in the ancient languages, and expert in writing Latin and elegiac verses.   They were powerful disputants, and much experienced in dogmatic controversy, stubborn and positive, and full of zealous indignation against the followers of Schwenkfeld, Theophrast, Rosenkreuz, and Weigelia, and their teaching was more full of hatred to heretics than love towards their fellow-creatures.   Their influence on the consciences of the laity had made them arrogant and imperious, and the most gifted among them were more occupied with politics than was good for their characters.   If an order may be considered responsible for the imperfection of the mental cultivation of the period, which it has not formed, but only represents, the Lutheran ecclesiastics were deeply and fatally guilty of the devastation of mind, the unpractical weakness, and the dry wearisome formalism which frequently appeared in German life. The ecclesiastics, as an order, were neither accommodating nor especially estimable, and even their morality was narrow-minded and harsh. But all these errors they atoned for in times of poverty, calamity, and persecution, more especially the poor village pastors. They were exposed to the greatest dangers, hated in general by the Imperial soldiers, and obliged by their office to bring themselves under the observation of the enemy; and the rough usage which they, their wives, and daughters had to suffer, fatally injured their consideration in their own parish. They were maintained by the contributions of their parishioners, and were not accustomed, and ill fitted to obtain their daily food by bodily labour; they were the greatest sufferers from any decrease in the wealth, morality, or population of their villages. One must bear witness that a very great number of them endured all these dangers as true servants of Christ. Most of them adhered to their parishes almost to the very last man. Their churches were plundered and burnt, chalice and crucifix stolen, the altar desecrated with disgusting ordures, and the bells torn from the towers and carried away. Then they held divine service in a barn, or an open field, or in the cover of a green wood. When the parishioners had almost perished, so that the voice of the singer was heard no more, and the penitential hymns were no longer intoned by the chanter, they still called the remains of their congregation together at the hour of prayer. They were vigorous and zealous both in giving comfort and in exercising discipline; for the greater the misery of their parishioners, the more reason they had to be dissatisfied with them. Frequently they were the first to suffer from the demoralization of the villagers: theft and insolent wantonness were willingly practised against those whose indignant looks and solemn admonitions had heretofore over-awed them. Hence their fate is particularly characteristic of that iron time, and we happily possess numerous records concerning them, frequently in church documents, in which they bemoaned their sufferings, when no one would listen to them. From such records of Thuringian and Franconian village pastors, only a few examples will here be given.

Magister Michael Ludwig was pastor at Sonnenfeld, about 1633; there he preached to his parishioners in the wood under the canopy of heaven; they were called together by the sound of the trumpet, instead of the bell, and it was necessary to place an armed watch whilst he preached; thus he continued for eight years, till his parishioners entirely disappeared. A Swedish officer then appointed him preacher to his regiment; he was afterwards made president of the army consistory at Torstenson, and superintendent at Wismar. Georg Faber preached at Gellershausen, read prayers daily to three or four hearers, always at the risk of his life: he rose every morning at three o'clock and learned his sermon entirely by heart; besides that, he wrote learned treatises upon the books of the Bible.

In the neighbouring towns of the interior, the clergy had as much to undergo. For example, the rector at Eisfeld, about 1635, was Johann Otto, a young man who had just married; he had in the worst times kept the whole school during eight years, with only one teacher, and provided the choir also gratis. The smallness of his income may be seen from the notes which the excellent man has written in his Euclid: " 2 days thrashing in autumn, 1 day working in the wood in 1646. 2 days thrashing in January, 1647. 5 days thrashing in February, 1647. 4 marriage letters written. Item, ½ day binding oats, and one day reaping," and so on. He persevered, and administered his office honourably for forty-two years. His successor, the great Latin scholar, Johann Schmidt, teacher of the celebrated Cellarius, had become a soldier, and when on guard at the Royal Castle was reading a Greek poet; this was perceived by his officer with astonishment, and was mentioned by him to Ernest the Good, who made him a teacher.

The superintendent at the same place, Andreas Pochmann, was, when an orphan, carried off with two little brothers by the Croats. He escaped with his brothers in the night. Later, when a Latin scholar, he was again taken prisoner by the soldiers, was made an officer's servant, and then a musketeer. But he continued to study in the garrison, and found among his comrades students from Paris and London, with whom he kept up his Latin. Once, when a soldier, he was lying sick by the watch fire, under his sleeve was the powder pouch, with a pound and a half of powder, the flames reached the sleeve and burnt half of it; the powder pouch was unconsumed. When he awoke he found himself alone, the camp was abandoned, and he had not a penny of money. Then he found two thalers in the ashes. With this he struck across to Gotha; on the way, he turned off to Langensalza, to a lonely small house near the walls : an old woman received the wearied man, and laid him on a bed. It was the plague nurse, and the bed was a plague bed, for the malady was then raging in the city; he remained unhurt. His life, like that of most of his cotemporaries, was full of wonderful escapes, sudden changes, and unexpected succour, of deadly perils, penury, and frequent changes of place. These times must be accurately observed, in order to understand how, just at a period when millions were brought to ruin and destruction, there was fostered in the survivors a deep belief in that Divine Providence, which, in a wonderful way, encompassed the lives of men.

From almost every village church one can obtain reminiscences of the sufferings, self-devotion, and perseverance of their pastors. It must be said, that only the strongest minds came out unscathed in such times. The endless insecurity, the want of support, the lawless proceedings of the soldiers and of their own parishioners, made many of them petty in their ideas, cringing and beggarly. We will give one example among many. Johanne Elfflein, pastor at Simau after 1632, was so poor that he was obliged to work as a day labourer, to cut wood in the forest, to dig and to sow; twice he received either alms from the poor-box at Coburg, or what was placed there at the baptism of children. At last the consistory at Coburg sold one of the chalices of the church to procure bread for him. He considered it an especial piece of good fortune, when he had once to perform the funeral of a distinguished noble, for then he got a good old rix-dollar, and a quarter of corn. When shortly afterwards he confidentially complained to a neighbour of his want of food, and the latter replied with desperate resolution, he knew well what he should do in such a case, then, firm in faith, Magister Elfflein said, " My God will provide means that I shall not die of hunger; He will cause a rich nobleman to die, that I may obtain money, and a quarter of corn." He considered it was ordained by Providence, when soon after, this melancholy event actually occurred. His situation was so pitiable, that even the rapacious soldiers, when they sent their lads in the neighbourhood after booty, emphatically ordered them to leave the pastor at Simau unmolested, as the poor simpleton had nothing for himself. At last he got another parish.

At the source of the Itz, where the mountains decline in high terraces towards the Main, lies the old village of Stelzen, a holy place even in heathen times. Close to the church, from the corner of a spacious cavern, overshadowed by primeval beech and lime trees, springs up a miraculous well; near the well, before the Reformation, stood a chapel to the Holy Virgin, and many a time did hundreds of counts and noblemen, with numberless other people, flock together there as pilgrims. The village was entirely burnt down at Michaelmas, 1632, only the church, the school, and shepherd's hut remained standing. The pastor, Nicholas Schubert, wrote to the authorities in the winter as follows: "I have saved nothing but my eight poor, little, naked, hungry children. I continue to dwell *ex mandato* in the very old, and on account of the want of a chimney, a floor and so forth, dangerous school-house, where I can neither attend to my studies, nor do anything for my support. For I have neither food nor clothes, *longe enim plura deficiunt.* . Given at my castle of misery, Stelzen, 1633. Your willing servant, and obedient poor burnt-out pastor, Nicholas Schubert." Shortly he was removed. His successor likewise was pillaged, and stabbed in the left hip with a rapier; he too was removed; a second successor also was unable to maintain himself there. After that, the parsonage house was uninhabited for fifteen years, but the neighbouring pastor, Götz of Sachsendorf, came every third Sunday, and performed service in the ruined village. For two years there came no pence to the church coffers. At last, in 1647, the church was entirely burned to the bare walls.

Gregory Ewald was pastor at Königsberg; in 1632, Tilly burnt down the city, and Ewald was taken prisoner in a vineyard by two Croats, and robbed; when they could not withdraw a gold ring from his finger they prepared to cut off the finger, but at last had so much consideration that they took only the skin with the ring, and demanded a thousand dollars ransom. Ewald released himself by this stratagem; he took the simple soldier, who was left with him to fetch the ransom, first to the door of a cellar in order to give him a drink of wine, and under the pretext of fetching the key he escaped. In his great necessity he took an appointment as Swedish army chaplain, and after the battle of Nördlingen, lived as an exile for a year in a foreign country, from thence he returned to his ruined parish, where for some years he and his family endured want and misery.

Among the most instructive of the biographical accounts of Protestant pastors, is that of the Franconian pastor, Martin Bötzinger. We see with horror, both the village life in the time of the war, and the demoralization of the inhabitants, distinctly portrayed in his narrative. Bötzinger was not a man of great character, and the lamentable lot he had to bear did not strengthen it; indeed, we can hardly deny him the predicate of a right miserable devil. Nevertheless he possessed two qualities which render him estimable to us, an indestructible energy with which there was not the slightest frivolity united; and that determined German contentment which takes the brightest view of the most desolate situations. He was a poet. His German verses are thoroughly pitiful, as may be seen by the specimen heading this chapter, but they served him as elegant begging letters by which, in the worst times, he endeavoured to procure sympathy. He celebrated all the officials and receivers of the parish of Heldburg in an epic poem, as also the melancholy condition of Coburg, where he tarried for a certain time as a fugitive.

Of the career which he noted down, the beginning and the last portion were already torn out when Krauss, in 1730, incorporated it in his history of the Hildburghaus church, school, and province. The following is faithfully transcribed from this fragment; only the series of events which are intermingled in his autobiography are here arranged according to years. Bötzinger was a collegian at Coburg and a student at Jena, during the *Kipper* time;* and in 1626, he became

---

* This was the time in the Thirty years' war when the German princes and dukes coined base money. When one prince had obtained possession of the coinage of another he melted it, and made it into new money by alloying it with copper and other metals.

pastor at Poppenhausen. In the spring of 1627, the young pastor entertained the idea of marrying the only daughter of Michael Böhme, burgher and counsellor at Heldburg, whose name was Ursula.

" In the year 1627, on the Tuesday after the Jubilate, all necessary preparations being made, on this very day, a body of eight thousand men, people from Saxe Lauenburg, together with the Prince himself, encamped before Heldburg ; pitched their camp on the cropped ground, and in eight days ruined the city and land belonging to the corporation, so that neither calf nor lamb, beer nor wine, could any more be procured. Provisions were brought from all the neighbouring districts, and yet even the royal officers and officials could hardly be maintained. They were, on account of the cold, quartered some days in the city and villages. It was then, for the first time, I was plundered in the parsonage house at Poppenhausen, for not only had I not secured anything, but rather had I made preparation as if I had to lodge an honourable guest or officer ; I lost my linen, bedding, shirts, and so forth, for I did not yet know that the soldiers were robbers, and took everything away with them. The prince of the country, Duke Casimir, was himself obliged to journey to Heldburg ; he ordered for the Lauenburger a princely banquet ; he presented him with fine horses and eight thousand thalers if he would only take himself away. After this misfortune, the blessing of God made itself miraculously visible everywhere. Owing to the thousands of huts, quarters and fires, which made the fields look like a wilderness, it was thought that the winter seed was lost in the ground. Nevertheless, there grew from these burnt huts and ditches so thick a crop, that in the same year, there was a superfluity of winter food. A miracle ! Thus my wedding could take place on the Tuesday after the *Exaudi*, and was celebrated at the Town Hall.

" For five years there was . rest in the land till 1632, except that several Imperial corps, consisting of two, three, or more regiments, passed to and fro, who often took up their quarters in the township of Heldburg, and exhausted it. I wanted for nothing at Poppenhausen. I could wish that I was now as well off as I was before the war. As, however, the fury of war at last arrived, the neighbouring bishops began to reform vigorously ; sent Jesuits and monks with diplomas into the country, and examined the ecclesiastical benefices and monasteries. The princes had their militia here and there, who now and then pilfered in the neighbouring Papal states, and stirred up the hornets there. Every intelligent person could discover that things would become worse. The noblemen also fled with their pastors, bailiffs, and all belonging to them, to our little towns and villages, hoping for greater security there than in their own places.

" In 1631, at Michaelmas, King Gustavus came from Sweden suddenly through the wood, just as if he had wings. He took Königshofen and many other places, and went on very flourishingly. Our nobles enlisted people for the king, who were as bad as the enemy in pilfering and robbing. They more especially took from the neighbouring Catholics their cows, horses, pigs, and sheep ; then was there a great sale ; a ducat for one cow, and a thaler for a pig. The Papists often came hither and saw how and who bought their cattle, and frequently redeemed them themselves. They were however so often taken, that they wearied of redeeming them, and it went ill with the poor neighbouring Papists. We all at Poppenhausen preserved for those in the neighbourhood, their bits of property in churches and houses, as far as we could. But when in the year 1632, the tables were turned, and the three Generals, the Friedlander, Tilly, and the Bavarian prince, took possession of Coburg and the country, the neighbouring Papists helped to rob and burn, and we found no faith or safety with them.

" When on the eve of Michaelmas, all the guns were heard from Coburg, as a signal that the enemy was approaching, and every one took care of himself, I went with all those whom I had lodged for some weeks, to Heldburg, where I had previously sent my wife and child.   The town was on its guard, but did not imagine what evil would betide it ; the burgomaster and some of the councillors ran away, my father-in-law of blessed memory, having the charge of the powder, lead, and linstocks, which he served out to the guard as need required, was obliged to remain in the town.   I had a great desire to leave the town with my wife and children, but he would not let me go, and still less his daughter, and bade us remain at home ; he had a tolerable purse of thalers with which he intended to make off in case of disaster.   But before midday on the feast of St. Michael, fourteen horsemen presented themselves ; they were supposed to be Duke Bernhard's people, but it was very far from the case.   These they were obliged to admit without thanks for it.   They were soon followed by some infantry, who from the beginning searched about everywhere, and knocked down and shot whoever resisted them.   In the middle of the market, one of these fourteen struck my father-in-law with a pistol on the head, so that he fell down like an ox.   The horseman dismounted, and searched his hosen, and our citizens who were at the Town Hall saw that the thief drew out from thence a large mass of money.   When the stupefaction from the blow had passed away, my father-in-law stood up : he was made to go to the Star Inn, where they found somewhat to eat, but nothing to drink ; then he said he would go home and bring some drink. Now as they thought he might escape them, they took the platters and food with them, and accompanied him to his house.   It was not long before one of them demanded money; and when he excused himself, the scoundrel stabbed him with his own bread-knife in the presence of his wife and mine, so that he sank to the ground. ' God help us!' screamed out my wife and child. I, who was hid in the bath-house, in the straw over the stable, sprang down and ventured amongst them. The wonder was that they did not catch me in the parson's cap. I took my father-in-law, who was reeling about like a drunken man, into the bath-room, that he might be bandaged. I was obliged to look on whilst they took off from your mother* her shoes and clothes, and laid hold of you, my son Michael, in their arms; hereupon they quitted the house and the street. I went from the little court of the bath-house to my father-in-law's room; I carried over there pillows and mattresses, whereon we laid him. I had to venture still further. I went into the cellar, wherein his brother, Herr George Böhm, pastor at Lindenau, had placed in three large butts, two tons of good wine. I wished to fetch a refreshing drink for my father-in-law, but the vent peg was so carefully and firmly driven into the butt that although I pulled out the spigot nothing would flow. I was obliged to stay a long time, at great risk, before I could get a spoonful. I had hardly gone over there, before a scoundrel went into the bath-house, threw the invalid off the bed, and searched everywhere. I had crept under the sweating bench, where indeed I got a good sweating, for the day before had been the bath day.

"As there was now a great butchery and shooting down in the town, so that no one was secure, divers citizens came at intervals to have themselves bandaged. Then my father-in-law consented that I should seek for a hiding-place and leave the town, but would not let my wife and children accompany me. So I went to the castle garden, and ascended the height behind the castle, that I might look out

* Bützinger gives this account to his children.

towards Holzhausen and Gellershausen, to see if it was safe.
Then the citizens and their wives came to me for comfort and
to journey with me. Thus I crossed over the Hundshanger
lake into the wood, and wished to go up to Strauchhahn.
When we came to the common, eight horsemen, who were
Croats, rode up the heights. As soon as they saw us they
hastily galloped up to us. Two citizens, Kührlein and
Brehme, escaped; I had most to endure. They took off my
shoes, stockings, and hosen, and left me only my cap. With
my hosen I had to give up my purse full of money, which I had
hid there three hours before, and thus had preserved from
the first pilferers. The danger was so urgent that I did not
think of my purse till I saw it for the last time. They
demanded first a thousand thalers, then five hundred, and
lastly a hundred, for my life. I had to go with them to their
quarters, and to run with them a whole hour barefoot. At
last they perceived that I was a *pap* or *pfaff*, which I also
confessed; then they began to thrust at me with their sabres
without discretion, and I held my hands and arms towards
them, and through God's protection only got a few wounds
on the wrist.

"Meanwhile they discovered a peasant who had hidden
himself in some bushes. It was the rich Kaspar of Gellershausen, so they all rode off to him, and only one remained
with me, who was by birth a Swede, and had been made
prisoner. This one said to me, 'Priest, priest, run, run,
otherwise you must die.' He was a good Swede: I placed
confidence in his counsel, and begged of him to feign to ride
after me, as if he would fetch me back. Thus it happened
that I escaped the Croats. But the rich Kaspar met a
miserable death at that place; for as he would not come
forth from thence, they hewed off his legs, as I saw, at the
knees. Therefore he was obliged to lie in that place, where
after their withdrawal he was found. But I ran through a

great oak wood for almost an hour, and could see no thick
bushes wherein to conceal myself, and fell at last into a pool
of water out of which an oak root had grown, and I was so
tired of running that I could go no further, and my heart
beat so that I knew not whether it was the horses' hoofs that I
heard, or my heart.

" Thus I sat till it was night ; then I rose up and continued
in search of a thick cover, till I came out and could see
Seidenstadt. I slipped into the village, and as I heard dogs
bark, I hoped to find people at home, but there was no one ;
I therefore went into a shed, and was desirous of passing the
night on the hay. But God granted that the neighbours,
who had hid themselves in Strauchhahn, had come together
behind this shed, and took counsel where they should reassemble, and where they should go to. This I could distinctly
hear. I therefore descended and went to the house. The
peasant had just come in, had struck a light, and was standing in the cellar taking the cream off the milk, which he
intended to drink. I was standing above the opening, spoke
to him and greeted him ; he looked up and saw the under
part of my body, namely, my shirt and naked legs, and it was
dark above. He was much frightened ; but when I told
him that I was the pastor at Poppenhausen, who had been
carried off by the soldiers, he brought the milk up, and I
begged him to procure me some clothes of his neighbours, as
I wished to accompany them wherever they were going. He
went out, and meanwhile I regaled myself on his pot of milk,
and entirely emptied it. In my whole life no milk had ever
tasted so good. He came back with others, and one of them
brought me a pair of old leather hosen, which smelt badly of
cart-grease, another a pair of old latchet shoes, and another two
woollen stockings, one green and one white. This livery was
not suitable either for a traveller or for a pastor ; yet I took it
with thanks, but could not wear the shoes, for they were frozen

too stiff. The soles of the stockings were torn, thus I went to Hildburghausen more barefooted than shod. When we looked around us we saw that many places in Itzgrund were in flames. At that time, Ummerstadt, Rodach, Eisfeld, and Heldburg were burnt to the ground.

" I was, on my arrival, such a spectacle as to create terror and fear at Hildburghausen; no one—though many thousand strangers had come there—felt secure, although the city had a strong guard. My only anxiety was to get a respectable dress, stockings, shoes, &c., before we departed from thence. I went, therefore, barefoot to the burgomaster, Paul Walz, and to the curate, and begged them to give me something to clothe me respectably. Herr Walz gave me an old hat which was almost an ell in height, which disfigured me more than anything else; nevertheless I put it on. Herr Schnetters Eidam, now curate at Römhild, gave me a pair of hosen, which came over my knees, these were still good, Herr Dressel a pair of black stockings, and the sexton a pair of shoes. Thus I was rigged out, so that I could appear without being ashamed before so many thousand strangers, who had sought security in the town; and could show myself amongst the citizens. But the hat disfigured me very much, therefore I sought an opportunity to obtain another. Now it came to pass that the whole ministry, the authorities of the high school and councillors, had agreed, without the knowledge of the citizens generally, that they would have the gates opened at nine o'clock at night, and go away with their wives and children : having learned this, I went to the lodging of the town-clerk, where the gentlemen were all assembled ; but no one knew or noticed me. I placed myself alone by a table in the dark ; there I discovered that a good respectable hat was hanging on a nail. I thought that if this should remain hanging on the breaking up of the assembly, it would suit me. What matter ; all would be ruined after the flight.

What I wished and thought came to pass : then there began a wailing and leave-taking on their departure, and I laid my head on the table as if I were asleep. Now when almost every one was gone, I hung the long stork on the wall, made the exchange, and went with the other gentlemen into the street.

"The arrangements for flight now became known to the people. Countless numbers therefore sat with their packages in the streets ; horses were put also to many waggons and carts, all prepared to go out of the gate with those who were departing. When we came into the open country we saw that the good people were all dispersed about the streets. There were thousands of lighted torches to be seen, some had lanterns, some burning wisps of straw, others links. In short some thousands came mournfully out. I and my flock came about midnight to Themar, the townspeople there rose up and joined us, so that some hundreds more were added to us. The march proceeded to Schwarzig and Steinbach, and when towards morning we arrived at a village, the people were so terrified that they abandoned their houses and farms and accompanied us. When we had been about an hour at an inn, the news came that the Croats had fallen upon Themar this very morning, had cut up the escort and plundered the carrier's goods ; had split the burgomaster's head, robbed the church, and carried the organ pipes off to the market ; and it was high time for us to have evacuated it. Hildburghausen had afterwards to ransom itself by a large sum of money and its chalices, otherwise the town would like all the others have been reduced to ashes. During this wandering I got also a present of a pair of gloves, a knife, and a sheath.

"This lasted five or six days, then came the news announcing that the enemy had departed from Coburg. Now I could not remain any longer. I went speedily to Römhild, where

lived my honoured godfather Cremer, the town clerk. I had
to report to the worthy magistrate what had happened to me.
This little town alone remained unplundered. The worthy
magistrate had ordered the enemy to be fired upon, and by
his foresight God preserved this little town. Meanwhile
Römhild became full of refugees, who were partly known and
partly unknown. But I did not then care for any society;
so I set off for Heldburg, and passing many hundred men,
arrived there first, just when the slain were being brought
on carts to the burial-ground. When I perceived this I
went to the burial-ground, and found seventeen persons lying
in one grave, among them were three councillors, one my
father-in-law, the precentor, some citizens, a tutor, the
country beadle, and town constable. They were all horribly
disfigured. After this I went to my mother-in-law's house;
I found her so ill and so disfigured from being broken on the
wheel, and pinched with pistol screws, that she could hardly
speak to me; she made up her mind that she should die. So
she desired me to seek my wife and children whom the enemy
had carried away with them. The children were you, Michael,
a year and a half, and your eldest sister, five years old. I
would gladly have eaten something at Heldburg, but there
was nothing either to eat or drink. I speeded therefore hungry and terrified to Poppenhausen, not only to refresh myself
there, but to procure a messenger who would seek and recover
my wife and children. But I learnt there that the Poppenhausen children had also been carried away, and that there
were marching columns on many roads, so that the life of a
messenger would be in deadly peril. Meanwhile my parishioners dressed a cow for me, which had escaped the soldiers;
this I looked for with a hungry stomach. So we had meat
enough to eat, but without salt and bread. After my repast I
learned by post that my wife was come, and thus it had come
to pass. She had been taken with her two children, by some

musketeers, to Altenhausen, where, from fear of dishonour, she and her children had sprung over the bridge into the water. From thence she was drawn out by the soldiers, and brought into the village, where she was made to help in the kitchen to prepare the supper.   Meanwhile there came another troop of soldiers who were higher in rank and more in number, and drove the others from their quarters.   My wife took this opportunity to escape.   She wended her way out, and left the two children with the soldiers.   A poor beggar-woman led her through secret byways out of the village, and brought her to an old cave in a wood, where she passed that night and remained the next day till evening.   On that day the people came forth from all quarters, and thus my wife set out and came safe and unharmed to me, so that we were all joyful and thankful to God.

" How murder and fire meanwhile had gone on at Heldburg, I will also relate.   The town of Heldburg had militia and trained bands, and it was ordered that if the enemy came there, the city should be defended.   For it was always hoped that Duke Bernhard's people were not far distant, and that the country would be relieved.   When therefore the town was fired, my honoured father-in-law, with many citizens and other folks, hastened out of the town, and arrived in the night with my wife and two children to Poppenhausen, and my wife prepared him a good invalid bed.   For my parsonage house had been filled with all kinds of furniture left by noblemen and magistrates in their flight; and although pilferers had been there, there was enough still left.   The following day a whole troop of horsemen came to the parsonage, examined my belongings, but let them alone because there was one there who was wounded ; they ordered supper and went out to plunder, and returned towards evening, bringing all kinds of booty ; then it was necessary to boil and roast, and the neighbouring women helped thereto with good will.   When the horsemen

were about to depart, they advised my father-in-law not to be
too confident, as this tumult would last yet eight days, and as
the road led past there, he and his daughter might suffer
violence, and as the neighbouring villages were Popish, he had
better remove to a Protestant one. This my father-in-law
did, and went at night in the fog for security to Gleichmu-
thrusen; but the ungodly neighbours screamed out that the
horsemen wished to burn and slay the Lutherans, but they
did it for their advantage, as the Papists had gone with the
troopers into our villages and houses and stolen as much as
others. Then my father-in-law did not like to remain there
any longer, he went with his belongings to Einöder wood and
remained there day and night. He occasionally went forth
to examine the road between Heldburg and Einöder. When
therefore one day he saw no one especial on the road, either
travelling or riding, and heard the little bell which was wont
to be sounded when children were baptized, he thought, such
being the case, he might creep nearer the town, and see
whether there was any hindrance along the road. As soon
as he came to the town his steps were watched. Then a
whole body of camp followers came and took him, my mother-
in-law, and my wife to the house of Herr Göckel. Ah! there
was banqueting and revelling! Being now urged to give
money and making various excuses, they singed and smeared
his eyes, beard, and mouth with tallow candles, and endeavoured shamelessly to maltreat my wife in the room before
every one, but she screamed so that her mother sprang violently into the room and drew her out through the door, which
indeed was fastened, but the under panel had been ingeniously
covered with list, and was fractured. Then the cook had compassion upon her, and brought her out of the house; and
when my wife gave him some ducats, which she had for a
whole week concealed in the cuff of her sleeve, he brought to
her my father-in-law, who however was horribly disfigured.

Thus they left the town more dead than alive, and being too weak to go further, went into the hospital. Not only the poor and sick were there, but many respectable citizens and women in hopes of finding it a safe asylum. But it was far from being the case. Although my father-in-law was lying on a bed nearly dying, and every one saw that he was labouring and had been evil treated, yet he was dragged hither and thither, some wicked people having believed that he was a rich man. They broke him on the wheel; they brought my wife and children prisoners into the town, where they had to make shirts for the soldiers. As she was sitting in the churchyard, one of them brought her a piece of linen to cut out, he said to one of his comrades: 'Go and make sure that the peasant, meaning my father-in-law, is dead.' He went and returned again, soon, having in his arms my father-in-law's bones and trousers, and said to my wife, 'Your father is done for.' What barbarity! When the officers had sufficiently pillaged the chests of clothes and linen, they left the town, and would carry my wife with them whether she would or no.

"Not long after they renewed their attack at Leuzen and Lützen, as now is read in what place. After this every one returned home, and people found each other again; but the sheep and cattle were all gone. I did but preserve three that three calves out of eight, without counting my forty-eight sheep which, with the whole herd, had been lost.

"Duke Adams Contare died in the year 1634, and was buried on the same day on which the funeral sermon was preached by Gustavus King of Sweden, in that country. At that time great robbing and plundering went on, amongst others by Duke Bernard's soldiers, the proportion of which was obtained at Regmont, to enable the country people to be buried in safety.

"In 1634 things became much worse, and one could well preserve that in a short time everything would be worse—

turvy. I therefore removed what I could to the parsonage at Steltzen, my beds, two cows, clothes, &c. But this being in the autumn, after Lamboy had quartered himself with every one and everywhere, my winter quarters cost me more than five hundred gulden in thirty-five weeks, which I had to settle with Captain Krebs. I had eleven persons in my house, not counting camp-followers and maid-servants. It is not to be described what I and my wife had to suffer and endure for a length of time. At last I could no longer feel secure on account of them; I ran away sick and came to Mitwitz and Mupperg, where I had as little rest as at Heldburg. My stepmother especially tormented me (she had been struck by lightning), she would not let me remain in my exile with my old father. I was obliged to go to Neustadt to the rector, M. Val. Hoffmann, now superintendent. But I was not only very poor, but became daily more ailing, therefore I only thought how I could return to Poppenhausen or Heldburg and die there, for I was weary of my life.

"It is miraculous how I passed along the roads and through the villages in the darkness of night, for it was still unsafe everywhere; at last I reached Poppenhausen. There my poor parishioners and schoolmaster were as joyful at sight of me, as if our Lord God had himself appeared among them. But we were all in such great weakness and want, that we looked more dead than alive. Many died of hunger; and we were frequently, each day, obliged to take to our heels and conceal ourselves. And although we hid our lentils, corn, and poor food in the ditches and old coffins, nay, under the skulls of the dead, yet all was taken away from us.

"Then were the survivors obliged to leave house and home, or die of hunger. At Poppenhausen most of the inhabitants were in their graves; there remained only eight or nine souls, who fled from it in the year 1636. The same circumstances occurred at Lindenau, the cure of which was committed to me vicariously in 1636, by the Royal Consistory. I could obtain no income; apples, pears, cabbage, turnips, &c., were my only pay. Thus I was pastor at Lindenau from 1636 to 1641. I had the parsonage arranged, but could not, on account of the insecurity and turmoil, dwell constantly there, and performed the duties from Heldburg. I have still the testimony of the Lindenauers, wherein they acknowledge that I did not in five years get ten gulden in money; but they have since honestly paid me the arrears in wood and apples.

"In the year 1640, between Easter and Whitsuntide, the Imperial and Swedish armies fought a battle at Saalfeld; and Franconia and Thuringia were devastated far and wide. At four o'clock in the morning of the Sunday before Whitsunday, strong bodies of Imperialists fell upon Heldburg, when most of the citizens were still resting in their beds. My whole street, in every direction, was full of the turmoil of horses and riders; just as if some one had taken pains to show them my house. I and my wife were taken prisoners five times in one hour; when I was released from one, I was taken by another. Then I took them into my room and cellar, that they might themselves seek what they required. At last they went off, leaving me alone in the house; yet my terror and anguish were so great that I never thought of my ready money, which I might have saved ten times over, if I had had sufficient confidence to take it with me. But all the houses and streets were full of horsemen; and if I had taken my Mammon with me, it might so have happened that I should have been caught. But in my dismay I thought not of money. Many men and women were convoyed out of the town by an escort of Hasisch horsemen, who had been quartered there. I then returned to my wife and children; we betook ourselves to the nearest wood towards Hellingen;

there old and young, ecclesiastics and laymen, remained day and night. Our chief sustenance was black juniper berries. Now certain of the citizens ventured into the town, and brought back with them food and other things that they required. I thought, ah! if thou also couldst go to thy house and get hold of thy small cash in pence, and therewith support thyself and thy children! I ventured it, slipped in, and went through the Spittel Gate to the Mühl Gate, which was closed in with palisades. Within, there were some who caught me by surprise, as a cat does a mouse; they bound me with new cords so that I could neither help myself with hands or feet, and must either give money, or betray rich people to them. The thieves obliged me to toss the fodder for their horses at the Herrnhof, to lead them to drink, and other odd work. Then imagining myself more at liberty, I ran from thence, being unaware that a whole troop of soldiers were standing at the gate of the courtyard, so I ran into their arms. They beat me well with their swords and bandoliers, kept me still more strictly with cords, led me from house to house, that I might tell them to whom this or the other house belonged. Thus I was also led to my own house, there I saw the copper water-can lying on the floor, in which had been placed my ready money, three hundred thalers, and I thought, hadst thou known that the birds and the foxes were in the way, thou wouldst have remained outside. Now because I would not betray any one, they put upon my head my own cap, which was lying on the ground in my house, and gave me a blow on the head with a cutlass, so that the blood ran down to my ears, but no hole was made in the cap, for it was of felt. Still more; the same man wantonly drew the cutlass across my stomach, in order to try whether I was invulnerable; he pressed tolerably hard, yet God willed not that he should draw more blood from me. Twice in one hour, namely, in Schneiderinn, at the farm of the tailor's wife Wittich, on the dung-heap, and in the forest ranger's stable, they gave me the Swedish drink mixed with dung water, whereby my teeth became all loose. I defended myself as well as a prisoner could, when they forced a great stick into my mouth. At last they led me along with cords, and said they would hang me up : they brought me out to the Mühl Gate on the bridge ; then one of them took the cord wherewith my feet were bound together, and another the cord on my left arm, and pitched me into the water, holding the cord so that they might draw me up and down. Now whilst I was groping around me in search of a support, I caught hold of a hay-rake, which however gave way with me, and I could find no help thereon ; but by God's providence an opening was made for me, so that I slipped under the bridge. Whenever I tried to hold on, they battered me with these said hay-rakes, so that they snapped in two like a school cane. When they were not only weary of their labour, but thought they had done for me, as I should drown in the water, they let go both cords, when I dived under the bridge like a frog, and no one could touch me. Then I searched the pocket of my hosen and found a little knife, such as could be closed, which they had not chosen to take, though they had often searched me ; I therefore cut the cord which bound my two feet, and sprang down to the floor of the mill, where lay the wheels. The water covered half my body ; then the rogues threw sticks, brickbats, and cudgels at me, in order to put an end to me completely. I was anxious to work my way to the miller's back door, but could not, either because my clothes being saturated with water held me back, or more likely, because God would not permit me to die there. For as a drunken man reels to and fro, thus did I, and came up on the other side at the back of the brewery. When they perceived that I was about to get into the narrow lane, they all ran into the town, collected more companions, and watched at the tan-house to see whether I would come thither. But as I perceived this, and was now left to myself, I remained lying in the water, and placed my head under a thick willow bush, and rested in the water four or five hours, till it was night and the town quiet; then I crept out half dead, and could hardly breathe, on account of the blows I had had. I went down to the tan-house and found that there was as yet no safety, as there was one there cutting grass, and another picking hides out of the tan-pits, and I almost stumbled upon them, so I was obliged to hide there till late in the night; I went then over the conduit, always following the course of the stream, and climbed over a willow stem by which I reached the other side, towards Poppenhausen.

" When I came to the Poppenhausen or Einöder road, it was strewed here and there with linen, which the soldiers had thrown away or lost, but I could not stoop to pick anything up. I came at last to Poppenhausen, and found no one at home but Claus Hön, whose wife was lying-in; he was obliged to cut the clothes from off my body, for I was swollen, and he put aside the wet clothes to be dried. He also lent me a shirt, and then examined my head, which was of all colours from the blows I had received; afterwards my back and arms became quite black and blue. The following day my parishioner bade me go away, for he feared they might lie in wait for me, and that he should get into trouble on my account. So with his assistance I put on my wet clothes, and went quite slowly to Lindenau, always through the densest thicket, and kept on the other side in the Lindenau garden, from which I could see the village. At last I discovered some people going into a house; I went thither, but they would not admit me, for they were too much afraid, but finally, when they saw through the window that it was I, their pastor, who had come, they admitted me, and I remained with them some days; for there was quartered there one who was a Lindenauer, which helped a little. But I met with a new misfortune. When those who were quartered here went to the castle of Einöd with the Lindenauers, to fetch away what could yet be found of their goods, the magistrate, the smith, and I were keeping guard the while on the tower; as we were all three performing this duty, certain horsemen came into the village, they saw us on the tower, went straight up to it, and found us there together. As they ascended the stairs we discovered from their blustering and talking that they were troopers, so, in bad plight as I was, I endeavoured, alas! to climb. I clambered up into the belfry and curled myself like a cat behind the clock; but one of the thieves climbed up at the same time and found me. My parishioners said I was their schoolmaster, and entreated for me, as I had already been badly beaten by the soldiers. It was however of no avail. They insisted on this schoolmaster descending. The magistrate went first, after him a trooper, the smith followed, then another trooper, and lastly I followed, lingering. Now when they all came out through the door of the church, I remained within, bolted the little door, and ran out of the other, and crept into a turnip pit. God help me! How woeful it was for me to be obliged to stoop and lie on all-fours for a whole hour! Thus I was saved, but my dear fellow-watchers were taken to a mill and obliged to fill the flour sacks.

"On the Friday before Whitsuntide I came with many citizens to Coburg. A thief had carried off my shoes, and left me a pair of old bad ones instead; I had nothing else to wear for almost a week, and both soles had fallen out, and when it became necessary to take to one's heels, the shoes turned round hindforemost, so that often I could not help laughing outright. Thus I came to Coburg. The news of my torments had reached Coburg some days before, together with the report that I had been killed; when therefore I came myself, the citizens and my old acquaintance were much astonished. Dr. Kesler, general superintendent, *item*, consul Körner, invited me several times during the Whitsuntide festival, and for a whole month the Coburgers showed great kindness to me, my wife, and children, which I lauded in print on St. John's day.

" Ah, how great was the grief and misery to be seen and heard in all the surrounding small towns at that time! the inhabitants of Eisfeldt, Heldburg, and Neustadt, together with the villagers, had to make shift miserably in the town. Asking and begging was no shame. Yet I did not wish to burden too much my good host, Herr Hoffman the apothecary. I went out into the wide world with the pastor of Walburg, Eisentraut, for three weeks, *victum quærendi gratia*, to Culmbach, Bayreuth, Hirschheid, Altorf, and Nuremberg, and again back to Coburg. I then found that my wife had returned to Poppenhausen, accompanied again by the Hasische trooper, but there was nothing to eat or reap there. What God had provided me with on my journey, I was obliged to carry to the town hall and give to the soldiers, and the children were well-nigh dying of hunger. They had not been able to buy bran enough for bread. My superintendent, Herr Grams, died from the effects of the Swedish drink, at the castle four or five weeks after this turbulent time.

" Now as exactions and extortions still continued, I could get no stipend, and yet had to assist in the superintendence of the parish of Heldburg, as well as my own, I went *cum testimonio et consilio* of Dr. Kesler, and also with letters of recommendation to Duke Albert, to Eisenach, and represented my poverty in divers ways to the Consistory. I got a presentment and other recommendations to their Princely Highnesses, the two brothers, that I might obtain advancement in their dominions. So I went from Eisenach to Gotha, just as our honoured prince and lord, Duke Ernest, fixed his residence at the Kaufhaus : for I was present when they paid him homage at Gotha. The royal Consistory soon offered to me the parish of Notleben ; but as the Notlebers were at strife with their old pastor, and there was to be a month's delay to carry on their contest, Dr. Glass persuaded me in the interim to go with my recommendation to Weimar, and to collect somewhat for my poor family. My wanderings, however, lasted till the year 1641. I returned on Tuesday the 18th of January to Gotha, and found the cure of that parish still vacant for me, which I undertook with the greatest humility and thankfulness, and preached my first sermon on the parable of the vineyard, from the 20th of Matthew. But I not only lived in great insecurity at Notleben, as one had daily to think of flight, but had also many disputes with the peasantry, who in church and school affairs had always a hankering after Erfurt, and to whom all royal ordinances with respect to the catechism were odious. I, the pastor, had to bear this from the council and peasants, and as all the stipend was paid in kind, and I was neither a tutor, nor had any other means whereby I could get on well, I humbly sought for a change of cure. When, therefore, our honoured lord, after the division of property, obtained the parish of Erock and the village of Heubach, he offered to me to become pastor there, which I had expected more than a year before. Thus in 1647, I in all humility accepted this removal, and preached my trial sermon on Judica Sunday, in the presence of the parishioners and commissaries. I received the call on the following day, and thus under God's providence brought hither my wife and child. This was my fourth piece of church preferment, where for my own part I desire, God willing, to live and die ; but my wife wishes herself away, in a better place in the plains, on account of the difficulty of getting servants. I leave it in the hands of God and my superiors."

Thus far extends what is preserved of Bötzinger's biography. He finally found rest at Heubach, and administered his office there for six-and-twenty years. He died in 1673, at the age of seventy-four, after having led for forty-seven years a life which cannot be designated as peaceful. Heubach was a new parish which had been formed at Gotha by Duke Ernest the Good, and Bötzinger was the first pastor. He was obliged to dwell in the royal shooting lodge, which had been built by Duke Casimir in the forest, for grouse shooting. In the neighbouring forester's house lived an insolent forester; the country was in a wild state, little inhabited, and the people, corrupted by the war, led a lawless forest life. It appears that the new pastor was not particularly welcome to these denizens of the woods, the forester especially was his vehement opponent, and the pastor secretly complained, in Latin distiches which he inscribed in the church records, to his successor, of the bitter sufferings which this servant of the woods occasioned him. He in a brotherly way warned his successor against the wickedness of the man and his bad wife. But in spite of this contention, it may be concluded that this long-tormented sufferer was not altogether unhappy, and a harmless self-contemplation is to be perceived in his Latin verses. When at last he died, laudatory poems by some of his noted clerical brothers were written, as was then the custom; some of them are extant both in Latin and German. Even Herr Andreas Bachmann, the court preacher at Gotha, a distinguished man, yielded a tribute of respect to his " Dear old, now deceased clerical brother;" it begins with the following verses, which will conclude this chapter :—

Martin Bötzinger, God's servant, faithful and true,
Upright as Job—was long time pastor I ween ;
A much tormented man with crosses not a few,
As will, in the record of his life, be seen.

CHAPTER IV.

THE THIRTY YEARS' WAR.—THE CLIPPERS OF MONEY, AND PUBLIC OPINION.

MONOTONOUSLY did the death wail sound in the chronicles and records of fellow-sufferers. Where thousands were saved, millions were ruined and destroyed. The war was destructive of house, wealth, and life, alike in town and country. Manifold was the work of the destroying forces, but a higher force was unceasingly at work to ward off final ruin.

It is a marvellous circumstance, that in the same year in which the war in Germany expired, the interest of the people in public affairs was so far developed as to originate the first newspapers. In matters of faith, moral feeling and the judgments of individuals had for a century worked, but in politics it was only rarely and feebly that serious diversity of opinion was ventured to be expressed by private individuals. It was just when the recruiting drums of the princes were beating at every muster-place that public opinion began its first political struggle in the press. On an important social question, the intellectual leaders of the people rose up against the immorality of their own Sovereigns. We shall endeavour here briefly to exhibit the course of public opinion, and show what was stirred up and carried away by it during the war. It may more especially be discovered in the literature of the flying-sheets, which contended for and against the Bohemian King, condemned the *Kipper* and *Wipper*, and did homage to the great Gustavus Adolphus, but at last became itself, like the nation, meagre and powerless.

It was after the beginning of the sixteenth century that the people began to receive news through the press, in a double form.   One of these forms was a single sheet printed on one side, almost always ornamented with a woodcut, and after the sixteenth century, with a copper-plate engraving, under which the explanatory text was generally rendered in verse.   In these flying leaves were communicated the appearances in the heavens, and comets; very soon also battles by land and sea, portraitures of the celebrities of the day, and the like. Much of the good humour, and coarse jests of the Reformation time are to be found in them.   The art of the wood carver was in constant activity, and we find many characteristic peculiarities of the talents of the great painters impressed upon it.   The other form was that of pamphlets, especially in quarto, frequently also ornamented with woodcuts.   They gave information of every novelty; coronations, battles, and newly discovered countries; by them every striking event flitted through the country.   After the Reformation, they increased enormously in number.   All printing-houses gave birth to them under the titles of newspapers, advices, reports, and couriers.   Besides these, there were the small controversial writings of the Reformers, sermons, discourses, and songs. Very soon also the Princes began to make use of the invention of printing, to inform the public of their quarrels, and to gain partisans.   Private individuals whose rights were injured contended with their opponents, whether city magistrates or foreign rulers, in pamphlets.   During the whole of the sixteenth century the aim of the small, not theological, literature, was first to impart news, and afterwards to serve the interests of individuals or princes, or to make known the views of those in power.   The opinions of individuals upon political affairs were principally conveyed in a form which was then considered particularly ingenious, as pasquinades or dialogues. These small news sheets were innumerable, and their spread was rapid ; after the Reformation it became a separate branch of industry.   The booksellers, or as they were then called, stationers, who offered these newspapers for sale in their shops and stalls, and introduced them to the markets of foreign cities, made a dangerous competition with the printers, bookbinders, and illuminators.   Important newspapers were everywhere pirated.   Along the great trade and post roads, more particularly of the Rhine and southern Germany, certain trading and printing establishments made special gains from the communication of the daily news ; for example, Wendelin Borsch, at the Tiler's Hut in Nuremberg, about 1571, Michael Enzinger at Cologne, at the end of the century, and others. These sheets at first were published very irregularly, but they already contained a correspondence from different cities, in which not only political, but mercantile intelligence was given.*   At last, in 1612, appeared here and there separate newspaper sheets in numbers, and in a certain degree of continuity.   Meanwhile it had been long the custom of the merchants to make such communications to their mercantile friends with some regularity, so that there already existed news-writers who were in the habit of forwarding written newspapers.   This method of spreading intelligence had come to Germany from Italy.   In Venice, from the year 1536, there were *Notizie Scritte*, written news in successive series, which continued there till the French Revolution.   There also, appeared the first regular newspaper shortly before 1600, which

---

* In a sheet of this kind, entitled, 'A Noteworthy Hungarian and the Netherlands New Newspaper,' 1599, has already the form and contents of a modern newspaper.   It contains a short correspondence with different cities, in the form of eleven letters ; amongst them reports of four vessels which had come to Amsterdam with spices, and of a new toll which the court at Brussels had levied on merchants' goods, of ten stivers on each pound of silk.

it is stated took the name of *Gazzetta* from a little coin which was the cost of the single numbers.

Soon after, the German newspapers began to appear regularly. In 1615 the first weekly newspaper was published at Frankfort-on-the-Maine, by Egenolf Emmel, bookseller and printer. In opposition to which, in 1616, the Imperial deputy postmaster Johann van der Brighden, published a competing paper called : Political Notices.' From these two undertakings resulted the oldest German newspapers, the 'Frankfort Journal,' and the 'Oberpostamts Zeitung.'

But these and other weekly papers were for a long time, only news sheets in which opinions on the facts communicated were carefully withheld. The great stream of public opinion still continued for two centuries to run in the old direction ; the flying leaves and occasional brochures.

At the beginning of the war even the distant readers were compelled to be violent partisans. Everywhere appeared controversial writings, opinions, councils, and deliberations. The nation was rent into large parties by this intellectual strife, and it is instructive to see how the writings of the disputants stand in exact relation to the success which their party had achieved. Till the battle of the Weissen Berge nine tenths of all the narratives and controversial writings are Protestant ; they reached full a thousand in number. Hatred to the Jesuits blazed fiercely ; bitter was the rancour against the Emperor, and incessant were the cautions against the League. After Prague, Strasburg was the centre of their warlike activity. Whilst at Prague the libel-writer von Rörig, as *Hussredivius*, made his voice heard vehemently in many 'Political Discourses' against his adversary Sturm : the *magisters* of Strasburg, after the fashion of Boccalini, made accusations against the same opponent, before Apollo and the high court of Parnassus ; but their Apollo had to deliver human and explicit oracles. The answers in defence are cautious and uncertain, as during the whole war the Catholic party were generally not a match for the Protestants in the serious warfare of the pen.   But the speedy flight of the new King of Bohemia suddenly changed the physiognomy of the literary market.   The secret writings obtained as booty from the Bohemian party were published by their opponents; and about these bulky quartos there raged for years a battle of petty flying sheets.   Revengeful, and joyfully triumphant, the Imperialists sounded their pæan.   It is true that in their brochures there was still some moderation, for they were obliged to spare the Lutheran Saxons; but so much the more irritably did they attack the enemy, in countless pictorial sheets and satirical verses.   Endless and merciless were the satires on the fugitive winter King, he, the proud and witless one, with his wife and children, were depicted in every kind of pitiful situation, seeking their bread, departing in bad waggons, and digging a grave for themselves.

This strife was interrupted by another, which will ever be of high interest.   It was the storm of the German press against the "*Kipper* and *Wipper*."

Of all the terrors at the beginning of the war, nothing gave such vague apprehension to the people, as the sudden depreciation of the coinage.   To the fancy of the suffering generation, the evil became so much the greater, as in the gloomy frame of mind of that period it appeared to occur suddenly, and everywhere roused the most frightful passions, discord in families, and hatred and strife between debtors and creditors, leaving behind, hunger, poverty, beggary, and immorality.   It made honourable citizens gamblers, drunkards, and profligates, it drove preachers and schoolmasters from their offices, brought opulent families to beggary, plunged every government into miserable confusion, and threatened the dwellers in cities, in a thickly populated country, with famine.

It was the third year of the war; its flames had already carried destruction over Bohemia and the Palatinate, and the ruins were still glowing, on which the Imperial troops erected the cross of the old faith. A sultry atmosphere loured over the country; throughout the empire, in every class, men armed themselves, and anxiety for the future pervaded all. But intercourse with the provinces in which the war was at first located, was then comparatively small. The countries exposed to its fury were, with the exception of the Palatinate, provinces belonging to the Emperor; and on the Elbe and lower Rhine, in Thuringia, Franconia, and the territories of lower Saxony, it was still a question whether the danger was approaching home. In August, 1621, the peasant had the prospect of a moderate harvest; in trade and commerce there was some degree of stagnation, but there was much of that excited eagerness which is the natural offspring of a great defensive movement, and manly youths were more allured than intimidated by the wild conduct of the soldiery. It had indeed been long remarked, that there was something unusual about the money which circulated in the country. The good heavy Imperial coin became more and more scarce, in its place much new money was current, badly coined, and of a red colour. The increasing rise in the price of foreign goods appeared still more strange. Everything became dearer. Whoever wished to make a present to a godchild, or to pay foreign tradesmen, had to give an increasing *agio* for his old pure Joachim's thaler. But in the local trade, betwixt town and country, the extensive new coinage was taken without hesitation, indeed it was exchanged or bartered with an increased activity. The mass of the people did not observe that the different kinds of coin with which it was the custom to pay, became in their hands, worthless lead; but the sharper ones, who had an inkling of the state of things, became, for the most part, accomplices in the dishonest usury of the Princes. It may be distinctly perceived how the people came to a knowledge of their situation, and we still feel dismayed at the sudden terror, anguish, and despair of the masses, and are struck by the anxieties and manly indignation of the thoughtful; and in reading the old narratives, we still feel somewhat of the indignation with which the guilty were regarded. When we consider the many wonderful errors of public opinion at that time, and the well-meaning zeal of individuals who gave good counsel, we may be permitted in this period of calamity and humiliation, to feel a proud satisfaction at the sagacity with which even then, some men of the people discovered the ground of the evil, and, in one of the most difficult national questions, found the right answer, and by it a remedy, at least for the worst misfortunes. Before we attempt to give a picture of the "*Kipper* and *Wipper*" years, we must make some remarks on the coining of that period.

In the olden time, all technical dexterity was environed with dignity, secrecy, and an apparatus of forms. Nothing is more characteristic of the peculiarity of the German nature, than its virtuosoship; even the most monotonous handicraft was ennobled by an abundance of lively additions. As soon as the spirit of the artisan was excited by the genial pleasure of creating, his imagination was occupied with images and symbols, and he turned his skill dexterously to high, nay even to holy things. What we have described as applicable to all the handicrafts of the middle ages, was so especially to the art of coining. A feeling of his self-importance was strong in the coiner; the work itself, the handling of the precious metals fresh from the fire, was considered ennobling. The obscure chemical processes, which were surrounded, through alchemy, with a wilderness of fantastic forms, had a far more imposing effect upon the workers, than can be understood by the rational fabricators of our century. To this was added the responsibility of the service. When the coiner took the assay weight out of its beautiful capsule, and placed the little acorn cup on the artistically worked assay balance, in order to weigh the remnant in it, he did this with a certain consciousness of superiority over his fellow-citizens.* When he purified the silver assay from lead in the cupel, and the liquid silver first overflowed, shining with delicate prismatic colours, and then, the variegated stream being rent, the bright gleam of the silver passed like lightning through the molten mass, this silver gleam filled him with reverential astonishment, and he felt himself in the midst of the mysterious creations of the spirits of nature, which, whilst he feared, he was yet able to control by the art of his handicraft, as far as his knowledge reached. After that period, in the order of things, the coiners formed themselves into a close corporation, with masters, associates, and apprentices, and held jealously to their privileges. Whoever was desirous of stamping the Holy Roman Imperial coin was first obliged to give proof of his free and honourable lineage, to do lowly service for four years, during this period to wear, according to custom, a fool's cap, and to allow himself to be punished and beaten when inexpert or in the wrong ; then at last he was admitted to the business of coining, and entered as an associate in the brotherhood of Imperial coiners.

But these strict regulations, which were again confirmed to the brotherhood by the Emperor Maximilian II., in 1571, had even then ceased to have the effect of making the corporation honourable and upright. Equally inefficient were the attempts at control, by the decisions of the Imperial Diet and the Sovereigns. At the inspection of every piece of coin the master of the mint had with him a warden,

---

* The sources of the following description were taken from the flying-sheets and brochures, first of the year 1620-24, and also from the later writings of the sixteenth century upon coinage, a rich literature.

who proved the texture and weight of the coin.   The ten
Circles of the Empire held yearly approbation days, in order,
mutually, to compare their coin and to reject the bad;
every Circle was to be represented by a warden-general;
for every Circle an appointed number of mints were established, in which the lesser rulers were to have their money
specially coined : but all these regulations were only imper-
fectly carried out.

There were undoubtedly some Sovereigns and mint-masters
then in the country who were faithful, but they were few in
number ; and generally a mint-master, who was considered
capable by a German Circle, and worked in a legal mint, was
concerned in many strange practices.   It was difficult to
exercise control over these imperfect coining proceedings ; the
temptations were great, and morality in general much lower
than now.   From the Sovereign down to the understrapper
and Jewish purveyor, every one concerned in coining deceived
the other.   The Sovereign allowed the master of the mint for
a series of years to work and become rich ; he perhaps permitted in silence the coin of the country to be debased, in
order at the right moment to proceed against the guilty,
from whom then he squeezed out by pressure, like a sponge,
all that they had sucked up for many years drop by drop.   It
did not avail them that they had long quitted the service, for
after many years greedy justice would reach them : but the
mint-master, who was not in the convenient position of the
lion, to be able to secure his booty by a single stroke of the
paw, was in the habit of industriously overreaching his
masters, the purveyors, nay even his cashiers, the associates,
and the apprentices, not to mention the public.   The other
assistants did no better ; every man's hand was against the
other, and the curse, which according to the proverb lies on
the gold of the German dwarf, appears in the seventeenth
century to have depraved all who transmuted the shining

metal into money. The common method of transacting the business was as follows.

The master of the mint purchased the metal, defrayed the costs of the stamping, and paid a tax to the Sovereign for every Cologne mark which he struck, which it appears amounted generally to about four good groschen: but he had to pay dear for fine silver, and the wages and other accessories were continually rising in price. If he paid the tax, from one to two thousand marks, weekly to the lord of the mint, he concealed from him the fifty marks which he had struck over and above, and retained the tax upon them for himself; furthermore, he was a sharp coiner, that is to say, he deducted from the money about half a grain in the amount of silver required by the law; he always struck a hundred marks in weight, two ounces too light, which was remarked by no one, and when he knew that the money was to be sent directly into foreign countries, especially to Poland, he was bolder in deducting from the weight. His dealings with the purveyors who procured the metal for him, were not more upright. There was carried on then, throughout the whole of Germany, a secret traffic, which was severely prohibited by the law, and traced with much sagacity by the gate-keepers of the cities, a traffic in false money. What was acquired by the soldier as booty, or stolen by the thief from the church, was smelted by the receivers of stolen goods into flat cakes or conical masses, which in the language of the trade were called "ingots" and "kings;" whatever was clipped from the money in diminishing the proper quantity of silver, or had otherwise to be carefully consigned under a false name, was poured out of the smelting crucible over moist birchen-twigs, and thus granulated: but besides this, by being incessantly bought up, the good coin was exchanged for bad, the small money-changers, most of them wandering Jews, journeyed from village to village far across the frontiers of the German Empire, and collected, as the ragmen do now, their wares from the soldiers, countrymen, and beggars. All the medals of distinguished persons, all coats-of-arms and inscriptions, horse and man, wolves, sheep and bears, thalers and hellers, the saints of Cologne and Treves, and the medallions of the heretic Luther, were bought up for the mint, collected and exchanged. The concealed wares were then packed into a vessel with ginger, pepper, and tartar, and paid toll duty as white lead, wrapped up in bales of cloth and frankincense. There were travelling waggons with false bottoms, which were specially prepared for such transports. A still better safeguard was an ecclesiastic as a travelling companion; but the best of all was a trumpeter, who gave the trader the appearance of being a prince's courier. If it happened that a distinguished lord was travelling towards the same country, it was expedient to bribe him, for he and his suite, their waggons and horses, were never examined at the city gates. Sometimes the agent disguised himself as a distinguished lord or soldier, and caused the burden to be conveyed by the trooper's horses or his servants. Sometimes the mint-master was obliged to travel to the frontier to meet the agent, under the pretext of paying a visit to some friend. Then the costly goods were carried far from the dwellings of men, across lonely heaths, or through the clearings of a wood, from one hand to another, on a merchant's parole.

Meanwhile the petty Jewish dealer carried at night, along byways over the frontier, his wallet full of old groschen, in the twofold fear of robbers and of the guardians of the law. The wallet, the broad-brimmed hat, and the yellow cloth border to the coat, the mark of a Jew of the Empire, was frequently seen at the mint. There existed between the dealer and the mint-master a confidential business connection, certainly not without a mental reservation; for it occasionally

happened to the Jew that false thalers were found in one of
the hundred marks which he delivered in thalers, or that the
wallet together with the coin had become moist during the
journey, which added some half-ounces to their weight,
or that fine white sand became mingled with the granulated silver, and was weighed with it. For this the mint-
master indemnified himself, by hanging the scales so that one
side of the beam was shorter than the other, by causing the
scales to spring up and descend slowly, notwithstanding the
perpendicular position of the balance, in order to make the
wares some half-ounces lighter, or by falsifying the weights
altogether. What the masters did not do, the apprentices of
the mint ventured upon. However cautious the purveyor
might be during the smelting assay, they understood how to
mix copper dust with the silver already weighed, in order to
make the assay worse than it really was. Such was the
state of the traffic even at those mints where there was still
some respect for the law.

Besides the licensed coiners, there were others in most of
the ten Circles, of easier conscience and bolder practice ; not
exactly false coiners in our sense of the term, although this
was carried on with great recklessness ; but nobles and corporations who had the right of coining, and prized it highly
as a source of income ; for, contrary to the Imperial decrees,
which imposed upon them the duty of having their money
coined in one of the approved mints of the Circle, they coined
actively in their own territory. Sometimes they let their
right of coining for a year's rent, nay, they even disposed of
their mints to other princes as a speculation. These irregular coining places were called hedge mints, and in them a
systematic corruption of money took place. No inquiry was
made as to the right of the coiners ; whoever knew how to
manage fire and metal, engaged in this kind of work. There
was little regard for the prescribed fineness of texture, and

weight of the money; it was coined with false stamps, and the head of the ruler, with the date of a better period, were stamped on light coin; nay, in regular false coining, the stamps of foreign mints were often counterfeited. The brightness of the new coin was removed by tartar or lead water; and all this took place under the protection of the Sovereign. The disposal of the money thus coined required all the cunning and circumspection of the agents, and a line of industry was in this way formed, which we may presume occupied many intermediate hands. Thundering decrees had been fulminated for seventy years at the Imperial Diets and Assemblages of the circles, against the hedge mints, but without success. Indeed, after the introduction of good Imperial money, they became more numerous and active, for the work paid better.

Such was the state of things even before the year 1618. The sovereigns, small and great, required more and more money. Then some of the Princes of the Empire—the Brunswickers, alas! were among the first—began to outdo the proceedings of the most notorious of the hedge mints; they caused the coin of the country, both heavy and light, to be struck of a bad mixture of silver and copper, instead of silver, and soon it was only copper silvered. At last, as for example at Leipzig, a small angular coin was issued by the city, no longer of copper, which was of higher value, but of pure tin. This discovery of making money at little cost spread like a pestilence. From both of the Circles of Saxony it spread to those of the Rhine and Southern Germany. Hundreds of new mints were established. Wherever a ruined tower appeared firm enough for a forge and bellows, wherever there was abundance of wood for burning, and a road to bring good money to the mint and carry away bad, there a band of coiners nestled. Electors and nobles, ecclesiastical communities and cities outvied each other in making copper money; even the people were infected with

it. For a century the art of making gold, and treasure digging had occupied the fancies of the people; now the happy
time appeared to have arrived, when every fish-kettle could
be turned into silver in the coiners' scales. A mania for money-
making began. Pure silver and old silver gilt became
continually and strikingly dearer in mercantile traffic, so that
at last it was necessary to pay four, five or more new gulden
for one old silver gulden, and the price of goods and the
necessaries of life slowly rose; but that signified little to the
multitude, so long as the new money, the production of which
seemed to increase without end, was willingly taken. The
nation, already excited, became at last madly intoxicated.
Every one thought they had the opportunity of becoming
rich without labour; all applied themselves to trafficking in
money. The merchant had money dealings with the artisan,
the artisan with the peasant. A general craving, chaffering,
and overreaching prevailed. The modern swindling in funds
and on 'Change, gives only a weak notion of the proceedings of
that time. Whoever had debts hastened to pay them; whoever could get money from an accommodating coiner, in exchange for an old brewing vessel,* could buy therewith house
and fields; whoever had to pay wages, salaries, or fees, found
it convenient to do so in plated copper. There was little
work done in the cities, and only for very high pay. Whoever had any old thalers, gold gulden, or other good Imperial
money lying in their chests as a store in case of need, as was
then the case with almost every one, drew out his treasure
and was delighted to exchange it for new money, as the old

* The new money was almost pure copper boiled and blanched; this
lasted a week, and then it became glowing red. The bottles, kettles, pipes,
gutters, and whatever else was of copper, were taken away to the mint, and
made into money. An honest man could not venture to lodge any one, as
he could not but fear that his guest might wrench away his copper in the
night, and carry it off. Wherever there was an old copper font in a church,
it was taken to the mint; its sanctity did not save it; those sold it who
had been baptized in it. Müller, 'Chronika von Sangerhausen.'

thalers, in a most remarkable way, appeared to be worth four, nay even six and ten times as much as formerly. That was a jolly time. If wine and beer were dearer than usual, they were not so in the same proportion as the old silver money. Part of the gains were jovially spent in the public-house. Every one was disposed to give, in those times. The Saxon cities readily agreed, at the Diet at Torgau, to a great addition to the land tax, as money was to be obtained everywhere in superfluity. People also were very ready to contract debts, for money was offered everywhere, and business could be done with it on favourable conditions; great obligations therefore were undertaken on all sides. Thus a powerful stream carried away the people to destruction.

But a counter stream arose, first gentle, then continually stronger. Those were first to complain who had to live on a fixed income, the parish priests most loudly, the schoolmasters and poor misanthropes most bitterly. Those who had formerly lived respectably on two hundred gulden, good Imperial coin, now only received two hundred light gulden, and if, as often undoubtedly happened, the salary of some were raised about a quarter in amount, they could not even with this addition defray half, nay even the fourth part, of the necessary expenses. Upon this unprecedented occasion the ecclesiastics referred to the Bible, and found there an indisputable objection to all hedge minting, and began to preach from their pulpits against light money. The schoolmasters starved in the villages as long as they could, then ran away and increased the train of vagabonds, beggars, and soldiers; the servants next became discontented. The wages, which averaged ten gulden a year, hardly sufficed to pay for their shoes. In every house there were quarrels between them and their masters and mistresses. Men and maid servants ran away, the men enlisted and the maids endeavoured to set up for themselves. Meanwhile the youths dispersed from the

schools and universities, few parents among the citizens
being sufficiently well off to be able to support their sons entirely during the period of education.   There were however a
multitude of scholarships founded by benevolent people for
poor students.   The value of these now suddenly vanished, the
credit of the poor scholars in foreign towns was soon exhausted,
many found it impossible to maintain themselves ; they sank
under poverty and the temptations of that bloody period.
We may still read in the autobiographies of many respectable
theologians, what distress they then suffered.   One supported
life in Vienna, by cutting daily his master's tallies for a four-
penny loaf ; another was able to earn eighteen batz * in the
week, by giving lessons, the whole of which he was obliged to
spend on dry bread.

There was increasing discontent.   First among the capitalists who lived on the interest of the money which they had
lent, which was then in middle Germany five, or occasionally six, per cent.   For a time they were much envied
as wealthy people, but now their receipts were often hardly
sufficient to maintain life.   They had lent thousands of good
Imperial thalers, and now a creditor would pay them on the
nail a thousand thalers in new money.   They demanded back
their good old money ; they squabbled and laid their complaints before the courts ; but the money which they had
received back bore the image of the Sovereign and the old
mark of value ; it was legally stamped money, and the debtor
could in justice allege that he had received similar money,
both as interest and capital and for labour.   Thus there arose
numberless lawsuits ; and the lawyers were in great per-
plexity.   At last the cities and even the Sovereigns were
embarrassed.   They had willingly issued the new money,
and many of them had coined it recklessly.   But now for all
their taxes and imposts they obtained only bad money, a

* A batz was four kreuzer.

hundred pounds of plated copper instead of a hundred pounds of silver, at the same time everything had become dear, even to them, and a portion of their expenses had to be paid in good silver.   Then the governments attempted to assist themselves by new frauds.   First they endeavoured to retain the good money by compulsion ; now they suddenly lowered the value of their own money, and again threatened punishment and compulsion to all who gave less value for it.   But the false money still continued to sink under the regulated value.   Then some governments refused to take for the payment of taxes and imposts, the money of their own country which they themselves had coined.   They declined taking back what they had stamped in the last year.   Now for the first time the people discovered the whole danger of their position.   A general storm broke loose against the new money ; it sank even in daily traffic to a tenth of its nominal value.   The new hedge mints were cried down as nests of the devil ; the mint-masters and their agents, the money-changers, and whoever else dealt in money concerns, were the general objects of detestation.   Then it was that they obtained in Germany the popular names of *Kipper* and *Wipper*.   These are Lower Saxon words : *kippen* comes equally from the fraudulent weighing, as from the clipping of the money ; and *wippen* from throwing the heavy money out of the scales.*   Satirical songs were sung about them ; it was supposed that their names were heard in the call of the quail, and the mob cried out after them " *kippe di wipp*," as they did " *hep* " after the Jews.   In many places the people combined together and stormed their dwellings.   For many a year after the terrors of the long war, it was considered a disgrace to have acquired money in the *Kipper-time*.   Everywhere disorders and tumults arose ; the bakers would no

* In the decrees of the Diet the words do not occur before the Thirty years' war ; they appear to be new in 1621.

longer bake, and their shops were destroyed; the butchers
would no longer slaughter, on account of the prescribed tax;
the miners, soldiers, and students raged about in a state of
wild uproar; the city communities, deep in debt, became
bankrupt, as for example the wealthy Leipzig. The old
joints of the burgher societies cracked and threatened to
burst asunder. The small literature urged on and excited
the temper of the public mind, and was itself still further
excited by the increasing discontent. The street songs
began it, and the pictorial flying-sheets followed. The
Kippers were unweariedly portrayed with the flames of
hell round their heads, their feet standing on an insecure
ball, surrounded by numerous gloomy emblems, amongst
which the cord and the lurking raven were not absent; or in
their mints collecting and carrying off money, and in contrast
to them the poor, begging; the different classes were depicted, soldiers, citizens, widows and orphans, paying to the
money-changers their hard earnings; the jaws of hell
appeared open, and the changers were assiduously shoved
down by devils; all this was adorned, according to the taste
of the times, with allegorical figures and Latin devices, made
comprehensible to every one by indignant couplets in
German.

As among the people, so also among the educated, a fierce
storm began to rage. The parish priests were loud in their
invectives and denunciations, not only from the pulpit but
also in flying-sheets. A brochure literature began, which
swelled up like a sea. One of the first that was written
against the new money was by W. Andreas Lampe, pastor
at Halle. In a powerful treatise, ' On the last brood and
fruit of the devil, Leipzig, 1621,' he proved, by numerous
citations from the Old and New Testament, that all trades
and professions in the world, even that of an executioner,
were by divine ordinance; but the *Kipper* was of the devil,

whereupon he characterizes in some cutting passages the mischief which they had caused. He had to suffer severe trials, and though he loyally spared the authorities, yet he was threatened with proceedings, so that he found it necessary to obtain from the sheriffs' court at Halle a justification. He was soon followed by many of his clerical brethren. The controversial writings of these ecclesiastics appear to us clumsy productions; but it is well to examine them with attention, for the Protestant priesthood are always representatives of the cultivation and the rectitude of the people.

The preachers exorcised the evil one, and the theological faculty soon followed with the heavy artillery of their Latin arguments, and how bitter was the priestly anger, was shown for example by the consistory of Wittemberg, when they refused the Lord's Supper and honourable burial to the *Kippers*. Lastly we have the lawyers with their questions, informations, detailed opinions on coining and recapitulations. The answers which they gave in thick brochures were almost always very diffuse, and their arguments frequently subtile; still they were necessary, for the disputes concerning *meum* and *tuum* between creditor and debtor appeared interminable, and numberless lawsuits threatened to prolong insupportably the sufferings of the people. The principal subjects of investigation were, whether those who had lent good money were to be repaid capital and interest in light money; and again, whether those who had lent light money had a claim for the repayment of the full capital in good money. It must be remarked here that, in many cases which the law and the acuteness of lawyers did not reach, the dispute was ended by that true feeling of equity which was inherent in the people. For when the governments were generally bad, and legal justice was very costly and difficult to be obtained, much had to be accomplished by the practical sense of individuals. A little flying leaf, in which is related how the sound common sense of the village magistrate administered justice, was certainly not less useful than a massive half-Latin, half-German " *Informatio.*"

In the flood of paper, which gives us information concerning the excitement of that period, there are certain sheets which more especially arrest our attention—the utterances of educated and experienced men, who know how to tell shortly and effectively in a popular form, from whence it all arose. Some of these flying-sheets, written at different periods of the Thirty years' war, have been preserved to us, in which we may even now behold with admiration, both energy of character, power of language, and genuine statesmanlike discernment. In vain do we inquire for the name of the author. We will only mention here one of these writings. Its title is, 'Expurgatio, or Vindication of the poor *Kipper* and *Wipper*, given by Kniphardum Wipperium, 1622. Fragfurt.'

The author has chosen the valiant Lampe as the object of his attack, as the cautious zeal of the Saxon ecclesiastic whose distinguished colleagues were accused of being Wippers—for example, the notorious court preacher Hoe, the subservient tool of the Elector—had excited the indignation of a powerful mind. A manly judgment, and a very just democratic tone appears in the strong expressions of this writing. We may judge of its peculiar tenour from the following passages :—

" I have never yet seen a single penny, and much less an inferior coin, on which was to be found the names, arms, or stamp of *Kipper* and *Wipper,* still less any inscription from the new quail call, *kippediwipp.* But one may truly see thereupon a well-known stamp or image, and the *Kipper* or *Wipper* will not appear even in the smallest letter of the alphabet.

" But if Herr Magister does not rightly understand the matter, let him ask who has bought the old saucepans at the highest price, in order to assist the coining; having done so, Herr Magister will truly learn who has coined the copper and tin money. For truly so many old pans in which so much good gruel or millet pap has been made, and so many coppers in which so much good beer has been brewed, are melted down and coined, and this not by the vulgar *Kipper*, but by the *Arch kipper*. For the others have no regale to coin, and if they, like the blood and deer hounds, have scented and hunted out such things, they have done so by the command of others, and thus are not to be so severely condemned as those (let them call themselves what they may) who have the regalie, and misuse it to the perceptible damage of the German States.

"No one now-a-days will bell the cat, or, like John the Baptist, tell the truth to Herod. Every one heaps abuse upon the poor rogues, the *Kippers* and *Wippers*, who nevertheless do not carry on this business by their own authority, for all that they do takes place with the knowledge, consent, and approbation of the government. And alas, they have now-a-days many competitors. For as soon as any one gets a penny or a groschen that is a little better than another, he forthwith makes with it usurious profit. Therefore, as experience teaches, it comes to pass as follows: the doctors abandon their invalids and think far more of usury than of Hippocrates and Galen; the lawyers forget their legal documents, lay aside their practice, and taking usury in hand, let who will peruse Bartholus and Balbus. The same is also done by other men of learning, who study arithmetic more than rhetoric and philosophy; the merchants, shop-keepers, and other traders acquire now-a-days their greatest gains by their hardwares which are marked by the mint stamp.

"From this we may perceive that the 'unhanged, thievish, oath-forgetting, dishonourable,' *Kippers* and *Wippers*, though not indeed to be quite exculpated, are not so much to be con-

demned as if they were the *causa principalis* of the ruin of
the German States.   I have, alas! assuredly great fears, that
if once there is a delivery to the devil or hangman, the
Kippers and *Wippers,* changers and usurers, Jews and Jew
associates, helpers and helpers' helpers, one thief with another,
will all be hurled off to the devil, or be hung up at the same
time together, like yonder host with his companions.   Yet
with a difference.   For their principals and patrons will justly
have the prerogative and pre-eminence, and indeed some of
them have been already sent there beforehand.   The others
will shortly follow to the above-mentioned place, and it will
then avail nothing on this journey downward, whether one
treats them with *carmina* or *crimina,* whether one passes
judgment on them as criminals, or gives them laudatory
poems—*facilis descensus Averni*—they will easily find the
way, for they need no good fortune for that; the devil will
couple them all with one cord, be the rogues ever so big.
Fiat."

It is not improbable that a similar view of their social
prospects in another world was impressed upon the rulers
from many quarters.   At all events, even they discovered that
they could only be saved by the most speedy help; nothing
would avail them but the reduction and hasty withdrawal of
the new coinage, and a return to the good old Imperial coin.
Thus the first fears of the princes and cities caused them to
depreciate their new money, and to make use of these verdicts
in order to express their abhorrence—not of very old date—
of the bad coin, and they forthwith had the coin stamped
honourably of due weight and alloy, as prescribed by the
Imperial law.   In order to put a stop to the excessive increase of prices, they hastened to put forth a tariff of goods
and wages, which decided the highest price to be permitted.
It is clear that this latter remedy could not be of more lasting
use than the famous edict of Diocletian, thirteen hundred

years before.   The compulsion which, for example, it exercised over the city weekly markets, day labourers, and guilds, was only a temporary help for restoring the overflowing stream to its old bed.

This state of intoxication, terror, and fury was followed by a dreary reaction.   Men gazed on one another as after a great pestilence.   Those who had rested secure in their opulence had sunk into ruin.   Many worthless adventurers now strutted, as persons of distinction, in velvet and silk.   The whole nation had become poorer.   There had not been any great war for a long time, and many millions in silver and gold, the savings of the inferior classes, had been inherited in city and village from father to son; the greater part of these savings had vanished in the bad times; it had been squandered on carousals, frittered away on trifles, and at last expended for daily food.   But this was not the greatest evil; it was a still greater, that at this time the citizen, and countryman had been forcibly torn from the path of their honest daily labour.   Frivolity, an unsettled existence, and a reckless egotism, had taken possession of them.   The destroying powers of war had sent forth their evil spirits to loosen the firm links of burgher society, and to accustom a peaceful, upright, and laborious people to the sufferings and mal-practices of an army which shortly overran all Germany.

The period from 1621 to 1623 was henceforth called the "Kipper and Wipper" time.   The confusion, the excitement, the trafficking, and the flying-sheet literature lasted till the year 1625.   The lessons which the princes had learnt from the consequences of their flagitious actions did not avail them against later temptations.   Even at the end of the seventeenth century it seems to have been impossible for them entirely to avoid hedge mints, and the continual recurrence of a depreciation of money.

Whilst Tilly was conquering Lower Saxony, and Wallenstein made great havoc in Northern Germany, small literature flowed in an under-current. After every engagement, and every capture of a city, there appeared copper engravings, with a text which described the position of the troops and the appearance of the city; irregular newspapers, and songs of lament conveyed the information of the advance of the Imperialists, and the destruction of the Mansfelders. In the midst of all this the people were dismayed by terrible decrees of the Emperor, who now from his secure position threw over the evangelicals, or compelled them by force to return to his Church, in spite of the fruitless intercessions of the Elector of Saxony. The Elector at last authorized the publication of a defence of the Augsburg confession, against the attacks of the Catholic theologians; this comprehensive work, called, 'The necessary Defence of the Apple of the Eye,' written in 1628, called forth immediately a theological war; both opponents and allies hastened in crowds to the field. 'Spectacles for the Evangelical Apple of the Eye;' 'A sharp round Eye on the Romish Pope;' 'Who has struck the Calf in the Eye?' 'The Catholic Oculist or Coucher;' 'Venetian Spectacles on Lutheran Nose,' &c. These are specimens of the defiant titles of the most readable of the controversial writings. But this literary strife was drowned in the burst of loud outcries against Wallenstein, which pierced from Pomerania through all the German States, on account of the battle near Stralsund, and his shameful conduct towards the Pomeranian Duke and his country, and finally the horrible ill treatment of the men and women of Pasewalk. Again these lamentations changed into a shout of joy from all the Protestants. Again hope and confidence revived; this time it was a man, whom the nation, with the genuine German longing to love and honour, welcomed with shouts of jubilee. What had been wanting to the Germans for a century, came to them from the North, an idol and a hero. But he was a foreigner.

Much of that halo of light still surrounds the figure of Gustavus Adolphus, which distinguished him in the eyes of his cotemporaries so immeasurably above all other generals and princes. It is not his victories, nor his knightly death, nor the circumstance that he appeared as the last help to a despairing people, which makes him the one prominent figure in the long struggle. It was the magic of his great nature, as he rode over the field of battle, firm, self-contained, and as confident as unerring; from head to foot he was dignity, decision, and nervous energy. If one examines more nearly, one is astonished at the strong contrasts which combined in this character to form an admirable unity. No General was more systematic, fertile in plans, or greater in the science of war. Discipline in the army, order in the commissariat, a firm basis, and secure lines of retreat in every strategical operation, these were the requisites he brought with him to the conduct of the German War. But even he, the powerful prince of war, was driven by an irresistible necessity from his good system, but with the whole power of his being he incessantly stemmed the tide of the wild marauding war that raged around him. And yet this same systematic man bore within him a rash spirit of daring against the greatest hazards; his bearing in the battle was wonderfully elevated, like that of a noble battle steed. His eyes lighted up, his figure became more lofty, and a smile played on his countenance. Again, how wonderful appears to men, the union in him of frank honesty and wary policy, of upright piety and worldly wisdom, of high-minded self-sacrifice and reckless ambition, of heartfelt humanity and stern severity! And all this was enlivened by an inward confidence and freedom of mind, which enabled him to look in a humorous point of view on the distracted condition of the decaying Princes of the country. The irresistible power which he exercised over all who came under his influence, consisted principally in the freshness of his nature, his surpassing good humour, and where it was necessary, an ironical bonhomie.   The way in which he managed the proud and wavering Princes, and the hesitating cities of the Protestant party, was not to be surpassed ; he was never weary of exciting them to war, and alliance ; he ever reverted to the same theme, whether to the Envoy of the Branden-burger, or when flattering the Nurembergers, or chiding the Frankforters.

He was closely allied, both by race and faith, to the Northern Germans ; but he was a foreigner.   This was thoroughly and constantly felt by the Princes.   It was not alone distrust of his superior power which, till the bitterest necessity compelled them to union, kept aloof from him the irresolute, but it was the discovery in him of a new master ; they revolted at the idea of this mighty non-German power, which so suddenly and threateningly arose in the empire. There was still to be found in a few of them somewhat of Luther's national idea of the empire.   They had no hesitation in negotiating with France, Denmark, the Netherlands, nay with the unreliable Bethlem Gabor ; all these were outside the Empire.   Within its boundaries there was the fanatical Emperor and his insupportable General ; they were new people to them, who might pass away as rapidly as they had become great ; but the sovereignty of the German Empire was old, and they were the pillars of it.   This con-ception was no longer in accordance with the highest policy, for the German Emperor had become the most mortal enemy of the German Empire.   But such a feeling is not deserving of contempt ; and the nation as well as most of the Princes, felt to the heart's core that their quarrel with the Emperor was in fact a domestic one, in which foreigners should have no concern.   But the people, blinded by their delight in the dazzling heroism of the Protestant King, lost sight of these considerations. For two years public opinion paid homage to him, as it has never done since, except to the Great Frederic of Prussia. Every word, every little anecdote was carried from city to city, and loud acclamations greeted every success of his arms. It was not only the zealous Protestants who thus felt; even in the Catholic armies and in the states of the League, the scorn was quickly silenced which had been called forth by the landing of the " Snow King," and the number of his admirers continually increased. Many characteristic traits of him are preserved to us; almost every conversation that he had with Germans, gives an opportunity of discovering something of his nature. We will give here a short conversation, after his landing in Pomerania, recorded by a clever negotiator.

The Elector of Brandenburg had sent his plenipotentiary, Von Wilmersdorff, to persuade the King to conclude an armistice with the Emperor; he further wished to negotiate a peace between them, although Wallenstein had already deprived him of his dominions, and the Emperor had shown him every kind of disregard. The conversation of the King with the Envoy gives a good picture of his method of negotiating. He is here concise, firm, and straightforward, in spite of some mental reservation; and so perfectly self-possessed that he can allow his lively temperament to break forth without danger. The Envoy relates as follows :—

" After his Kingly Majesty had listened graciously to me, though when I came to the proposition of an armistice he rather smiled, he, no one being present, answered me circumstantially.

" ' I had expected a different kind of embassy from my loving cousin; that is to say, that he would rather have come to meet me and united himself with me for his own welfare; and not that my loving cousin should be so weak as to lose this opportunity so providentially sent by God. My loving cousin will not comprehend the clear and evident intentions of his enemies; he does not discern the difference between pretexts and truth, nor consider that when this pretence shall cease, that is to say, when they have no longer anything more to fear from me, another will soon be found to establish himself in my loving cousin's country.

" ' I had not expected that my loving cousin would have been so much terrified at the war as to remain inactive notwithstanding all the consequences to himself. Or does not my cousin yet know, that the intention of the Emperor and his allies is not to desist till the evangelical religion is entirely rooted out of the empire? my loving cousin must be prepared either to deny his religion or abandon his country. Does he think that anything else can be obtained by prayers, entreaties, or the like means? For God's sake let him reflect a little, and for once take *mascula consilia.* You see how this excellent prince the Duke of Pomerania was in the most innocent way,—having really committed no offence but only peaceably drunk his beer,—brought into the most lamentable condition, and how wonderfully he was saved under God's providence, *fato quodam necessario*—for he was constrained to do so—by making terms with me. What he did from necessity my loving cousin may do willingly.

" ' I cannot withdraw, *jacta est alea, transivimus Rubi-conem.* I do not seek my own advantage in this business; I gain nought but the security of my kingdom; beyond this I have nothing but expenses, trouble, labour, and danger to body and soul. They have occasioned me enough; in the first place they have twice sent help to my enemies the Poles, and endeavoured to drive me away; then they have endeavoured to possess themselves of the harbours of the Baltic, whereby I could well perceive what their intentions towards me were. My loving cousin the Elector is in a similar case, and it is

now time that he should open his eyes and give up somewhat
of his easy life, that he may no longer be a Stadtholder of the
Emperor, nay even an Imperial servant in his own country :
" Qui se fait brebis le loup le mange."

" ' This is now precisely the best opportunity, when your
country is free from Imperial soldiers, to garrison and defend
your fortresses. If you will not do this, deliver over one
to me, if it be only Küstrim. I will defend it, and you may
then remain in the inactivity which your Prince so dearly
loves.

" ' What other will you do ? For I declare to you distinctly, I will not hear of neutrality, my loving cousin must
be either friend or foe. When I come to your frontier you
must show yourselves either cold or warm. This is a struggle
between God and the devil ; if my loving cousin will hold to
God, let him unite with me ; but if he would rather hold to
the devil, he must henceforth fight against me, *tertium non
dabitur*, of that he may be assured.

" ' Take this commission upon you to inform my loving
cousin secretly of it, for I have none with me whom I can
spare to send to him. If my loving cousin will treat with
me, I will see if I can go to him myself ; but with his present
arrangements I will have nothing to do.

" ' My loving cousin trusts neither in God nor to his good
friends. It has gone ill with him therefore in Prussia and this
country. I am the devoted servant of my loving cousin, and
love him from my heart : my sword shall be at his service, and
it shall preserve him in his sovereignty and to his people, but
he must do his part also.

" ' My loving cousin has great interest in this dukedom of
Pomerania ; this will I also defend for his advantage, but on
the same condition as in the book of Ruth the next inheritor
is commanded to take Ruth for his wife, so must my loving
cousin take to him this Ruth ; that is, unite himself with

me in this righteous business if he wishes to inherit the country. If not, I here declare that he shall never obtain it.

" ' I am not disinclined to peace, and have conformed myself to it contentedly. I know well that the chances of war are doubtful ; I have experienced that, in the many years in which I have carried on war with various fortune. But as I have now, by God's grace, come so far, no one can counsel me to withdraw, not even the Emperor himself if he were to make use of his reason.

" ' I might perhaps allow of an armistice for a month. It may appear fitting to me that my loving cousin should mediate. But he must place himself in a position, arms in hand, otherwise all his mediation will avail nothing. Some of the Hanse towns are ready to unite with me. I only wait for some one in the Empire to put himself prominently at the head. What might not the electors of Saxony and Brandenburg together with these cities, accomplish ? Would to God that there were a Maurice !'

" Thereupon I replied that I had no commands from his Electoral Highness to confer with his Majesty, touching an armed alliance. But in my poor opinion, I doubted much whether his Electoral Highness would be able to come to an understanding without detriment to his honour and truth, *salvo honore et fide sua.*

" Then his Majesty interposed promptly : ' Yes, they will honour you when they have deprived you of your land and people. The Imperialists will keep faith with you as they have kept the capitulation.'

" I : ' It is necessary to look to the future, and consider how all will fall to ruin if the undertaking does not prosper.'

" The King : ' That will happen if you remain inactive, and would have done so already if I had not come. My loving cousin ought to do as I have done, and commend the result to God. I have not lain on a bed for fourteen days. I might have spared myself this trouble and sat at home with my wife if I had had no greater considerations.'

" I : ' As your Kingly Majesty is content that his Electoral Highness should become mediator, you must at least allow his Electoral Highness to remain neutral.'

" The King: ' Yes, till I come to his country.   Such an idea is mere chaff, which the wind raises and blows away. *What kind of a thing is that Neutrality ?   I do not understand it !'*

" I : ' Yet your Kingly Majesty understood it well in Prussia, where you yourself suggested it to his Electoral Highness and to the city of Dantzic.'

" The King : ' Not to the Elector, but certainly to the city of Dantzic, for it was to my advantage.'

" After this he returned again to the subject of the Duke of Pomerania, saying that the good prince had been well content with him.   He would have restored him Stralsund, Rügen, Usedom, Wollin, and all the rest.   The Duke had desired that his Majesty should be his father.   ' But I,' said his Majesty, ' answered, I would rather be his son, as he has no children.'

" Thereupon I answered : ' Yes, Kingly Majesty, that might very well be, if his Electoral Highness could only maintain the law of primogeniture in Pomerania.'

" The King : ' Yes, that may be very easily maintained by my loving cousin ; but he must defend it, and not, like Esau, sell it for a mess of pottage.' "

Thus far goes the narrative.

When the great King, the lord of half Germany, sank into the dust in battle, the wail of lamentation broke forth in all the Protestant territories.   Funeral services were performed in the towns and country, endless elegies poured forth ; even the enemy concealed their joy under a manly sympathy, which at that time was seldom accorded to opponents.

His death was considered as a national misfortune; the deliverer and the saviour of the people was lost: we also, whether Catholic or Protestant, should not only regard with heartfelt sympathy that pure hero life, which in the prime of its strength was so suddenly extinguished, but we should also contemplate with the deepest gratitude the influence of the King upon the German war; for he had, in a time of desperation, defended that which Luther had attained for the whole nation,—freedom of soul, and capacity for the development of national strength against the most fearful enemy of the German national existence, against a crushing despotism in Church and State.   But we must also observe concerning him, that the fate which he met strikes us as more peculiarly tragical because he drew it upon himself.   History makes us acquainted with some characters which, after mighty deeds, are suddenly struck down at the height of their fame by a rapid change of fate in the midst of powerful but unaccomplished conception.   Such heroes have a popular mixture of qualities of soul, which make them the privileged favourites both of posterity and art.   Such was the case with the almost fabulous hero, the great Alexander; and thus it was, in a more limited sphere, with smaller means, with the Swedish King Gustavus Adolphus: but however accidental the fever or the bullet which carried them off may appear to us, their destruction arose from their own greatness.   The conqueror of Asia had become an Asiatic despot before he died; the deliverer of Germany was shot by an Imperial mercenary when he was rushing through the dust of the battle-field, not like a General of the seventeenth century, but like a " Viking " of the olden time, who fought their battles in wild excitement under the protection of the battle-maidens of Odin.   Often already had the incautious heroism of the King led him into rash daring and useless danger, and long had his faithful adherents feared that he would at some time meet his end

thus.   It was a wise policy which led him to establish himself on the German coast, in order to secure to his Sweden
the dominion of the Baltic, also to draw the sea-ports to his
interests, and to desire firm points of support on the Oder,
Elbe, and Weser.   But what duty did he owe to the German
Empire, whose own Emperor wished to suppress the national
life and popular development by Roman money, and calling
thither hordes of soldiers from half Europe ?   When Gustavus
Adolphus conceived the idea of making himself lord para-
mount over the German Princes, when he proceeded to form
an hereditary power for himself in Germany, he was no longer
the great cotemporary of Richelieu, but again the descendant
of an old Norman chieftain.   It is possible that the power of
the man, during a longer life and after many victories, might
have brought under his sway, with or without an Imperial
throne, the greater part of Germany ; but that Sweden, the
foundation of his power, was not in a position to exercise a
lasting supremacy over Germany, a small ·distant country
over a larger, must have been obvious even then to the
weakest politician.   The King might still for some years
longer have sacrificed the peasant sons of Sweden on the
German battle-fields, and corrupted the Swedish nobility by
German plunder ; but he could not build up an enduring
dynasty for both people, whatever his genius might have
accomplished for a time.   Men of ordinary powers would soon
have restored things to their natural condition.   We are
therefore of opinion, that he died just when his lofty desires
were beginning to contend against a fundamental law of the
new state life, and we may assume that even a longer life of
success would not have made much alteration in our position.
When he died, his natural heir in Germany was already
twelve years of age : this heir was Frederic William, the
great Elector of Brandenburg.   Gustavus Adolphus was the
last but one of the northern princes to whom the old Scan-

dinavian expedition to the south proved fatal.   Charles XII.,
dying before Friedrichshall, was the last.

As the funeral lament died away in Germany, there began
a reaction in public opinion against the foreigners.   The
Catholic faction had, during the whole war, the doubtful
advantage that their quarrels and private dissensions were
not brought to light by the press, but their Protestant opponents were broken into parties.   It was more especially after
Saxony, in 1635, had endeavoured, at Prague, to make an
inglorious reconciliation with the Emperor by a separate
peace, that there arose both in the north and south an Imperial and a Swedish party, and much weak dissension besides.
The French endeavoured, but without success, to gain by
means of the press, adherents on the Rhine.   Bernhard von
Weimar found warm admirers, who foresaw in him the successor of Gustavus Adolphus.   He possessed great talents as
a General, and some of the winning qualities of the great
King ; but he was only in one respect his successor, that he
carried on in the most dangerous way the too great political
daring of his instructor.   He wished to make use of, and
at the same time deceive, a foreign power which was greater
and stronger than himself : it was an unequal struggle, and
he, as the weaker party, was soon put aside by France, and
these foreigners possessed themselves of his political legacy,
his fortress and his army.

While love and hate were thus divided in this gloomy
period, there arose among the better portion of the nation a
characteristic patriotism, which the German people, in the
midst of their great need and sufferings, opposed to the egotistic interests of the rulers who helped to destroy each other.
There no longer existed any party to which a wise man could
from his heart wish success.   Differences of faith had diminished, and the soldiers complained, without scruple, of confession.   Then began for the first time a new political system,

called a constitution founded on reason, in opposition to the reckless selfishness of the rulers.   But even this constitutional principle, the basis of which was the advantage of the whole, as it was then understood, was still without greatness of conception or any deep moral purport ; and there was no repugnance to the employment of the worst means in carrying it out.   Still it was an advance.   Even the peaceful citizen, after eighteen years of troubles, was obliged to take an interest in this political system.   The character of the ruling powers and their interests became everywhere a subject of deliberation. Every one was terrified out of his provincial narrowness of mind, and had urgent reasons for interesting themselves in the fate of foreign countries.   Thousands of fugitives, the most powerful members of the community, had scattered themselves over distant provinces, the same misfortunes had befallen them also.   Thus, amidst the horrors of war, was developed in Germany a feeling of distrust of their rulers, a longing for a better national condition.   It was, a great but dearly bought advance of public opinion ; it may be discerned more particularly in the political literature after the peace of Prague.   A specimen of this tendency is here introduced from a small flying-sheet, which appeared in 1636 under the title of ' The German Brutus : that is, a letter thrown before the public.'

" You Swedes complain that Germany is ungrateful, that it drives you away with violence, that the good deeds, done with God's power by Joshua, are forgotten, the alliance no longer thought of, in short, that you are less valued, like an old worn-out horse, or decrepit hound, both of which, when no longer useful, get such thanks as the world gives.   Thus you are treated with great injustice before God and the world.

'⋆Be of good comfort : there are many remaining who wish you well from their heart, who pray for you, and show their devotion to you in every possible way. A country where such people are to be found cannot be accused of ingratitude ; and that there are yet many thousand such people, even your enemies know right well. But that selfishness, secret envy, hidden counsels, and clandestine negotiations are stirred up against you, must not be ascribed to the whole of this praiseworthy German nation, but only to the causes which have led to such results ; for you have on your part shown a double amount of selfishness.

" In the first place, in raising at your pleasure the toll on the Baltic ; for I have been told by honest trustworthy seafaring folk, that you have exacted from people, not only from fifteen to thirty, but up to forty, nay, even to fifty out of a hundred, and have troubled all hearts by this rapacity ; and as no improvement has taken place, but commerce has been thereby miserably straitened, and many honest people have been lamentably brought to beggary, the minds of men being thereby much embittered, your best friends began at first to condemn you secretly, and at last through their falling fortunes were made your worst enemies. Would you throw the blame on the toll gatherers ? They are your servants. It is a well-known rule of law : what I do by my servant is as though done by myself. You appear to me exactly like him who carried off a pair of shoes secretly and offered them afterwards to the holy Benno.

" The states and cities of the Empire, so long as they were in your hands, contributed fully and sufficiently to your maintenance ; many, nay too many, to say the least of it, as a proof of their fidelity, have lost soul and body, wealth and life, nay all their privileges, and, in a great measure, religion itself. Ratisbon testifies to this. Augsburg laments over it. All grieve together over it. You have allowed the old regiments to dissolve, have completed no companies, nor paid either new or old, notwithstanding you have demanded, and in fact received large sums of money from many Diets ; I say nothing of what you have extorted from your enemies in their own countries.   How has this money been spent ?   In super-fluous pomp and luxury which is hateful to every one.   We have observed this silently, and made a virtue of necessity. The children of Israel, when they had intercourse with the daughters of their enemies, and afterwards boasted of their victory, and tormented their brethren of Judah with the hardest yoke of bondage, were both times severely punished by God.   And shall it fare better with you who have exer-cised more than Turkish cruelty in many evangelical places ? The corn from the monastery of Magdeburg, the Dukedom of Brunswick and other places, has been thrashed out and carried off in heaps from the country, sold at a very high price, and the money spent for your own use, nothing given to the poor soldiers ; the country people, harassed to death, are dying of hunger ; and many fortresses, from avarice, either not supplied with provisions, or not amply provided with powder and shot, and, in short, general mismanagement.   Now we see ourselves everywhere abandoned by fortune, so that at last we discover there is no money in hand, and no people to be got, as those who were available have run away, and the remainder will no longer be restrained by martial law.   Dear friends, think you of the saying of Boccalini : ' When the prince leads the life of Lucifer, what wonder that the subjects become devils !'

"Our politicians know well that the Electors hold kingly rank in the Empire.   But who has exalted himself above them with kingly magnificence, a great retinue and boundless ex-pense, is it not your chief (Oxenstiern) ?   Do you think that this has not been complained of at every court ?   His Kingly Majesty of Christian memory never did the like.   From these and countless other reasons the Princes, states, and cities have become first secretly, and then publicly offended with you ; to this may be added a conduct towards the established inhabitants which they cannot well bear, when foreigners place themselves higher than their native princes.

" You say that electoral Saxony should have made peace by force of arms. Let us leave that uncertain. It is known to every one that certain persons have helped to shove the cart into the mud, and afterwards left it there. If electoral Saxony has been wrong, you with your procedures are not less guilty. In short, every one, be he who he may, has sought his own advantage ; therefore Magdeburg lies in ashes, Wismar is in ruins, Augsburg is bound with the fetters of servitude, Nuremberg is in peril of death, Ulm is in quotidian fever, Strasburg has passed to the French, Frankfort has the jaundice, and the whole Empire is consumed. The enemy have beaten with rods, but you have chastised with scorpions. The Wallensteiners inflicted wounds, and you physicians have applied drawing plasters as a remedy instead of oil, have corrupted the blood and fastened yourselves on like a crab ; such a crab must either be cut out by force, or satisfied daily by inordinate sums of money. The last is out of our power, the first we do not wish to do to you, but cannot help it. If God thus harasses you it is your own fault. Meanwhile, do you think that God has a flaxen beard, and will allow himself to be led by the nose ? Oh, no, He sees well that you shelter yourselves under the name of freedom, that you make use of the cloak of the gospel, and at the same time live as Turks.

" You cry out much about the Spanish monarchy. I have no fears of it. Give me one of the best chemists who is sufficiently scientific to know how to mingle earth and ores, so that they will hold together firm and infrangible, and then let us see whether we have to fear the Spanish monarchy. But I am afraid that France will be to us Germans, the broken reed of Egypt, which will pierce the hand of whoever leans on it. All empires have their fixed time appointed by God, and a boundary across which they cannot pass. First they arise, then grow like boys; some improve as youths, remain for a time at a standstill in their manhood, then decline, become old, languish and at last die; nay, are so utterly annihilated, that one scarcely knows that they have existed.   This course of things cannot be prevented by any human wisdom.   The wise man sees this, and prepares himself beforehand; the fool does not believe it, and is ruined, like the surviving Generals of Alexander the Great, who so long divided his conquests, till the Romans became their masters. And truly the Empire has great need to rid herself at last of foreign physicians.

"I have been severe, but a steel axe is necessary to sever such a hard knot, one cannot cut with a fur coat.

"It is asked what will be the issue?   It rests with God. Have you had too little bloodshed?   Let God be the judge, and fly ye from his wrath.   Although the Church still suffers, it is not yet dead.   You cannot complain that you have gained nothing for the money you have spent and the dangers you have undergone.   You have brought copper out of your country, but carried silver and gold back to it.   Sweden, before this war, was of wood thatched with straw, now it is of stone, and splendidly adorned, and that you have obtained from the abducted vessels of Egypt.   This no one would grudge you if you would only thank God yourselves for it. The Germans have indeed been excited to rise against their Emperor, but they will take no one who is not of their race and language.   If the house of Austria has done evil, God will truly search it out.   As concerns the French, I know well that God will, through them, punish Germany; for we have daily imitated in manners, ceremonies, demeanour, and entertainments, in language and clothing, together with music, this nation of apish behaviour and dress, and frivolous manners.   How can we expect better than to fall into their hands?   But the Frenchman will not therefore become our

Emperor. To him belongs the Lily, the Eagle to the Germans, the East to the Turks, and the West to the Spaniards. None among them can reach higher.

"I must hope that it will not be taken amiss of me, that I have so roundly described these transactions. But frankness suits a German well. Would to God that any one had in good time thus placed the matter before you. Now we can indeed complain, but help, none either will or can give. God alone will and can help us; to Him we must pray that He may at last have compassion on us, and turn the hearts of the high potentates to love and long-wished-for peace."

Here ends the flying-sheet. The author, without putting sympathy with the Imperialists in the foreground, evidently belongs less to the Swedish party than we do now. Undoubtedly the Swedish soldiers and officers had become merciless devils, like the Imperialists, and, like them, they ruined the country and people. But it was not their exorbitant demands which hindered the peace, but the injustice of the Emperor, who still continued to raise the execrable pretension to subdue the life and freedom of the nation to his interest. Had it been possible for the Hapsburgers to assure freedom of faith, and the independence of the Imperial tribunals, almost all the German princes would have succumbed to him to drive away the foreigners. But the struggle stood thus: either the nation must be crushed, and all the ideas suppressed, which had grown up in the German soil for one hundred and forty years, or the pretensions of the Imperial House must be certainly and fundamentally overcome. The last was impossible to the Germans without the help of Sweden. Thus on a retrospect of those years, every one will be well disposed to Sweden, who does not consider it a mere accident that well-known men of later times, like Lessing, Goethe, Schiller, Kant, Fichte, Hegel, and Humboldt did not blossom out of the country in which hundreds of thousands were driven from Church and school, by the Jesuits of Ferdinand II. But at that period the patriot undoubtedly felt the weakness of the Empire more than all the fearful misery of the people. And great ground there was for anxiety about the future. From this point of view this brochure is to us the first expression of that feeling which still, in the present day, unites hundreds of thousands of Germans. That love of Fatherland took root in the oppressed souls of our ancestors during the Thirty years' war, which has not yet attained to political life by a unity of constitutions. Such a feeling indeed only existed then in the minds of the noblest. But we must honour those who, in a century poor in hope, left in their teaching and writings, as an inheritance to their descendants, the idea of a German Empire.

After Banner's devastating expedition all was quiet in Germany. Almost all the news and State records which the war had left, flowed from the press. In the last years thousands of printed sheets were filled with the negotiations for peace. Finally the peace was announced to the poor people in large placards.

CHAPTER V.

THE THIRTY YEARS' WAR.—THE CITIES.

WHEN the war broke out, the cities were the armed guardians of German trade, which was carried on with wealth and bustle, in narrow streets between high houses. Almost every city, with the exception of the smallest market towns, was shut out from the open country by walls, gates, and moats. The approaches were narrow and easy to defend; there were often double walls, and in many cases the old towers still overtopped the battlements and gates. Many of the more important of these middle-age fortifications had been strengthened in the course of the century, the bastions of stone and brick-work, as well as strong single towers, were mounted with heavy artillery; and frequently the old castle of some landed proprietor, or the house of some former magistrate or count appointed by the Emperor, were fortified. They were not fortresses in our sense, but they could, if the walls were thick and the citizens stanch, resist even a great army, at least for a long time. Thus Nördlingen maintained itself in 1634 for eighteen days, against the united Imperial armies of King Ferdinand, Gallas, and Piccolomini—forming together more than 60,000 men: the citizens repulsed seven assaults, with only five hundred men, Swedish auxiliaries. For a defence like this, earth sconces were thrown out as outworks, and rapidly united by trenches and palisades. Many places, however, far more than at present, were r.l fortresses. Their chief strength consisted in their outworks, which were planned by Flemish science. It had long been known that the balls of carronades were more destructive to stone and breast-works than to earth-works.

In the larger cities the cleanliness of the streets was much attended to; they were paved, even in the carriage ways; the pavement was raised in the centre for carrying away the water; the chief market-place, as for example in Leipzig, was already paved with stone. Great efforts had long been made to procure for the cities a certain and abundant supply of drinking-water; under the streets ran wooden conduits; stone cisterns and fountains often decorated with statues, stood in the market-places and principal streets. The streets were not as yet lighted; whoever went out by night required torches or lanterns; later, however, torches were forbidden; but at the corner houses were fixed metal fire-pans, in which, in case of uproar or fire at night, pitch rings and resinous wood were burnt. It was the custom on the breaking out of a fire to allow the water to run from the cisterns or the fountains to the streets which were endangered. For this purpose flood-gates were hung, and it was the duty of par-ticular trades—in Leipzig, the innkeepers—to dam up the water with these flood-gates at the burning-places; at the same time from dung that was heaped up, they formed a traverse. The street police and patroles had been improved in the course of the last sixty years. The Elector Augustus of Saxony had organized this department of administration with no little skill. His numerous ordinances were used as models by the whole Empire, according to which the princes and cities regulated their new social life.

The chief market was on Sunday the favourite resort of the men. There, after the sermon, stood the citizens and journeymen in their festival attire, chattering, interchanging news, and conferring together on business. In all commercial cities the merchants had a special room where they met, which was even then called the Bourse. On the tower of the Council House, over the clock, there was always a gallery, from which the warder kept a look out over the city, and where the city piper blew the trombone and cornet.

The city communities kept beer and wine cellars for the citizens, in which the price of the retailed drink was carefully fixed; there were special drinking-rooms for persons of distinction to hold agreeable intercourse. In the old Imperial cities, the patricians had generally, like the guilds, their especial club-houses or rooms, and the luxury of such a society was then greater in proportion than now. There were also numerous hotels, which, in Leipzig, were already famed for their grandeur, and splendidly arranged. Even the apothecaries were under regulations; they had special rules and prices; they sold many spices and delicacies, and whatever else was agreeable to the palate. Bath rooms were considered greater necessaries than now. Even in the country there was seldom a little farm-house without its bath-house, and there was a bath-room in every large house in the city. The poor citizens went to the barbers, who acted as surgeons, and kept bagnios. But besides these the cities maintained large public baths, in which, gratis, or for a very small payment, warm and cold bathing could be had with every convenience. This primitive German custom was almost abandoned during the war, and is not yet restored to its old extent.

In more important cities the houses of the inner town, in 1618, were for the most part built of stone, three, and more stories high, and roofed with tiles; the rooms in the houses were often noted for their cleanliness, decoration, and elegance; the walls were generally adorned with worked and embroidered carpets, even of velvet, and with beautiful costly inlaid wainscoting and other decorations; and this not only

in the large old commercial cities, but also in some that were
in more youthful vigour.   The household gear was elegant
and carefully collected.   There was as yet no such thing as
porcelain in use.   Rich plate was only found at the courts of
great princes, and in a few wealthy merchant families.   In
choice pieces of the noble metals, the artistic work of the
goldsmith was of more value than its weight.   Among the
opulent citizens, the place of silver and porcelain was supplied by pewter ; it was displayed in great abundance,
shining with a bright polish ; it was the pride of the housewife, and together with it were placed fine glasses and pottery
from foreign countries, often painted and ornamented with
either pious or waggish inscriptions.   On the other hand the
dress and adornments of the men were far more brilliant and
costly than now.   The feeling of the middle ages was still
prevalent, a tendency of the mind for outward display and
stately representations directly opposed to ours, and nothing
tended so much to preserve this inclination, as the endeavours of the authorities to meet it, by regulating even the
outward appearance of individuals, and giving to each class of
citizens their own peculiar position.   The endless sumptuary
laws about dress gave it a disproportionate importance ; it
fostered more than anything else vanity and an inordinate
desire in each to raise himself above his position.   It appears
to us a ludicrous struggle, which the worthiest magistrates
maintained for four centuries up to the French Revolution,
against all the caprices and excesses of the fashion, and
always without success.

   Surrounded by these forms and regulations, lived a rich,
vigorous, laborious, and wealthy people ; the citizens held
jealously to the privileges and dignity of their cities, they liked
to exhibit their riches, capacity, and enterprise among their
fellow-citizens.   Handicraft and trade were still very prosperous.   It is true, that in wholesale commerce with foreign

countries Germany had already lost much. The splendour of
the Hanse towns had faded. The great commercial houses of
Augsburg and Nuremberg even then existed, only as heirs of
the great riches of their fathers. Italians, French, and above
all, English and Flemish, had become dangerous rivals, the
Swedish, Danish, and Dutch flags floated on the Baltic more
triumphantly than those of Lubeck and other Baltic ports,
and the commerce with the two Indies ran in new currents
and into foreign marts. But the German herring fishery was
still of great importance, and the vast Sclave lands of the East
were still an open market to the commerce of the country.
But throughout the whole width of the Empire industry
flourished, and a less profitable but sounder export of the products of the country had produced a general and moderate
degree of wealth. The manufactures of wool and leather, and
linen, harness, and armour with the ornamental industry of
Nuremberg were eagerly desired by foreign countries. The
chief cause of disturbance was the insecurity of the ratio of
value. Almost every town had then its special branch of industry, solidly developed under the restrictions and control of
guilds. Pottery, cloths, leather work, mining, and metal
work, gave to individual places a peculiar character, and
even to smaller ones a reputation which reached through the
country and excited in the citizens a well-justified pride. But
in all, scarcely excepting the greatest, agriculture was deemed
of more importance than now, not only in the suburbs and
farms of the city domains, but also within the towns; many
citizens lived upon the produce of their fields. In the smaller
towns most persons possessed portions of the town lands, but
the richer had other property besides. Therefore there were
many more beasts of burden and of draught than now, and
the housewife rejoiced in having her own corn-fields, from
which she made her own bread, and if she was skilful, prepared
fine pastry according to the custom of the country. The

with mistrust, as it was difficult to restrain the recklessness of wild boys. They wished to dance without mantles; they lifted up, swung, and twirled about their partners, which was strictly forbidden, and the thronging of the gaping domestics into the saloon was displeasing to the authorities. At twilight all dancing amusements were to cease.

The larger cities had lists where the sons of the patricians held their knightly exercise and ran at the ring, also shooting galleries, and trenches for crossbow and rifle practice. The shooting festivities were a great source of enjoyment throughout the country, and on these occasions booths, tents, and cook-shops were erected. The people also took a lively interest in the festivals of particular guilds, and almost every town had its own public feast; for example, Erfurt had yearly prize races for the poorer classes; the men ran for stockings and the women for fur cloaks. Tennis was a favourite game of the young citizens, which unfortunately in the troubles of the century almost disappeared. There were special tennis courts, and a tennis-court master, of the town. If any gentlemen of distinction came into the town, a place in the market was strewed with sand, and a playground marked off with pegs and cords. There these distinguished persons played, and the citizens watched with pleasure from the windows, to see how a young Prince of Hesse threw the ball, and how one of Anhalt did his best. At the great yearly markets, for more than a century, Fortune's urn was a favourite game. Sometimes it was undertaken by the town itself, but generally it was granted to some speculator. How much the people were interested in this, we learn from the fact that the town chronicles frequently reported the particulars concerning it. Thus, in 1624, at Michaelmas, at Leipzig a Fortune's urn of seventeen thousand gulden was prepared; each ticket cost eighteen pfennige; there were seventeen blanks to one prize; the highest prize was three hundred and fifty gulden, and there were three hundred thousand blanks. The students at last became angry at the number of blanks; they attacked and broke down the lottery booth. The pleasure of the people in spectacles was greater than now, at least more easily satisfied; processions and city solemnities were frequent; plays undoubtedly were still a rare enjoyment, in these the children of the citizens had always the pleasure of representing the characters themselves, as bands of travelling players were still new and rare. The clerical body was already unfavourably disposed to what were called profane pieces, therefore ecclesiastical subjects and allegories with moral tendencies were always interspersed with burlesque scenes, and great was the number of the actors. At the yearly markets the play booths were more abundant than now. At the Easter fair at Leipzig in 1630, was to be seen, amongst other things, a father with six children who performed beautifully on the lute and violin, a woman who could sew, write, and convey her food to her mouth with her feet, a child of a year old quite covered with hair and with a beard; and of strange animals, there were two marmoset monkeys, a porpoise, and a spoonbill, and, as now, these monsters were recommended to the people by large pictures. Besides these there were ropedancers, fire-eaters, jugglers, acrobats, and numerous ballad singers and vendors.

But what gave the greatest feeling of independence to the citizen in 1618 was his martial aptitude—almost every one had some practice in the use of weapons. Every large city had an arsenal; even the heavy artillery on the fortifications were served by the citizens, who, as a body, were under ordinary circumstances superior to the young companies of besieging soldiers. Magdeburg would have made a stronger resistance, if feeling of duty and discipline had not already become weaker among the citizens than in former sieges, in one of which the maiden of the City Arms so valiantly defended her garland.

Besides the city train bands, there was in most of the Circles of the Empire a regular militia for the defence of the country. About every tenth man in the city or country was drawn, regularly armed, paid during service, and appointed for the internal defence of the frontiers of the country. The beginning of the Landwehr dates from the sixteenth century. This regulation was recommended by military theorists as most efficient, and from time to time it was renewed. It was introduced by the States in Saxony in 1612, and renewed in 1618; there were to be altogether in the Electorate nine thousand men. The privates were to receive a daily pay of four groschen, and the serjeants ten and a half, and the cost was distributed among the houses. But this militia was found very useless in the war. The discipline was much too lax; the industrious citizen endeavoured to withdraw himself when danger did not threaten his own city; the consequence was, that many unsettled people were scouring the country in arms. If they were required by the community to defend the ploughs in the field against roving marauders, they demanded a special gratification, or they evaded it, and very soon they became more a plague than a benefit to their own country.

What ruin the war brought upon the towns may be learned from every town chronicle. First, the disorders of the *Kipper* time inflicted deep wounds on their morality and prosperity. Then came the sufferings that even distant war brought upon the citizens, the scarcity and dearness of provisions. Everything became so insecure that nothing was thought of but the enjoyment of the day. Rough and wild was the love of pleasure; and foreign modes, which had been learned from the travelled courtiers and soldiers became prevalent. From 1626 dandyism began in Germany after the French fashion; the *Messieurs à la mode* strutted about, molesting every one on the paved footpaths of the streets. They had short pointed beards, long hair in frizzled locks, or cut short on one side, and on the other hanging on the shoulder in a queue or lock, a large flapped hat, spurs on their heels, a sword on the left side, dresses slashed and jagged, a coxcombical bearing, and added to all this, a corrupt language full of French words. The women were not behindhand; they began to carry foreign masks before their faces, and feather fans in their hands; they wore whalebones in their dresses, and repudiated sables, gold and silver stuffs, and, above all—what appeared very remarkable—silver, and at last, indeed, white lace. This conduct raised the indignation of the authorities and pastors, as being fantastic and immoral. To us it appears as the characteristic evil of a time when the old independence of the German citizen was crushed.

When an army approached a town, the traffic with the country almost entirely ceased, the gates were carefully watched, and the citizens maintained themselves on the provisions that had been collected. Then began the levying of contributions, the passage and quartering of friendly armies, with all its terrors. Still worse was the passage of the enemy. They uselessly endeavoured to purchase safety—it was a favour if the enemy did not set fire to the town woods or cut them down for sale, or carry off the town library on his baggage waggon; everything that was inviting to plunder, such as the organ or church pictures, had to be ransomed, even to the church bells, which, according to the custom of war, belonged to the artillery. The cities were not in a position to satisfy the demands of the Generals, so the most considerable of the citizens were dragged off as hostages till the sum exacted was paid.

If a town was considered strong enough to resist the enemy's army, it was always filled with fugitives at the approach of the enemy, the number of whom was so great that the citizens could not think of providing for them. There came to Dresden, for example, in 1637, after the capture of Torgau in the course of three days, from the 7th to the 9th of May, twelve thousand waggons with fugitive country people. The enemy surrounded the over-filled place; round the walls the battle raged, and within, not less voracious, hunger, misery and sickness. All the fugitives who were capable of bearing arms were employed in severe siege service; the nobility also of the neighbourhood sometimes assisted. If the siege lingered long, the high prices were followed by shameless usury, the millers ground only for the rich, and the bakers made exorbitant demands. The pictures of famine, such as was then experienced in many towns, are too horrible to dwell upon. When at Nördlingen a fortified tower was taken by the besiegers, the citizens themselves burnt it down, hungry women fell upon the half-roasted bodies of the enemy and carried pieces home for their children.

But if a town was taken by storm it experienced the fate of Magdeburg; the mowing down of masses, the dishonouring of women, horrible torments and mutilations; and, added to all this, pestilence. To what an extent pestilence then raged in the cities is scarcely credible; it frequently carried off more than half the inhabitants. In 1626 and the following years, it depopulated wide districts; from 1631 to 1634 it returned again, and still worse in 1636.

At all events it gave to each town for years plenty of space, and proportionate peace; and the places—not very numerous—which were only once destroyed in the course of the war, were able to recover themselves. But the most fearful cases of all, were those where the same calamities were two, three, and four times repeated. Leipzig was besieged five times, and Magdeburg six, and most of the smaller towns were more frequently filled with foreign soldiers ; thus both large and small towns were equally ruined.

But this was not all ; over wide territories raged a plague of quite another kind,—religious persecution,—which was practised by the Imperial party wherever it established itself. The army was followed everywhere by crowds of proselytizers, Jesuits, and mendicant monks on foot. These performed their office by the help of the soldiers. Wherever the Roman Catholics had a footing, the leaders of the Protestant party, and above all the shepherds of souls, were swept away, more especially in the provinces which were the Emperor's own domains. Much had been done there before the war, but still in the beginning of the war in upper Austria, Moravia, Bohemia, and Silesia, the active intelligence of the country and the greater part of the community were evangelical. Their general character was improved. Whoever, after imprisonment and torture, would not give up his faith was obliged to abandon the country, and many, many thousands did so. The citizens and country people were driven in troops by the soldiers to confession. It was considered a favour when the fugitives were allowed a short insufficient delay for the sale of their movable goods.

The fate of a small town in one of these provinces, the only one which was restored at a later period to the spiritual life of Germany, is here given, not on account of the monotony of misery, but because other characteristic points of the old burgher life are displayed.

Where the Riesengebirge descend into the Silesian plain, in a fruitful valley on the shores of the Bober, lies the old town of Löwenberg, one of the first places in Silesia which was brought under the regulations of the German law ; it had already in the middle ages become a powerful community, and numbered in 1617, in the city and suburbs, 738 houses and

at least 6500 inhabitants.*   It rose stately, with its strong
walls, moats, and gate-towers, amidst woods and meadows;
it had in its centre, like almost all the German cities in
Silesia, a large market-place, called the 'Ring,' which included
the council-house and fourteen privileged inns and licensed
houses of traffic; the houses within the town were of stone,
high gables projected over the streets, and they were from
four to five stories high.   Originally the under story had
been built with trellised porches; these covered passages,
however, had been removed sixty years before; on the under
floor the houses had a large hall, and a strong vault, behind
these a spacious room, in which was the baking oven, and
over this a wooden gallery which occupied the back portion
of the room, a staircase led up to it; the forepart of the
room was the sleeping-room of the family, and the gallery was
the eating-room.   On the floor above was a good apartment
wainscoted with wood work, all the rest were chambers and
lofts for wares, superabundant furniture, corn and wool.   For
Löwenberg was a celebrated cloth-manufacturing town; in
the year 1617, three hundred cloth factories fabricated 13,702
pieces of cloth, and traders carried their strong work far into
Bohemia and the Empire, but especially into Poland.   The
city seal, a lion in the town gate, was of pure gold.

In 1629, the town had already suffered much from the
war.   The citizens, demoralized and tortured, had lost the
greater portion of their old spirit.   Lichtenstein's dragoon
regiment—Imperialists—were quartered in the neighbouring
city, and supported the proselytizing Jesuits by sword and
pistol.   The burgesses of the town of Löwenberg, dreading
their arrival, were obliged to dismiss their old pastors; they
separated from them with tears, the populace followed them
weeping to their dwellings, bearing with them their last

* In 1770 the population was only 2126; but in 1845 it had increased
again to 4500.

parting gifts as an expiation. The Jesuits succeeded them; the night before they came, a horned owl took up its abode in the church tower, to the terror of the citizens, and alarmed the town all night long by its hootings. The Jesuits preached after their fashion daily, promising freedom from all contributions, and from the infliction of billeting, and special favour and privileges from the Emperor; but to the refractory temporal destruction. They went so far, that the intimidated burgesses were driven to the determination of accepting confirmation; most of the men of the community took the Lord's Supper according to the Roman Catholic custom, unblessed by the cup. The more steadfast of the citizens, however, were compelled to go away in misery. Hardly had the Jesuits left the town, when the people fell back again, the citizens rushed to the neighbouring villages, where there were still evangelical pastors, and were there married and baptized; their churches standing empty under a Roman Catholic priest. There were new threatenings, and new deeds of violence. The upright burgomaster Schubert was carried off to severe imprisonment, but the Council now declared boldly that they would die for the Augsburg Confession; the burgesses pressed round the governor of the province in wild tumult. The executioners of the Emperor, "*the beatifiers*," rode through the gates; great part of the citizens flew with their wives and children out of the town; all the villages were full of exiles, who were brought back with violence by the soldiers and apostate citizens, and put into prison till they could produce certificates of confession; those who fled further, were driven into Saxony. A new Council was now established—as was the custom in those times—of unworthy and disreputable men. The houses abandoned by the citizens were plundered; many waggons heavily laden with furniture were bought of Roman Catholic neighbours, by the soldiers, and carried off. The new

Council lived in a shameless manner. The King's judge—an apostate Löwenberger advocate—and the Senators, ill treated the secret Protestants, and endeavoured to enrich themselves from the town property. Two hundred and fifty citizens lived in exile with their families ; one side of the market-place was entirely uninhabited, long grass grew there, and cattle pastured upon it. In the winter, hunger and cold drove the women and children at last back to the ruined houses. The leading spirit of the new Council was one Julius, who had been a Franciscan, a desperate fellow, not at all like a monk, who wore under his capoche golden bracelets. Then a Roman Catholic priest, Exelmann, son of an evangelical preacher, was established there. But however crushed and dispersed the citizens were, the offices of the priest and the new town council were not undisputed. All the authorities of the town were not yet under constraint. How the opposition resisted, will be learned from the narration of a cotemporary, which was printed by the industrious Sutorius in his history of Löwenburg, 1782.

"On the ninth of April, 1631, early in the morning, the following gentlemen met at the council-house : first, the priest, secondly, the King's judge, who was Elias Seiler, an advocate ; thirdly, George Mümer, a woollen wiseacre and cloth factor ; fourthly, Schwob Franze, also a cloth factor ; fifthly, Dr. Melchior Hübner, who had been a miller's man, and a broken down baker ; sixthly, Master Daniel Seiler, a joiner ; seventhly, Peter Beyer, the town clerk ; all these took possession of the councillors' chairs. The worshipful burgomaster was ill of the gout. Then the priest who had the upper-hand in the council made a proposal in the following words : 'My beloved children in the Church, hearing that you intend sending an embassage to the court of his Kingly* Majesty at Vienna, I and the worthy King's judge have, on

* The Emperor was sovereign of Silesia, as King of Bohemia.

mature consideration, come to the conclusion, that before you break up it would be well for you to compel all the women to adopt our religion. You would thereby obtain for yourselves great favour at court. Also I will not fail to give you letters of recommendation, to my highly esteemed honourable cousin Herr Pater Lemmermann, now confessor to his Kingly Majesty, who certainly has much influence in all secret deliberations, representing to him how indefatigable and zealous you have been, and have brought the women into the right way, so that all you who are now here together may receive a special gratulation. Therefore proceed zealously; if they are not willing, you have towers and prisons enough to compel them.'

"On this proposition votes were taken all round, and first the King's judge spoke: 'Yea, gentlemen, as I am willing to undertake such a journey for the advantage of the town, it seems good to me that this project should be carried out with zeal and earnestness. If they are not willing, let the most distinguished of them be put in confinement. I wager that the others will soon give in. They will come and beg that they may be let out. Many will be glad that their wives run away and they be quit of them. If we have been able to bring the men into the right path, why should we not be able to deal with these little brutes ?'

"Herr Mümer, 'the woollen wiseacre,' said: 'I have been a widower six weeks; I can well tell what cross a man must bear when his conscience is moved on account of his wife day and night. It would truly be good if man and wife had one faith and one paternoster; as concerns the Ten Commandments, it is not so pressing. It would also be good that the women should do like us, as they enjoy our income, and become councillors' wives. Only I fear it will be difficult to manage. I would almost rather consult with the honourable captain-general of the province hereupon, how he would deal

with his own wife.   One should be able to act with better
effect when one has a decided command thereunto.   I could
never have succeeded with my wife !'

"Now Schwob Franze said: 'Gentlemen, my wife, as you
know, died a few days ago, so that I am now free and a
widower ; I have also somewhat to say on this matter, as I
have been plagued by my bad wife concerning the Papacy.
Nevertheless I know not how to handle this business rightly.
There are many beautiful women and widows among the
Lutheran heretics.   Would it be well, and could one make
up one's mind to confine, or drive them all away at once ?
Gentlemen, you may do it if it seems good to you.   I am of
the same opinion as my honourable colleague, Mümer.   If I
marry to-day or to-morrow, my wife must have the like faith
with me, or hold her tongue upon the same.'

"Hereupon Dr. Melchior began: 'Gentlemen, God's
sacrament, im-m-imprison them all together till they assent ;
le-le-let none out, though they should all rot alike in prison.
I yesterday thrashed my domestic plague concerning this.
The de-e-vil ta-a-ta-ake me, she must do it or I will drive
her entirely away.'

"Master Daniel Seiler said: 'My high and most gracious
gentlemen, you can proceed in such a good work with force
alone.   The captain-general of the province can give us no
commands herein ; let him see to himself how he can bring
his heretical wife into the right way, who is no small vexation
to him, and a mirror to our wives.   Therefore I beg of you
proceed with speed against the women.'

"The honourable town clerk Peter Beyer's vote, was as
follows : 'Gentlemen, I know not what to say in this matter.
I have a notable shrew, who snaps about her like the devil.   I
cannot trust myself to be able to restrain her.   If you can do
it, try.   But I advise, that we should begin to speak kindly
with the women.   Let benches be placed in the council-room,

desire them to sit them down, and see whether it be possible
to convert them by good words, or afterwards by threats.
Perhaps they will take it into consideration.'

" Hereupon the priest and the King's judge came to a conclusion.   They said : ' The time is short, much delay cannot
be given ; it is a saying here, eat or die.'

" So the King's judge spoke to the town clerk saying :
' Are the women without ?'   He answered : ' No, there are as
yet none there.'   Then the judge said : ' Go, and you will
find them either at my house or with Frau Geneussin.'   The
town clerk found no one at the house of the King's judge, but
at that of Frau Geneussin there were about fifteen.   To these
he said : ' His reverence the priest, together with his honour
the King's judge, and the honourable council, send greeting
to the ladies, and beg that they will come to the council-
house, where the gentlemen are assembled.'

" Then the wife of the King's judge answered : ' Yea, yea,
greet them in return, and we will come soon.'   So the women
went two and two, the judge's and burgomaster's wives fore-
most, and ascended the stairs of the council-house, but the
other women who had collected at the bread tables or elsewhere, or in houses, came after them in great numbers, by
troops.   Now when the servant had announced to the council
that the women were there, the King's judge said : ' Let them
in.'   The servant replied : ' Sir, there will not be room here
for them all ; I believe that there are five hundred of them
together.   The council-house is full of them, part of them
are already sitting on the musicians' stools.'

" Then the priest began : ' Indeed, we must pause awhile,
this is not well.   I only intended at first that the most distinguished wives, such as those of the council, the justices,
and jurymen should be called.   Ay, ay, what have you done ?'
The servant answered : ' Your reverence must be informed,
that yesterday the King's judge commanded that all the

women who had not been converted, or would not be so, should be summoned, and to begin with his wife; this I have done, and because it was rather late, I told most of those whom I met that they should notify this to the others, that they were to come on the morrow without fail on pain of punishment. I believe I have done no wrong.'

" The priest spoke again: ' Ay, ay, gentlemen, gentlemen, this is not well. I know not how we shall manage to be rid of a portion of these women.'

" Thereupon the King's judge said to the priest: ' Let your reverence be content; we will arrange the business, and in the beginning we will only call in the women of distinction. When they see that they must really give in or be imprisoned, the others will soon withdraw themselves and run away.'

" It was therefore determined, and made known to the servant, that the above-mentioned ladies only should enter.

" Now when the servant announced this, the wife of the King's judge began: ' We will by no means allow ourselves to be separated; where I remain, there shall my train remain also. Say that we only beg they will allow us to enter.' The servant reported this again to the council. Then the King's judge waxed wrath and said with great vehemence: ' Go out again and tell these simple women that they must not show themselves disobedient and refractory, or they will learn how they will be treated.' Then the servant went out again and delivered the command seriously, but the good-wives held to their former opinion, and said that they wished to know why they had been summoned, that none would separate from the others; as it fared with one so should it fare with all. On this there was great confusion and murmuring among the women, which was heard by the gentlemen in the council-room.

" When the servant returned with this answer, they were sore afraid, and would rather have seen the women I know not where. They therefore determined unanimously to send out his honour the town-clerk, that he might persuade them with earnest yet friendly words, that the most distinguished of the women should enter, and the others return home, and none should suffer. But it was all in vain. The women remained firm not to separate from one another. And the judge's wife began, and said to the town-clerk: ' Nay, nay, dear friend, do you think we are so simple, and do not perceive the trick by which you would compel and force us poor women, against our conscience, to change our faith ? My husband and the priest have not been consorting together all these days for nothing ; they have been joined together almost day and night ; assuredly they have either boiled or cooked a devil, which they may eat up themselves ; I shall not enter there. Where I remain, there will my train and following remain also.' She turned herself round to the others and said : ' Women, is this your will ?' Then once more there were loud exclamations from the women : ' Yea, yea, let it be so ; we will all hold together as one man.'

" Hereupon his honour the town-clerk was much affrighted ; he went hastily back to the council, and reported woefully the state of affairs, adding, that the council was in no small danger, for he had observed that almost every woman had a large bunch of keys hanging at her side.* Upon this their courage utterly and entirely evaporated ; they hung their heads and were at their wits' end ; one wished himself here, another out there. Dr. Melchior took heart and said to the priest : ' *Potz-Sacrament !* Most reverend sir, if I had now but two hundred musketeers, I would soon mow down the whole pa- pa-pack, even those who would fall down on their knees.'

" At last his honour the town-clerk bethought himself of a device. ' Gentlemen, I know a way by which we can

---

* The bunch of keys in the middle ages was not only an important symbol of right, but also the popular weapon of women.

VOL. II.   N descend and escape from the women. If the gentlemen will close both doors of the council-house, we will silently make off with ourselves by the under council-room, through the doors of the tower; thus they will not be aware what has become of us. But I do not know where the keys of the tower are to be found.' This good counsel pleased them all well, and the keys were sought for carefully, but meanwhile the town-clerk was called in, and commanded to signify to the women, that they should have a little patience. And the town-clerk was to see how one could slip round to the front, and the other to the back door, that they might suddenly run out and close the doors behind them.

"This plan succeeded with the good-wives, of whom two hundred and sixty-three were thus imprisoned. The town-clerk speedily opened the tower gates, which had not been done for several years, and running back exclaimed : ' Away, gentlemen, away, the coast is clear ; but silence, for God's sake silence, that the women may not become aware of it, otherwise there will be the devil to pay.'

" Thereupon they ran away as fast as they could, part of them without hats or gloves ; some ran home, others to a neighbour's, each, where in his hurry he thought he should be secure. All could confess to a state of frightful terror. The priest ran at full trot up the church lane, looking more behind than before him, to see whether the women were following and would shake their keys at him during mass ; he closed the parsonage-house behind him, as the town-clerk had done the council-house. He was so exhausted that he could neither eat nor drink ; both his ladies had enough to do to cool him.

" Now when the imprisoned women, most of whom sat by the window, heard the rumour which was noised about the town, that the honourable gentlemen had so cunningly gotten off, the wife of the King's judge ran to the council-door, unlatched it, and called out with great amazement : ' The devil has carried away the rogues ; see, there lies a hat, a pocket-handkerchief and a glove, and all the doors are open. Come, let us sit in council ourselves and send for our husbands ; they shall come on pain of punishment, and hear our behests.' Thereupon there was great screaming and laughter amongst the wives, so that they might be heard over the whole ' Ring.'

" At last the women divided into small parties by tens and twelves, they pitied their husbands, children, and babies, who would have nothing to eat. So they agreed, by means of certain women who were outside the door, and desirous of joining the prisoners, to beg the King's judge to free them, and to notify to them wherefore they had that day been summoned to the council-house.

" In the meanwhile, however, the King's judge discovered, that he had returned from the council-house a wiser man than when he had entered it in the morning, and it struck him that all husbands might not be so evil disposed towards their wives as he was. He saw also a tolerable concourse of children and mob collecting round the council-house, who were disposed to carry food and drink to the women ; nay, some good friends had already prepared a whole quarter cask of beer for the refreshment of the dear women. Besides this also, a number of men had collected together, desiring to know what their wives had done, that they should be thus locked up. Then the King's judge took heart again, and invited the gentlemen *cito citissime* to his house for a necessary conference. The four gentlemen of the council and the town-clerk were found, but with great difficulty ; but the priest had thoroughly concealed himself, and sent to excuse himself on account of his exhaustion and his need of rest. But it was determined to send another embassage to him, to call to his mind that he must appear without fail, as he had occasioned this transaction.

" Meanwhile the usher of the council came running to the council-house, at whose bidding no one knows, and called through the closed door to his wife, who was in conclave, and said to her : ' Tell the other women that the gentlemen have reassembled at the house of the King's judge ; they will soon send out and open the council-house, that every one may return home.' Thereupon the judge's wife answered : ' Yea, we will willingly have patience, as we are quite comfortable here ; but tell them they ought to inform us why we were summoned and confined without trial.'

" The priest at last allowed himself to be prevailed on, and came to the judge's house. They all began by complaining bitterly of their exhaustion on account of the great anguish and danger they had undergone, therefore a refreshing drink of wine was speedily passed round amongst them ; but what plans they afterwards made I have not been able to gather distinctly, because all passed standing, and there was no protocol concerning it. But certain it is, that as is usual with such ragamuffins, the biters were bitten, and one threw dirt into the face of the other. At last, however, they became unanimous to send an embassage to the imprisoned ladies, to release them from the *cito*, and to bespeak them in all friendship, that they might be induced to quit the council-house. The persons empowered for this embassage were Herr Mümer, Master Daniel, and Herr Notarius.

" When these arrived the doors were immediately opened, and the envoys entered into the midst of the circle of women.

" Then began the town-clerk thus : ' Honourable, very honourable, excellent, and most especially gracious and dear ladies ! his reverence the priest, together with his honour the King's judge and very wise council, send greeting to the ladies assembled ; they greatly wonder that the women have so ill conceived and misunderstood their intentions ; and as they have so earnestly desired to know wherefore this has happened, the aforesaid gentlemen have sent us to explain this in all truth. First, as now the holy week is approaching, in which there will be held by the Church special preachings on the Holy Sacrament, it has been thought advisable to admonish the women christianly and faithfully, to present themselves zealously thereat. Secondly, it is requested that at the approaching Easter festival the women will likewise present themselves collectively and show their benevolence, as his reverence the priest's dues will be so poor in amount, owing to the small number of citizens present.'

" After this harangue of the town-clerk, Master Daniel the joiner, wishing to improve the matter, said : ' My very gracious ladies ! Let it be understood by the women that this is a friendly conference, and that no constraint will be used ; for it is not customary with my masters and the very wise council to hang a man before they have caught him.'

" At this inconsiderate and incautious speech, which did not in the least serve the council, Herr Mümer and Herr Notarius pushed him away ; but among the assembled wives there was great laughter and uproar. ' Yea ! yea ! we understand well enough now ; they compare us to people who are to be hanged. What fellows you are, one with the other ! Oh you faithless rogues ! you usurious corn-dealers ! you woollen thieves ! Thereupon the judge's wife called out : ' Silence ! silence, you women !' and said to Master Daniel : ' Hear, dear brother-in-law, you do not understand the matter, and are also too few to compel us against our conscience. Oh, how God will punish you, and my husband also, who so openly acts against his conscience ! Your dear deceased father, a dignified Lutheran ecclesiastic, taught you both very differently. Now you say you are good Roman Catholics. Your new faith is necessary for your roguish tricks ; when you are drunk you speak shamelessly enough of the mother of God

herself, and when you go to your bad women you speak
of yourselves as the brothers of the Virgin Mary. Oh, if
your gains were taken away from you, which you make from
your offices and the common property of the town, and consume again in eating and drinking ; if you were obliged to
resume your joiners' trade again, and work vigorously to keep
yourselves warm, how soon you would give up your Popery.
May God punish you ! Never shall you deprive us of our
faith, you yourselves will yet be hanged on that account.'

"The burgomaster's wife said : ' If you had nothing else to
say to us, the priest might have done that from the pulpit,
and it would not have been necessary to confine us on that
account. It is not thus I could be compelled to go to church.
Under our former pastors and preachers it was a great pleasure to me to go to church, for I received there comfort from
the word of God; now I am only scandalized and troubled
when I go there. So that it cries out to God in heaven. As
concerns the Easter offerings, every one is free ; he who has to
give may do so.' Hereupon the other women screamed out
loudly : ' Yea, we will give to the priest, the devil, as his
due.' The honourable envoys were terrified at such discourse,
and begged to be allowed to withdraw, and said not a word
further, but departed.

"Now when the honourable envoys returned to the King's
judge, the priest and the other gentlemen had already gone
away; they made their report, and also went home. The
women were now released from their arrest. But this affair
worked seriously in the head of the King's judge ; he took it
to heart that he had been so ignominiously led astray by his
ideas, and feared that the upshot would bring him to eternal
ridicule. He páced up and down the room, murmuring to
himself; at last he said : ' Give me somewhat to eat.' When
the table was spread, and dinner served up by his maid-servant
and children,—a dish of crab, a piece of white bread and

cheese and butter,—the worthy gentleman waxed wrath, took first the good bread, then the tin butter-mould with the butter, and threw them out of the window into the market-place ; he threw the crab also all about the room, and seized upon the sausage which was also on the table, which the children would gladly have had, being hungry, as they had eaten nothing the whole day. Nay, he was so furious that he ran out of the room, dashing down the dishes and saucepans, and all that came to his hand, so that a great concourse of neighbours was brought together. After that, he ran up to his room and went on calling out and conducting himself as if it was full of people. The following morning he rose betimes and stole away, having delivered over his office to Dr. Melchior.

"That day the other gentlemen rested till towards evening ; then the priest sent for the beadle, and commanded him to summon in his name and that of Dr. Melchior, as the vice King's judge, the wife of the burgomaster and the frau Geneussin to come to him at the parsonage early in the morning after mass. This the beadle did. The burgomaster's wife answered : ' Yea, yea, I will come, but I will first tell my lord.' But when the beadle came to Frau Geneussin, and announced the same to her, her son-in-law was with her, Herr Krekler, who was afterwards burgomaster, who thus answered for her : ' Are the priest and Dr. Melchior your masters ? Are they the masters of my honoured mother-in-law ? Reply that she will not come without the commands of the burgomaster.' This the beadle told to the burgomaster, who reflected thereupon, and at last said : ' For my part they may go, I am content, so the blame cannot be laid upon me.'

"On Friday morning, at the appointed hour, the wife of the burgomaster went to the priest and likewise the judge's wife, who however was not summoned, together with Frau Geneussin. Then the priest began to speak with them in the most friendly way ; he begged them very politely to conform and accept the only holy religion which could make them blessed, as their lords had done. They would see what comfort they would find in it, and how well it would fare with them. To this the women forthwith replied : 'No, we were otherwise instructed by our parents, and former preachers ; according to that we find ourselves right comfortable. We cannot reconcile ourselves to your religion.' Thereupon the priest said : 'You women may come to church or to me as oft as you please, when you have anxieties or scruples, and I will assuredly instruct you assiduously.' The women answered : 'Your reverence need not give yourself any trouble on our account, as we will not do so.' 'Ay,' said the priest, 'then set the other women a good example, and at least go to church and mass, and do not be a cause of offence to others who have already declared that they would go if the women went.' The women replied : 'We will not do it ourselves, but we will not prevent others from doing so ; these are matters of conscience whereof none can judge but God.' Now when the priest saw that all was in vain, he entreated them thus : 'Ay, ay, yet at least tell the other women that you have begged for, and also obtained, fourteen days for consideration.' Then answered the women almost with indignation : 'No, dear sir, we were not taught to lie by our parents, and we will not learn it from you; we beg you will excuse us.' So they departed therefrom.

"But whilst the three women were with the priest, a great multitude of women collected together with marvellous rapidity, many more than on the first occasion. Herr Schwob Franze perceiving this, came running panting with haste to the burgomaster and said : 'Sir, I pray you for God's sake have a care, and prevent the priest from meddling with the women ; they have assembled together again in a great multitude, the whole of the bread-market and all the houses in Kirchgasse are full of them ; God help us, they will slay us, together with the priest.   I made the best of my way out from them.'

" The good burgomaster was so ill in bed that he could neither move hand nor foot.   He sent hastily to the priest and told him in plain German what a hazardous business he had begun, the like of which had never been heard of in any town. If he were to meet with any annoyance from the women the fault would be his own.

" Thereupon the priest said : ' Ah no ! Herr Burgomaster, let not your worship be thus angered.   I see that I have been led astray by that inconsiderate man Dr. Melchior, who represented the matter quite otherwise.   I beg that your worship will signify to the women, that they may return to their homes ; assuredly what has happened shall not happen again, of that I hereby assure your worship.'   When the women heard this, and that nothing further had happened to the ladies, as has been related above, the women were well content, went home and laid aside their bundles and bunches of keys, nevertheless, not out of reach, that they might have them at hand day or night in case of need."

Here ends the old narrative.   The priest was obliged the following year to leave Löwenberg ignominiously, as he would not desist from his scandalous proceedings.   Amongst other things he had a public chop and beer-house erected for the old Silesian beer.   The spiteful Dr. Melchior became afterwards in esperation a soldier, and was hanged at Prague.   And the valiant women,—we hope they took refuge with their husbands at Breslau or in Poland.

After 1632, the town decayed more and more every year, now under Swedish or Imperial, now under Evangelical, or Roman Catholic ministers ; in 1639, the town contained only forty citizens, and had a debt of a ton and a half of gold ; in 1641, the citizens themselves unroofed their houses in order not to pay taxes, and dwelt in thatched huts.

When the peace came, the town was almost entirely in ruins. Eight years later, in 1656, there were again one hundred and twenty-one citizens in Löwenberg and about eight hundred and fifty inhabitants ; eighty-seven per cent. of the population had perished.

CHAPTER VI.

THE THIRTY YEARS' WAR.—THE PEACE.

THE peace was signed; the ambassadors had solemnized the ratification by shaking hands, and trumpeters rode about the streets announcing the happy event.

At Nuremberg the Imperialists and the Swedes held a peace banquet in the great saloon of the council-house; the lofty vaulted hall was splendidly lighted; betwixt the chandeliers hung down thirty kinds of flowers and real fruits, bound together with gold tinsel; four choirs were stationed for festive music, and the six classes of invited guests were assembled in six different rooms. On the table stood two prodigious show dishes, a triumphal arch, and a hexagonal mound covered with mythological and allegorical figures with Latin and German devices. The banquet was served up in four courses, in each course were a hundred and fifty dishes, then came the fruits in silver dishes, and on real dwarf trees by which the whole table was covered; amidst all this, fine frankincense was burnt, which produced a very agreeable odour. Afterwards the upper leaves of the table were taken away by pieces, then the table was covered again with napkins, and plates strewed over with flowers made of sugar, and now came the confectionery; among these there were gigantic marchpanes on two silver shells, each of which weighed ten pounds. And when the health of his Imperial Majesty of Vienna and his Kingly Majesty of Sweden was drunk, to-

gether with the prosperity of the peace which had been concluded, fifteen large and small pieces were discharged from
the citadel.   When this peace banquet had lasted far on into
the night, the Field-marshals and Generals present, wished on
parting to play once more at being soldiers.   They caused
arms to be brought into the hall, chose the two ambassadors
as captains; his Illustrious and Serene Highness Herr Carl
Gustav, Count Palatine on the Rhine, afterwards King of
Sweden, and his Excellency General Piccolomini; but for a
corporal they chose Field-Marshal Wrangel; and all the
Generals, colonels, and lieutenant-colonels were made musketeers.   Thus these gentlemen marched round the table, fired
a salvo, went in good order to the citadel, and there fired off
the pieces many times.   On their return they were playfully
discharged by Colonel Kraft and dismissed the service, as now
there was to be peace for ever.   Two oxen were slaughtered
for the poor, and there was a great distribution of bread, also
for six hours red and white wine flowed from a lion's jaw.
For thirty years had tears and blood flowed from a greater
lion's jaw.

   Like the honourable ambassadors, the people prepared
a festive celebration in every town, nay in every half-
destroyed village.   Howg reat was the effect of the intelligence
of peace on the German nation may be learned from some
affecting details.   To the old country people the peace appeared as a return of their youth; they looked back to the rich
harvests of their childhood, thickly populated villages, the
merry Sundays under the hewed-down village lindens, and
the happy hours which they had passed with their ruined and
deceased relations and companions.   They saw themselves
happier, more manly, and better than they had been during
thirty years of misery and degradation.   But the youth of
the country—a hard war-engendered demoralized race—discovered in it the approach of a wonderful time which appeared

to them like a legend from a distant country. The time
when on every acre of field, the thick yellow ears of corn would
wave in the wind; when in every stall the cows would low,
and in every sty a fat pig would be lying; when they themselves should drive with two horses in the fields, merrily
cracking their whips, and when there would be no enemy's
soldiers to snatch rough caresses from their sisters or sweet-
hearts; when they would no longer have to lie in wait in the
bushes, with pitchforks and rusty muskets, for the stragglers,
nor to sit as fugitives in the dismal gloom of the wood by the
graves of the slain; when the village roofs would be without
holes, and the farm-yards without ruined barns; when the howl
of the wolf would not be heard every night at the yard gate;
when their village churches would again have glass windows,
and beautiful bells; when in the soiled choir of the church,
there should arise a new altar with a silk cover, a silver crucifix and a gilt chalice; and when one day the young lads would
again lead their brides to the altar, bearing the virgin wreaths
in their hair. A passionate, almost painful joy palpitated
through all hearts; even the wildest brood of the war, the soldiery, were seized with it. The stern rulers themselves, the
Princes and their ambassadors, felt that this great boon of peace
would be the salvation of Germany. The festival was celebrated with the greatest fervour and solemnity of which the
people were capable. From the same circle of village recollections from which examples have already been taken, the
following description of a festival is placed, in juxtaposition
to that of the Princes and Field-marshals.

Döllstedt, a fine village in the dukedom of Gotha, had suffered severely. In 1636 the Hatzfeld corps had fallen upon
the place, had committed great damage, plundered the church,
burnt and broken off the woodwork, as had been prophesied
by the pastor Herr Deckner shortly before. "This dear
man," thus writes his successor, the pastor, Herr Trümper,

" had rebuked his flock with righteous zeal on account of their sins ; but they had laughed at his rebukes and warnings, had treated him with anger and ingratitude, and as he lamented in 1634, with weeping eyes, had cut down his hops from the poles, and carried off the corn from his fields.   Thus he could only proclaim to them God's righteous judgment on such hardened hearts.   Not only publicly from the pulpit, but also a few hours before his blessed departure, he had thus lamented : ' Ah ! thou poor Döllstedt ! it will go ill with thee after my decease !'   Thereupon he turned, with the assistance of the attendants, towards the church, and raised his weary head, struggling ineffectually with death, as if he wished once more, from the corner of his room, to see the church, in the service of which his life had been passed, and said : ' Ah ! thou dear, dear church !   How will it fare with thee after my death ? They will sweep thee up with a besom.' "

His prophecy was fulfilled.   The village in 1636 had to liquidate war damages to the amount 5500 of gulden, and between 1627 and 1637 it amounted altogether to 29,595 gulden, so that the inhabitants by degrees disappeared and the place remained quite desolate; in 1636 there were only two married couple in the village.   In the year 1641, after Banner and, again in the winter, the French had been quartered in it, half an acre of corn was sown, and there were four couple dwelling there.   By the zealous care of Duke Ernest the Good, of Gotha, the deserted villages in his country were comparatively quickly occupied by men.   In 1650, therefore, the jubilee and peace festival could be solemnized in Döllstedt.   The description of it is given, as it is recorded in the church books, by the then Pastor Trümper.

" On the 19th of August, at four o'clock in the morning, we, together with our coadjutors and some of the householders of Gotha, mounted our tower, and celebrated with music our morning prayer.   Towards six o'clock, as happened the preceding day at one o'clock, they began to ring the bells for a quarter of an hour, and again, for the same length of time, at half after seven. Meanwhile, the whole population, man and woman, young and old, except those who assisted at the ringing, assembled before the gate : 1st, the women-folk stood on one side ; before them was a figure of Peace, which the noble maidens had dressed up beautifully, in a lovely green silk dress and other decorations ; on her head was placed a beautiful green wreath intermingled with gold spangles, and in her hand a green branch. 2nd. On the other side towards the village stood the men, and in front of them Justice in a beautiful white garment, with a green wreath round her head, and bearing in her hands a naked sword and gold scales. 3rd. Towards the fields on the same side, stood the young men with guns, and some with naked swords, and before them Mars, dressed as a soldier, and bearing in his hands a cross-bow. 4th. In the middle near me, stood the scholars, house-holders, and the coadjutors. Then did the recollection come across me, of how often we had been obliged to quit our homes and flee from our gates, our eyes overflowing with tears, and when the storm was passed, had returned home again with joy, notwithstanding that we found all devastated, ruined, and turned topsy-turvy. Now we thought it fitting thus to honour our dear God, going out in front of our gates, and as He had preserved us from the like devastation and necessity for flight and escape, by the gracious boon of the noble and long-desired peace, we desired now to go to his gates with thanksgiving, and into his courts with praise, and would for that raise our voices with one accord and sing : ' To God alone most high be honour, &c.' 5th. Whilst these strophes were being chanted, Peace and Justice approached one another nearer and nearer. At the words : ' All feuds are now at an end,' those who held naked swords sheathed them, and those who had guns fired some salvos and turned themselves round.

Peace beckoned to some who had been hereto appointed; these took from Mars, who appeared to defend himself, his cross-bow, and broke it in twain; Peace and Justice met together and kissed each other. 6th. Thereupon the chanting, which had been begun, was continued, and we prepared to go. Before the scholars, went Andreas Ehrhardt, adorned to the utmost, with a staff in his hand wound round with green garlands. Then followed the scholars with green wreaths on their heads and green branches in their hands, and they wore short white garments; then came the assistants and musicians; after these, I, the Pastor, together with the Herr Pastor of Vargula, who had come to me. After us came the maidens, the little ones in front, and the taller ones behind, all adorned to the utmost, and green wreaths on their heads. After these went Peace, and behind her the boys, who carried a basket of rolls and a dish of apples, which were afterwards distributed among the children; item, all kinds of fruits of the field.

" These were followed by the noble maidens, together with their relations, whom they had bidden; after them nobles from Seebach, Saxony, and others who had accompanied them. After these came Justice, and behind her, magistrates and assessors, all bearing white staves in their hands, twined with green garlands. Then followed the Ensign Christian Heum, in his best attire, with a staff in his hand, on which he leant, but it was encircled with a green garland. Afterwards came the men in pairs with green bouquets in their hands; the men were followed by Mars bound, then the young lads with their guns reversed. There followed the Sergeant-major Herr Dietrich Grün in his finery, with a staff in his hand like the Ensign; and after him the women-folk, all also in pairs in their order, and all passed singing through the village to the church. When the aforesaid song was finished wassang, ' Now Praise the Lord, O my soul.'

"In the church there was preaching and singing conformable to the royal ordinance. After the service was completed, we went in the former order from the church to the Platz in front of the inn; there the men on one side, and the women on the other, in half-circles, closed in, forming a fine wide circle, and during their progress they sang, 'Now rejoice together, dear Christians.' When the circle was formed I gave thanks to all collectively, that they had not only, according to the proclamation of the high and mighty princely government, obediently observed this solemnity, but also had gone out at my desire, all together, noble and humble alike, to the gates, and had followed me in such beautiful order to church, &c., and I admonished them to attend again zealously the afternoon service. And truly, as I said that it would be well for every one to come from their houses to church in the afternoon, they did all reassemble as before in front of the inn; Peace and Justice also were there again in their dress, but Mars had disappeared. When I was informed of this, I went during the last peal of the bells with the scholars, the coadjutors, and the householders out by the back gate through the church lane to the church, when every one again, as before, followed me into the church. There we then sang, 'Now let us sing unto the Lord,' &c. From the church we returned in the same order, again singing, 'Praise the Lord, praise the Lord,' &c., to the above-mentioned place, where I again gave thanks both to strangers and townspeople, with heartfelt wishes for peace. And here the six groschen, rolls, and ripe apples were distributed among the children."

It is known that the great peace came very slowly, like the recovery from a mortal illness. The years from 1648 to 1650, from the conclusion of the peace to the celebration of the festival, were among the most grievous of that iron time; exorbitant war taxes were imposed, the armies of the different countries lay encamped in the provinces till they could be paid off, the oppression which they exercised on the unhappy inhabitants was so fearful, that a despairing cry arose from the people, which mingled itself with the wrangling of the negotiating parties. To this was added a plague of another kind; the whole country swarmed with a rabble that had no masters; bands of discharged soldiers with the camp followers, troops of beggars, and great hordes of robbers, roved about from one territory to another; they quartered themselves by force on those villages which were still inhabited, and established themselves in the deserted huts. The villagers also, provided with bad weapons and disused to labour, thought it sometimes more satisfactory to rob, than to till the fields, and made secret roving expeditions into the neighbouring territories, the Evangelical into the Catholic countries, and vice versâ. The foreign children of a lawless race, the gipsies, had increased in number and audacity; fantastically dressed, with heavily laden carts, stolen horses, and naked children, they encamped in great numbers round the stone trough of the village green: whenever the ruler was powerful and the officials active, the wild rovers were encountered with energy. The villagers of the dukedom of Gotha were still obliged, in 1649, to keep watch from the church towers, to guard the bridges and fords, and to give an alarm whenever they perceived any of these marching bands. A well-regulated system of police was the first sign of that new feeling of responsibility which the governments had acquired: every one who wished to settle down was encouraged to do so. Whoever was established, had to render an account of how much land he had cultivated, of the condition of his house and farm, and whether he had any cattle. New registers of the farms and inhabitants were prepared, new taxes on money and on natural products were imposed; and by the severe pressure of these, the villagers were compelled to labour.

The villages were gradually reinhabited; many families who had fled to the towns during the war repaired their devastated farms; others returned from the mountains or foreign countries; disbanded soldiers and camp followers sometimes bought fields and empty houses with the remainder of their booty, or returned to their native villages. There was much marrying and baptizing.

But the exhaustion of the people was still lamentably great. The arable land, much of which had lain fallow, was sown without the necessary manure; not a little remained overrun with wild underwood and weeds, and long continued as osier land. The ruined districts were sometimes bought by the neighbouring villages, and in some places two or three small communities united themselves together.

For many years after the war, the appearance of the villages was most comfortless; one may perceive that this was the case in Thuringia, from the transactions with the Government. The householders of Siebleben and some other communities round Gotha, had held, from the middle ages, the right of having timber free from the wooded hills. In 1650, the government demanded from them, for the exercise of this right, a small tax upon oats: some of the communities excused themselves, as they were too poor to be able to think of rebuilding their damaged houses. Ten years after, the community of Siebleben had forty boys who paid small school fees, and the yearly offering in the church amounted to more than fourteen gulden. A portion of this offering was spent in alms to strangers, and it is perceptible, from the carefully kept accounts, what a stream of beggars of all kinds passed through the country; disbanded soldiers, cripples, the sick and aged; amongst them were lepers with certificates from their infirmaries, also exiles from Bohemia and Hungary, who had left their homes on account of their religion, banished noblemen from England, Ireland, and

Poland, persons collecting money for the ransom of their relatives from Turkish imprisonment, travellers who had been plundered by highwaymen, and others, such as a blind pastor from Denmark with five children; the strangers came prepared with testimonials. The governments, however, were unwearied in their efforts against harbouring such vagrants.

Much has been written concerning the devastation of the war; but the great work is still wanting, that would concentrate the statistical notices which have been preserved in all the different territories: however enormous the labour may be, it must be undertaken, for it is only from this irrefragable computation, that the full greatness of the calamity can be understood. The details hitherto known scarcely amount to a probable valuation of the loss which Germany suffered in men, beasts of burden, and productive power. The following inferences only attempt to express the views of an individual, which a few examples will support.

The condition of the provinces of Thuringia and Franconia is not ill adapted for a comparison of the past with the present; neither of them were more afflicted by the visitation of war than other countries; the state of cultivation of both provinces, up to the present time, answers pretty accurately to the general average of German industry and agriculture: neither of them are on the whole rich : both were hilly countries, without large rivers, or any considerable coal strata, with low lands, of which only certain tracts were distinguished by especial fertility, and were up to modern times devoted to agriculture, garden culture, and small mining industry. Thus this portion of Germany had known no powerful stream of human enterprise or capital, nor, on the other hand, was it the theatre of the destructive wars of Louis XIV.'s time, and the rulers, especially the grandson of Frederic the Wise, were even in the worst times tolerably sparing of the national strength.

There have been preserved to us from these districts, amongst other things, accurate statistical notices of twenty communities, which once were in the Hennebergen domain; but now, with the exception of one that is Bavarian, belong to Saxe Meiningen. It is nowhere mentioned, and from their condition need not be concluded, that the devastation in them had been greater than in other portions of the province. The government in 1649 ordered an accurate report to be given of the number of inhabited houses, barns, and head of cattle that existed when the worst sufferings of the war began in 1634. According to the reports delivered by the magistrates of the places, there had perished in the twenty communities more than eighty-two per cent. of families, eighty-five per cent. of horses, more than eighty-three of goats, and eighty-two of cows, and more than sixty-three per cent. of houses. The remaining houses were described as in many places damaged and in ruins, the still surviving horses as lame and blind, and the fields and meadows as devastated and much overgrown with underwood; but the sheep were everywhere altogether destroyed.*

It is a bloody and terrible tale which these numbers tell us. More than four fifths of the population, far more than four fifths of their property were destroyed. And in what a condition was the remainder!

Precisely similar was the fate of the smaller provincial

* We have to thank Professor Brückner of Meiningen, for the communication of the following summary: it is printed in 'Memorials of Franconian and Thuringian History and Statistics,' 1852.

In nineteen villages of the former domain of Henneberg there were in the years—

				1634	1649	1849
	Families	.	.	1773	316	1916
	Houses	.	.	1717	627	1558
In 17 villages—Cattle	.	.	.	1402	244	1994
13 „	Horses	.	.	485	73	107
12 „	Sheep	.	.	4616	. .	4596
4 „	Goats	.	.	158	26	286

towns, as far as one can see from the preserved data. We
will give only one example from the same province. The old
church records of Ummerstadt, an agricultural town near
Coburg, famed, from olden times, throughout the country for
its good pottery, report as follows :—" Although in the year
1632 the whole country, as also the said little town, was very
populous, so that it alone contained more than one hundred
and fifty citizens, and up to eight hundred souls, yet from
the ever-continuing war troubles, and the constant quartering
of troops, the people became in such-wise enervated, that
from great and incessant fear, a pestilence sent upon us by
the all-powerful and righteous God, carried off as many as
five hundred men in the years 1635 and 1636 ; on account of
this lamentable and miserable condition of the time, no children were born into the world in the course of two years. Those
whose lives were still prolonged by God Almighty, have from
hunger, the dearness of the times, and the scarcity of precious
bread, eaten and lived upon bran, oil-cakes, and linseed husks,
and many also have died of it ; many also have been dispersed over all countries, most of whom have never again seen
their dear fatherland. In the year 1640, during the Saalfeldt
encampment, Ummerstadt became a city of the dead or of
shadows ; for during eighteen weeks no man dared to appear
therein, and all that remained was destroyed. Therefore the
population became quite thin, and there were not more than
a hundred souls forthcoming." In 1850 the place had eight
hundred and ninety-three inhabitants.

Still more striking is another observation, which may be
made from the tables of the Meiningen villages. It is only
in our century that the number of men and cattle of all kinds
has again reached the height which it had already attained in
1634. Nay, the number of houses was still in 1849 less than
in 1634, although there the inmates of the smallest village
houses, even the poorest, still anxiously endeavour to preserve

their own dwellings. It is true that there is a trifling increase of the number of inhabitants in 1849 over that in 1634; but even this increase is dubious when we consider that the number of inhabitants in 1634 had probably already experienced a diminution from sixteen years of war. Thus we are assuredly justified in concluding that two centuries were necessary, at least for this tract of Germany, to restore the population and productive power of the country to its former standard. These assumptions are supported by other observations. The agriculture of the country, before the Thirty years' war, nay even the relative proportion of the value of corn to that of silver, at a time when the export of corn was only exceptional, lead to the same conclusions.

It is true that during the last two centuries, agriculture, owing to the mighty effects of foreign traffic, has developed itself in an entirely new direction. The countryman also now cultivates field vegetables, clover, and other herbage for fodder, which were unknown before the Thirty years' war, and agricultural produce is more lucrative for an equal amount of population. Perhaps our ancestors lived in a poorer style, and farmed less. We can compare the stock of cattle. The number of cattle kept now in the villages is precisely the same as before the war; they have still the short, thick, curly-woolled Spanish herds, which used to be reared in the pens of the peasants; the old wool fell in long locks; but judging from the value of the cloth and stuffs woven from it, and the price of sheep at that time, it must have been good.

On the other hand, the stock of horses has diminished by three fourths in comparison with 1634. This striking circumstance can only be thus explained: that the traditions of the troopers of the middle ages exercised an influence even upon agriculture; that the rearing of horses was more profitable than now, on account of the bad roads which made a distant transport of corn impossible, whilst the lowing of cattle in the narrow farm-yards of the towns was so general that the sale of milk and butter paid little ; and finally, that a larger portion of the country people were better able to maintain teams. The breaking up of the ground was then, as may be seen from the old farm books in Thuringia, somewhat—but not considerably—less than now. In the present day the number of goats and of cattle belonging to small farmers has increased, as also the number of oxen, which probably in Middle and Southern Germany are now finer and higher bred than formerly. This is a decided progress of the present day. But on the whole, reckoning the amount of fodder required, the number of beasts which are maintained with advantage is very inconsiderably larger at present than in 1634.

Thus Germany, in comparison with its happier neighbours in England and the Low Countries, was thrown back about two hundred years.

Still greater were the changes which the war made in the intellectual life of the nation. Above all among the country people. Many old customs passed away, life became aimless and full of suffering. In the place of the old household gear the rudest forms of modern furniture were introduced ; the artistic chalices, and old fonts, and almost all the adornments of the churches, had disappeared, and were succeeded by a tasteless poverty in the village churches, which still continues. For more than a century after the war the peasant vegetated, penned in, almost as much as his herds, whilst his pastor watched him as a shepherd, and he was shorn by the landed proprietors and rulers of his country. There was a long period of gloomy suffering. The price of corn in the depopulated country was, for fifty years after the war, even lower than before. But the burdens upon landed property rose so high, that for a long time, land together with house and farm, bore little value, and sometimes were offered in vain as acquit-

tance for service and imposts. Severer than ever was the
pressure of vassalage, worst of all in the former Sclave countries, in which the peasantry were kept down by a numerous
nobility.   With respect to their marriages, they were placed
under an unnatural and compulsory guardianship ; strict care
was taken that the son of the countryman should not evade
by flight the servitude which was to weigh down his future.
He could not travel without a written permission ; even ship
and raft masters were forbidden under severe penalties to take
such fugitives into their service.

Much to be lamented is the injury to civilization which
took place in the devastated cities, especially the return to
luxury, love of pleasure, and coarse sensuality, the want of
common sense and independence, the cringing towards
superiors and heartlessness towards inferiors.   They are the
ancient sufferings of a decaying race.   That the self-government of cities was more and more infringed upon by the
princes, was frequently fortunate, for the administrators
were too often deficient in judgment and feeling of duty.

The new constitution of governments which had arisen
during the war, laid its iron hands on town and country. The
old territories of the German empire were changed into
despotic bureaucratic states.   The ruler governed through his
officials, and kept a standing army against his enemies ; to
maintain his " state," that is, his courtiers, officials and
soldiers, was the task of the people.   But to make this possible,
it was necessary to promote carefully the increase of the
population, and the greater tax-paying capacity of the subject.   Some princes, especially the Brandenburgers, did this
in a liberal spirit, and thus in this dark period, by increasing
the power of their new state, laid the foundation of the
greatness of their houses.   Others indeed lavished the
popular strength, in coarse imitation of French demoralization.

It was a mortal crisis through which Germany had passed, and dearly was the peace bought.   But that which was most important had been preserved, the continuity of German development, the continuance of the great inward process, by which the German nation raised itself from the bondage of the middle ages to a higher civilization.

The long struggle, politically considered, was a defensive war of the Protestant party against the intolerance of the old faith and the attacks of the Imperial power.   This defensive struggle had begun by an ill-timed offensive movement in Bohemia.   The head of the House of Hapsburg had law and right on his side, so long as he only put down this movement.   His opponents put themselves in the position of revolutionists, which could only be vindicated by success.   But from the day when the Emperor made use of his victory to suppress by means of Jesuits and soldiers the sovereignty of the German princes, and the old rights of the cities, he became in his turn the political offender whose bold venture was repulsed by the last efforts of the nation.   But here we must take a higher point of view, from which the proceedings of Ferdinand II. appear still more insupportable.   Just a hundred years before his reign, all the good spirits of the German nation fought on the side of the Emperor, when he, in opposition to existing rights and old usages, had founded a German Church and German state.   Since that, the family of Charles V. had for a century, a short time excepted, done much by laborious scheming, or listless indifference, to destroy the last source of this new life, independence of spirit, thought and faith : it was for a century, a short time excepted, the opponent of the national German life ; it had its Spanish and Italian alliances, and had arrayed the Romish Jesuits against the indigenous civilization of the nation, aided, alas ! by some of the German princes.   It was by such means that it had endeavoured to become great in Germany, and in the same spirit, an overzealous Emperor called forth the bloody decision. On his head, not on the German people or Princes, lies the guilt of this endless war. The Protestant chiefs, with the exception of the lesser rulers, only sought to submit and make peace with their Emperor. It was only for a few years they were led into open war, by the arrogance of Wallenstein, the scorn of Vienna, and the warlike pressure of Gustavus Adolphus ; the alliance of the great electoral houses of Saxony and Brandenburg with Sweden did not last four years ; at the first opportunity they receded, and during the last period of the war, neutrality was their strongest policy.

The princes obtained by the peace the object of their defensive opposition ; the extravagant designs of the Imperial Court were crushed. Germany was free. Yes, free ! Devastated and powerless, with its western frontier for a century the fighting-ground and spoil of France, it had still to bear the out-pouring of an accumulated measure of humiliation and shame. But whoever would now clench their hands at this, let them beware of raising them against the Westphalian peace. The consequences that followed, the laying in ashes of the Palatinate, the seizure of Strasburg, the loss of Alsace and Lorraine, were not owing to this peace. The cause of all this, was long before the Thirty years' war ; it had been foreseen by patriotic men long beforehand. Since the Smalkaldic war the sovereignty of the German Princes, and the independence of portions of the empire, were the only guarantee for a national progressive civilization. One may deeply lament, but can easily understand this. Now at last this independence had been legally established by streams of blood. Whoever considers the year 1813,—the first kindling of the people since 1648,—as full of glory ; whoever has at any time ennobled himself by a sense of duty and enlarged moral sentiments, acquired from the severe teaching of Kant and his followers ; whoever has at any time derived pleasure from the highest that man is capable of understanding, and from the nature and souls of his own and foreign people ; whoever has at any time felt with transport the beauty of the new German poetry, the Nathan, Faust, and Guillaume Tell ; whoever has taken a heartfelt participation in the free life of our science and arts, in the great discoveries of our natural philosophers, and in the powerful development of German industry and agriculture, must remember, that with the peace of Munster and Osnaburg began the period in which the political foundation of the development of a higher life was in a great measure secured.

The war had nevertheless consequences which we must still deeply deplore ; it has long severed the third of Germany from intellectual communion of spirit with their kindred races. The German hereditary possessions of the Imperial family have ever since been united in a special state. Powerfully and incessantly has the foreign principle worked which there prevails. For a long time the depressed nation scarcely felt the loss. In Germany the opposition between Romanism and Protestantism had been weakened, and in the following century it was in a great measure overcome. Even those territories which were compelled by their rulers to maintain their old faith, had participated in the slow and laborious progress which had been made since the peace. It is not to be denied that the Protestant countries long remained the leaders, but in spite of much opposition, those of the old faith followed the new stream, and the results of increasing civilization flowed in brotherly union from one soul to another ; joy and suffering were in general mutual, and as the political requirements and wishes of the Protestant and Roman Catholics were the same, the feeling of intellectual unity became gradually more active. It was otherwise in the distant countries which Ferdinand II. and his successors had bequeathed as conquered property. The losses which the

German races had experienced were great, but the injury to
the Austrian nationalities was incomparably greater. To
them had happened what must now appear, to any one who
examines accurately, most terrible. Almost the whole
national civilization, which in spite of all hindrances had been
developed for more than a century, was expelled with an iron
rod. The mass of the people remained ; their leaders—opulent
landed proprietors of the old indigenous race, manly patriots,
men of distinguished character and learning, and intelligent
pastors, were driven into exile. The exiles have never been
counted, who perished of hunger, and the horrors of war ;
those also who settled in foreign countries can scarcely be
reckoned. Undoubtedly their collective number amounted
to hundreds of thousands. It is thanks to the Bohemian
exiles, that Electoral Saxony recovered its loss in men and
capital quicker than other countries. Yet it is not the
numbers, however great, which give a true representation of
the loss. For those who fell into calamity on account of their
faith and political convictions were the noblest spirits, the
leaders of the people, the representatives of the highest civilization of the time. But it was not the loss of them alone
that made the Emperor's dominions so weak and dormant ; the
millions also that remained behind were crushed. Driven by
every low motive, by rough violence or the prospect of earthly
advantage, from one faith to another, they had lost all self-
respect and the last ideal which even the most common-
place man preserves, the feeling that he has a place in his
heart that cannot be bought. Everywhere throughout
Germany in the worst times after the war, there were thousands who were fortified by the feeling that they also, like
their fathers and neighbours, had resisted armed conversion
to the death. In the converted Austrian territories of the
Emperor, this feeling was rare. For almost a century and a
half the Bohemian and German races vegetated in a dreary

dream life.   The Bohemian countryman hung the various
saints of the restored church by the side of his pictures of
Huss and Zisko, but he kept a holy lamp burning before the
old heretic; the citizen of Vienna and Olmutz accustomed
himself to speak of the Empire and Germany as of a foreign
land; he accommodated himself to Hungarians, Italians, and
Croats, but at the same time he remained a stranger in the
new state in which he was now domiciled.   Little did he care
for the categorical imperative, imposed by the new worldly
wisdom; later he learned that Schiller was a German poet.
Only then did a new spring begin for the Germans, in which
freedom of mind and beauty of soul were sought for as the
highest aim of earthly life; when the new study of antiquity
inspired them with enthusiasm, when the genius of Goethe
irradiated the court of Weimar, then sounded from dormant
Austria, the deepest and most mysterious of arts, a fullness of
melody.   There also the spirit of the people had found
touching expression in Haydn, Mozart, and Beethoven.

CHAPTER VII.

ROGUES AND ADVENTURERS.

THE war had fearfully loosened the joints of burgher society. The old orderly and disciplined character of Germans appeared almost lost. Countless was the number of unfortunates who having lost house and farm, maintenance and family, wandered homeless through inhospitable foreign countries; and not less numerous were the troops of reprobates who had habituated themselves to live by fraud, extortion, and robbery. Excitement had become a necessity to the whole living race, for thirty years the vagrant rabble of all Europe had chosen Germany as their head-quarters.

Thus it happened that after the peace the doings of the fortune hunters, adventurers, and rogues increased to an extraordinary extent. A contrast of weakness and roughness is, in the following century, a special characteristic of the needy, careworn family life, into which the spirit of the German people had contracted itself. Some particulars of this wild life will be here related, which will denote the gradual changes it underwent. For like the German devils, the children of the devil have also their history, and their race is more ancient than the Christian faith.

People are hardly aware of the intimate connection between German life and Roman antiquity. Not only did the traditions of the Roman empire, Christianity, Roman law, and the Latin language become parts of the German civilization, but

still more extensively were the numerous little peculiarities
of the Roman world preserved in the middle ages.   German
agriculture acquired from the Romans the greater part of its
implements, also wheat, barley, and much of the remaining
produce.   The most ancient of our finer kinds of fruit are of
Roman origin, equally so our wine, many garden flowers, and
almost all our vegetables ; also the oldest woollen fabrics,
cotton and silk stuffs, and all the oldest machines, as for example, watermills, and the first mining and foundry works ;
likewise innumerable other things, even to the oldest forms of
our dress, house utensils, chairs, tables, cupboards, and even
the panels of our folding doors.   And if it were possible to
measure how much in our life is gathered from antiquity, or
from primitive German invention, we should still, after the
lapse of fifteen centuries, find so much that is Roman in our
fields, gardens, and houses, on our bodies, nay, even in our
souls, that one may well have a right to inquire whether our
primeval ancestors were more under the protection of Father
Jove or of the wild Woden.

Thus amongst numberless others, the despised race of
Gladiators, Histrions, and Thymelei—or jesters, were preserved throughout the storm of migration, and spread from
Rome among the barbarian races.   They introduced amongst
the bloody hordes of Vandals the dissolute Roman pantomime ;
they stood before the huts of the Frank chiefs, and piped and
played foreign melodies, which had perhaps once come with the
orgies of the Asiatic gods to Rome ; they intermingled with
the Gothic congregation, which poured out of the newly built
church into the churchyard, and there opened their chests in
order to show a monkey in a red jacket as a foreign prodigy,
or produced the grotesque figures of old Latin puppets, the
maccus, bucco, papus, and whatever else the ancient fathers
called our jack-puddings, for the amusement of the young
parishioners, who opened wide their large blue eyes at these

foreign wonders.   Meanwhile other members of the band of
jugglers offered on payment, to execute gymnastic games before the warriors of the community, which they performed
with sharp weapons and all the artifices and cunning of the
Roman circus ; then these foolhardy men formed a ring and
carried on with passionate eagerness, for the sake of pay, the
dangerous hazards of the combat, which the spectators admired the more, the bloodier it became, whilst they held the
unfortunates, who thus struggled for money, in no greater
consideration than a couple of wolves or hungry dogs.
But for the distinguished spectators there were other more
enticing artists.   Women also roved with the men amongst
the German tribes, dexterous and bold, dancers, singers, and
actresses, in brilliant cavalcades.   When they shook the Greek
tambourine or the Asiatic castanets, in the licentious mazes of
the bacchanalian dance, they were generally irresistible to the
German barons, but were extremely offensive to serious people.
In the year 554 a Frank king interposed with his authority
against the nuisance of these foreign *rovers*, and the worthy
Hinkmar, paternally warned his priests also against these
women, whose foreign sounding designation was expressed by
the true-hearted monk with a very well known but bitter
word.

To these foreign jugglers were speedily added numerous
German recruits.   The German races had had wandering
singers from the primitive times, bearers of news, spreaders of
epic songs and poems.   These also moved from farm to farm,
highly welcome in the large houses of persons of distinction,
honoured guests, trusted messengers, who often received from
their hosts a more affectionate reward than golden bracelets
or new dresses.   They had once upon a time sung to the harp
by the fireside, of the adventurous expedition of the thunder
god to the world of giants, and of the tragic fall of the Nibelungen, then of Attila's battle, and the wonders of southern

lands.   But to the new Christian faith, this treasure of old
native songs was obnoxious.   The high-minded Charlemagne
made a collection of the heroic songs of the German race, but
his Popish son Louis hated and despised them.   These songs
undoubtedly were so thoroughly heathen, that the Church had
reason to remonstrate against them in synodical resolutions
and episcopal decrees.   Together with them, the race of singers
who carried and spread them, fell into disfavour with the
church.   The songs did not however cease, but the singers
sank to a lower scale, and finally a portion of them at least
fell into the class of vagrants, and the people were accustomed
to hear the fairest heritage of their past from the lips of despised players.

Another heritage also from German heathendom fell to
these strollers.   Even before the time of Tacitus there were
simple dramatic processions in Germany ; on the great feast
days of the German gods, there already appeared the humorous ideas of the pious German regarding his world of deities,
associating with them comic processions of mummers, the
figures of goblins and giants, gray winter and green spring,
the bear of Donar, and probably the magic white horse of
Woden, which in the oldest form of dramatic play opposed
each other either in mimic combat, or for their rights.   The
wandering jugglers, with great facility, added these German
masks to the grotesque Roman figures which they had
brought into the country ; and in the churchyard of the new
Christian congregation, the bear of the bacchanalian Asen
bellowed beside the followers of the Román god of wine, and
the satyr with his goats' feet and horns.

Thus this race of wanderers soon Germanized themselves,
and during the whole of the middle ages roved about amongst
the people—in the eye of the law homeless and lawless.
The Church continued to rouse suspicion against these strollers
by repeated decrees ; the clergy would on no account see or

listen to such rabble, nay, they were denied the right of taking a part in the Christian sacraments. The old law books allowed hired pugilists to kill each other without penance, like stray dogs; or what was almost worse, they granted to the injured vagrant only the mockery of a sham penance. If a stroller was struck by a sword or knife, he could only return the thrust or blow upon the shadow of his injurers on the wall.

This ignominious treatment contrasted strongly with the favour which these strollers generally enjoyed. Singly, or in bands, they went through the country, and streamed together by hundreds at the great court and Church fêtes. Then, it was the general custom to distribute among them food, drink, clothes, and money. It was thought advisable to treat them well, as they were well known to be tale-bearers, and would publish in satirical songs throughout the whole country the scandalous conduct of the niggardly man, with a vindictiveness which was sharpened by the feeling that such revenge was the best means of making themselves feared. It was rarely that a prince like Henry II., or a pious bishop, ventured to send away these bands from their fêtes without a reward. Almost everywhere, till quite into the fifteenth century, they were to be found wherever a large assemblage of men sought for amusement. They sang ballads, satirical songs and love songs, and related heroic tales and legends from foreign lands, on the stove-bench of the peasant, in the ante-room of the burgher, or the hall of the castle. From the latter its lord is absent perhaps on a crusade, and his wife and servants listen anxiously to the fables and lies of the wandering player. To-day he is the narrator of foreign tales of marvel, and to-morrow the clandestine messenger betwixt two lovers; then he again enters for a time the service of knightly minne-singers, whose minne-songs he accompanies with his music, and undertakes to spread them through the country, as a journal does now; or he dresses himself up more strikingly than usual, takes his bauble in his hand, places a fool's cap on his head, and goes as travelling fool to some nobleman, or follower of some distinguished ecclesiastic.

Wherever his fellows collected together in numbers, at courtly residences and tournaments, or in churchyards at great saints' feasts, he quickly pitched his tent and booth by the side of those of traders and pedlers, and began his arts; rope-dancing, jongleur exercises, sham-fights, dramatic representations in masks, shows of curiosities, songs, masked artistic dances, and playing for dances and festive processions. In the churchyard itself, or within the boundaries of some castle, were heard the sounds of noisy pleasure; and the sun-burnt women of the band slipped secretly through side doors into the castle or the priests' house.

Only some of the practices of these vagrants deserve special mention. The influence which these musicians exercised on the progress of epic and lyrical popular poetry, has been already mentioned; it is even now discerned in heroic poetry, for the players often endeavoured to introduce fellows of their own class into the old poetry, and took care that they should play no contemptible rôle. Thus in the Nibelungen, the brilliant form of the hero Volker the fiddler, is the representation of a musician; similar figures, grotesque in appearance, but rougher and coarser, hectored in the later poems and popular legends, as for example the monk Ilsan in the Rosengarten.

But it was not only in the German epos, that the strollers smuggled in, beautiful copies of their own life; despised as they were, they contrived, with all the insolence of their craft, to introduce themselves into the nave and choir of the church, though almost excluded from its holy rites. For even in the first strict ecclesiastical beginnings of the German dramas, they crept into the holy plays of the Easter festivals. Already in the beginning of the middle ages the history of the crucifixion and resurrection had assumed a dramatic colouring; alternate songs between Christ and his disciples, Pilate and the Jews, were sung by the clergy in the church choir; a great crucifix was reverently deposited in an artificial grave in the crypt, and afterwards there was a solemn announcement, on Easter morning, of the resurrection, songs of praise by the whole congregation, and the consecration of psalms. They began early to bring forward more prominently, individual rôles in dramatic songs, to put speeches as well as songs into their mouths, and to distinguish the chief rôles by suitable dress and particular attributes. On other Church festivals the same was done with the legends of the saints, and already in the twelfth century whole pieces were dramatically performed in the German churches, first of all in Latin, by the clergy in the choir. But in the thirteenth century the German language made its way into the dialogue; then the pieces became longer, the number of rôles increased, the laity began to join in it, the dialogues became familiar, sometimes facetious, and contrasted wonderfully with the occasional Latin songs and responses, which were maintained in the midst of them, and which also gradually became German. The personages in the Biblical plays still appear under the same comic figures, with the coarse jokes and street wit which the roving people had introduced into the churchyards. Generally the fool entered as servant of a quack. From the oldest times these strollers had carried about with them through the country, secret remedies, especially such as were suspicious to the Church, primitive Roman superstitions, ancient German forms of exorcism, and others also which were more noxious and dangerous. At the great Church festivals and markets, there were always doctors' booths, in which miraculous remedies and cures were offered

for sale to the believing multitudes. These booths also of
the wandering doctors are older than the Augustine age ; they
are to be seen depicted on the Greek vases, and came to
Germany through Italy, with the grotesque masks of the
doctors themselves and their attendant buffoons, and were the
most profitable trade of the strollers. These doctors and
their servants were introduced as interludes to the spiritual
plays, with long spun out episodes of the holy traffic, in
which ribaldry and drubbing are not wanting.

But the strollers introduced another popular person into
the holy plays, the devil, probably his first appearance in the
church. Long had this spirit of hell spit out fire under the
tents of the churchyard, and wagged his tail, and probably he
had often been beaten and cheated, to the delight of the spectators, by clever players, before he assisted in the thirteenth
century as a much-suffering fellow-actor, in the holy Easter
dramas, to the edification of the pious parishioners.

Such was the active industry carried on by these strollers
through the middle ages. Serving every class and every
tendency of the times, coarse in manners and morals, as
privileged jesters both cherished and ill treated, they were
probably united amongst themselves in firm fellowship, with
secret tokens of recognition ; they were distinguished by their
outward attire, and chiefly by fantastic finery, and by the
absence of long hair and beard, the honourable adornment of
privileged people, which they were forbidden to wear.

In the fifteenth century the severity of the laws against
them were relaxed, for the whole life of all classes had become
more frivolous, daring, and reckless ; an inordinate longing
after enjoyment, an excessive pleasure in burlesque jesting,
in music and dancing, in singing and mimic representations,
was general in the wealthy towns. Thus many of the race of
strollers contrived to make their peace with the burgher
society. They became domestic fools in the courts of princes,

the merry-andrews of the towns, associates of the town pipers, and players to the bands of Landsknechte.

But besides the players and their followers, there appeared along the roads of the armies, and in the hiding-places of the woods, other children of misfortune less harmless and far more awful to the people, first of all the gipsies.

The gipsies, from their language and the scanty historical records that there are of them, appear to be a race of northern border Indians, who lost their home, and their connection with their Indian relatives, at a time when the transformation of the ancient Sanscrit into the modern and popular languages had already begun. In their wanderings towards the west, which had gone on for centuries, they must have lived in continual intercourse with Arabians, Persians, and Greeks, for the language of these people has had a marked influence on their own. They were possibly, about the year 430 but more probably about 940, in Persia. They appeared about the twelfth century as Ishmaelites and braziers,* in

* Brazier here means tinker and scythe-sharpener. The oldest accounts of them are in a free paraphrase of the 1st Book of Moses, in rude verses, which were at all events written before 1122 ; printed in 'Hoffmann's Fundgrubben,' 2. There they are represented as foreign Jew traders. These remarkable verses are as follows :—

> "From Ishmael come the Ishmaelitish people ;
> They go peddling throughout the wide world ;
> We call them braziers.
> Oh ! what a life and habits are theirs !
> On all they have for sale
> There is a blot, and it is unsound.
> If he, the brazier, buys anything,
> Good or bad, one must give him somewhat over ;
> And if he sells his wares
> He never replaces the damaged ones.
> They have neither house nor home—
> Every place is alike to them ;
> They rove through the country,
> And cheat the people with their tricks :
> Thus they deceive mankind.
> They rob, but not openly."

Upper Germany. They were settled in the fourteenth century in Cypress, and in the year 1370, as bondsmen in Wallachia. The name of Zingaro or Zitano, is a corruption from their language; they still call themselves Scindians, dwellers on the banks of the Indus; their own statement also, that they came from Little Egypt, may be correct, as Little Egypt appears then to have denoted, not the valley of the Nile, but the frontier lands of Asia.

In the year 1417, they came in great hordes, with laughable pretensions and grotesque processions, from Hungary, into Germany, and shortly afterwards into Switzerland, France, and Italy. A band of three hundred grown-up persons, without counting the children, proceeded as far as the Baltic, under the command of a duke and count, on horseback and on foot; the women and children sitting with the baggage on the carts. They were dressed like comedians, and had sporting dogs with them as a sign of noble birth; but when they really hunted, they did so without dogs, and without noise. They showed recommendations and safe-conducts from princes and nobles, and also from the Emperor Sigismund. They asserted that their bishops had commanded them to wander for seven years through the world. But they were great swindlers, and passed their nights in the open air, for better opportunities of stealing. In 1418, they appeared in many parts of Germany, and the same year went under the command of Duke Michael, from Little Egypt into Switzerland. A rendezvous of many hordes seems to have taken place before Zurich. They numbered according to the lowest computation a thousand heads. They had two dukes and two knights, and pretended to have been driven from Egypt by the Turks; they carried much money in their pockets, and maintained that they had received it from their own people at home; they ate and drank well, and also paid well, but they have never shown themselves again like this.

disappeared.   They themselves were thoroughly decimated by their wandering lives, and the persecutions of the local inhabitants.

Their language gives the best explanation of their past. The original homogeneousness of the gipsy language is distinctly visible amidst the various changes which it has gone through in many countries.   It appears to be the mode of speech of a single and special Indian race.   The gipsy is apparently not the descendant of a mixed Indian people, or of a single low caste of Indians, but of a distinct race of people. The men call themselves everywhere, *rom ;* and in contradiction to the western nations, also *calo,* black : their wives, *romni,* and their language *romany-tschib.*   The names which their race have had in different countries are numerous and various.

Their language is in its origin and internal structure a genuine daughter of the distinguished Sanscrit, but it has become for many centuries like a beggar and thief ; it has lost much of its beauty, its elegance, and its resemblance to its mother and sisters ; instead of which it has appropriated something to itself from every country in which these people have tarried in their wanderings, and its dress appears covered with the tatters of all nations, so that it is only here and there that the genuine gold threads are still visible.   The race have lost a great portion of their own words, more especially those, that express ideas which they could not preserve in their paltry miserable life in foreign countries. They have lost the Indian expression for parrot, elephant, and lion, also for the tiger and buffalo snake, but sugar —*gúlo,* silk—*pahr,* and grapes—*drakh,* they call by their Indian, and wine—*mohl,* by its Persian name.   Nay, they have also lost the Indian words for many current terms : they no longer call the sparrow by its Indian name ; no fish, and hardly any plants ; but undoubtedly they retain those of many

large and small animals, amongst others *dschu*, the louse.
But in all countries, new representations, images, and ideas
offered themselves, and too lazy and careless to form words of
their own, they took those of every foreign language and
adapted them to the necessities of their own tongue.   The
result was, that even the gipsies who were in bands, being
without firm union, were split in pieces among the various
people, so that what they still possessed did not remain
common to all, and there arose in every country a peculiar
gipsy idiom, in which old recollections were mixed up with
the language of the country, in an original way.   Finally the
rom appropriated to himself almost everywhere, besides the
common language of the country that of the rogues, the
thieves' dialect, to which he imparted, in friendly exchange,
words from his own language.   In Germany he understood
gibberish, or *Jenisch ;* in Bohemia, *Hantyrka ;* in French,
Argôt ; in England, Slang ; and in Spain, *Germania.*

It is instructive to observe how their hereditary language
became corrupted ; for the decadence of one language,
through the overpowering influence of another, proceeds
according to fixed laws.   First, foreign words penetrate in a
mass, because foreign cultivation has an imposing effect ; next
the formation of sentences is taken from the foreign language,
because the mind of the people accustoms itself to think after
the method of the foreigners ; and thirdly, they forget their
own inflections ; then the language becomes a heap of ruins,
a weather-beaten organism, like a corroded mass of rock
which crumbles away into sand or gravel.   The gipsy language has gone through the first and second stages of decadence, and the third also in Spain.

The life of this race in Germany was far from comfortable.
As their hands were against the property of every one, so
did the popular hatred work against their lives.   Charles V.
commanded them to be banished, and the new police ordinances

of the Princes allowed them no indulgence. Yet they were able to gain money from the country people by soothsaying and secret arts, by doctoring man and beast, or as horse-dealers and pedlers. Often, united with bands of robbers, they carried on a new service during the long war, as camp followers. Wallenstein made use of them as spies, as did the Swedes also later. The women made themselves agreeable to the officers and common soldiers. The cunning men of the band sold amulets and shod horses.

After the war they went about through the country audaciously, the terror of the countryman. In 1663 a band of more than two hundred of them invaded Thuringia, where they distributed themselves, and were considered as very malevolent, because it was reported of them that they reconnoitred the country probably for an enemy. They had in fact become a great plague throughout the country, and the law thundered against them with characteristic recklessness. Orders were issued everywhere for their banishment; they were considered as spies of the Turks, and as magicians, and were made outlaws; even after the year 1700, in a small Rhenish principality, a gipsy woman and her child were brought in amongst other wild game which had been slain. A band again broke into Thuringia in the eighteenth century, and a law in 1722 declared all the men outlawed. In Prussia, in 1710, an edict was promulgated, commanding the alarm to be sounded, and the community to be summoned together against them, whenever they should make their appearance. On the frontiers, gallows were erected with this inscription: " The punishment for thieves and gipsy rabble, both men and women." As late as the year 1725 all the gipsies in the Prussian states, over eighteen years of age, were to be hanged whether they had a passport or not. Even in 1748 Frederick the Great renewed this strong edict. The conduct of the civilized nineteenth century forms a pleasing contrast to

this.   In 1830 at Friedrichslohra in Thuringia, a philan-
thropic endeavour was made, and warmly promoted by the
government, to reform a band of about one hundred men,
by the maintenance of the adults and education of the
children.   The attempt was continued for seven years, and
completely failed.

The name of Stroller disappeared, and the occupation of
these possessionless rovers became to a certain degree free
from the old defect; but the great society of swindlers maintained a certain organization.   Their language also remained.
The gibberish, of which many specimens remain to us from
the latter end of the middle ages, shows already, before the
demoralization of the people by the Hussite war, a full development of old German rogues' idioms.   It consists for the
greater part of Hebrew words as used by persons who were
not themselves Jews; together with these are mingled some
of the honoured treasures of the German language, beautiful
old words, and again significant inventions of figurative expressions, for the sake of concealing the true sense of the
speech by a deceptive figure: thus, windgap for mantle,
broadfoot for goose.   Few of their words lead us to expect
an elevated disposition; the rough humour of desperadoes
breaks out from many of them.   The practice, like the language of these rogues, developed itself in greater refinement.
The usual form in which the resident inhabitants were plundered was begging.   The works of holiness of the old Church
—an irrational alms-giving—had spread throughout christendom an unwieldy mass of mendicancy.   In the first century
of German christendom it is the subject of complaint of pious
ecclesiastics.   In churchyards and in public places lay the
beggars, exposing horrible wounds, which were often artistically inflicted; they sometimes went naked through the
country with a club, afterwards clothed, and with many
weapons, and begged at every homestead for their children,

or for the honour of their saints, or as slaves escaped from
the Turkish galleys, for a vow, or for only a pound of wax, a
silver cross, or a mass vestment.   They begged also towards
the erection of a church, producing letters and seals ; they
had much at heart to obtain special napkins for the priest,
linen for the altar cloth, and broken plate for the chalice ; they
rolled about as epileptics, holding soap lather in their mouths.
In like manner did the women wander about, some pretending
to give birth to monsters (as for example a toad) which lived
in solitude as miraculous creatures, and daily required a
pound of meat.   When a great festival was held they flocked
together in troops.   They formed a dangerous company, and
even iron severity could scarcely keep them under restraint.
Basle appears to have been one of their secret meeting-places ;
they had there their own special place of justice, and the
famed " *Liber Vagatorum* " also, seems to have originated
in that neighbourhood.   This book, written by an unknown
hand about 1500, contains, in rogues' language, a careful
enumeration of the rogue classes and their tricks, and at the
end a vocabulary of jargon.   It was often printed ; and Pam-
philus Gengenbach of Basle rendered it into rhyme.   It
pleased Luther so well that he also reprinted the clever little
book, after one of the oldest impressions.

To the order of beggars belong also the travelling scholars,
who, as treasure diggers and exorcists, made successful attacks
on the savings of the peasants and on the provisions in their
chimneys.   " They desired to become priests," then they
came from Rome with shaven crowns and collected for a
surplice ; or they were necromancers, then they wore a yellow
train to their coats and came from the Frau Venusberg ;
when they entered a house they exclaimed, " Here comes a
travelling scholar, a master of seven liberal sciences, an ex-
orciser of the devil, and from hail storms, fire, and monsters ;"
and thereupon they made " experiments."   Together with them

came disbanded Landsknechte, often associated with the dark race of outlaws, who worked with armed hand against the life and property of the resident inhabitants.

Throughout the whole of the middle ages it was impossible to eradicate the robbers. After the time of Luther they became incendiaries, more particularly from 1540 to 1542. A foreign rabble appeared suddenly in middle Germany, especially in the domains of the Protestant chiefs, the Elector of Saxony and Landgrave of Hesse. They burned Cassel, Nordheim, Göttingen, Goslor, Brunswick, and Magdeburg. Eimbech was burned to the ground with three hundred and fifty men, and a portion of Nordhausen; villages and barns were everywhere set on fire; bold incendiary letters stirred up the people, and at last also the princes. The report became general that the Roman Catholic party had hired more than three hundred incendiaries, and the Pope, Paul III., had counselled Duke Henry the younger, of Brunswick, to send the rabble to Saxony and Hesse. Undoubtedly much wickedness was laid to the credit of the unscrupulous Duke; but it was then the interest of Pope Paul III. to treat the Protestants with forbearance, for earnest endeavours were being made on both sides for a great reconciliation, and preparation was made for it at Rome, by sending the Cardinal Contarini to the great religious conference at Ratisbon. The terror, however, and anger of the Germans was great and enduring. Everywhere the incendiaries were tracked, everywhere their traces were found, crowds of rabble were imprisoned, tried for their lives, and executed. Luther publicly denounced Duke Henry as guilty of these reckless outrages; the Elector and Landgrave accused him of incendiarism at the Diet before the Emperor; and in vain did he, in his most vehement manner, defend himself and his adherents. It is true that his guilt was pronounced by the Emperor as unproved; but then he was desirous, above all, of internal peace and help against the

Turks.   In the public opinion, however, the stain on the prince's reputation remained.   It is impossible to discover how far the strollers of that time were the guilty parties. The depositions of those arrested are inaccurately given, and it cannot be decided how much of it was dictated by torture. One thing is quite clear, they did not form into any fixed bands, and their secret intercourse was carried on through the medium of signs, which were scratched or cut on striking places, such as inns, walls, doors, &c.   These signs were partly primitive German personal tokens, which, as house-marks, may still be found on the gables of old buildings, but partly also in rogues' marks.   Above all, there was the cha-racteristic sign of the Strollers, the arrow, once the signal announcing enmity ;   the direction of his arrow shows the way which the marker has taken ;   small perpendicular strokes on it, often with ciphers above, give probably the number of persons.   These signs are to be found sometimes still on the trees and walls of the high-roads, and it betokens now, as it did then, to the members of the band, that the initiated has passed that way with his followers.

In addition to the indigenous rovers came also foreign ones ; as in the middle ages, a stream of Italian adventurers again flowed through Germany.   Together with the German player rose the cry of the Italian orvietan (Venice treacle) vendor, and side by side with the Bohemian bear were the camels of Pisa.   The marvellous Venetian remedies and the harlequin jacket, mask, and felt cap of the Italian fool wan-dered over the Alps, and were added as new fooleries to our old stock.

The Italian, Garzoni, has given a lively picture of the pro-ceedings of these strollers in his book, ' Piazza Universale,' a description of all the arts and handicrafts of his time.   His work was translated in 1641, into German by Matthäus Merian, under the title of ' General Theatre of all Arts, Professions, and Handicrafts.' The description of the Italian portrays also in its chief features the condition of Western Germany after the war. The following extract is given according to Merian's German translation :—

"The wandering comedians in their demeanour are uncivil asses and ruffians, who consider that they have performed beautifully when they have moved the mob to laughter by their coarse sayings. Their *inventiones* are such, that if the toads acted thus we might forgive them, and they all tally together without rhyme or reason; they do not care whether they are sufficiently polished and skilful so long as they can only obtain money. Though they could easily curtail or cloak whatever is coarse, they imagine that they give no satisfaction in their business if it is not set forth in the coarsest manner; on this account comedy and the whole comic art has fallen into the greatest contempt with respectable people, and even the high comedians are banished from certain places, are treated with contumely in public laws and statutes, insulted and derided by the whole community. When these good people come into a town they must not remain together, but must divide themselves among divers inns; the Lady comes from Rome, the Magnificus from Venice,* Ruffiana from Padua, the Zany from Bergamo, the Gratianus from Bologna, and they must lurk about for certain days, till they have begged and obtained permission if they wish to maintain themselves and carry on their profession; they can with difficulty obtain lodgings where they are known, every one being disgusted with their filth, as they leave for a length of time a bad smell behind them.

"But when they come into a town and are permitted to perform their tricks, they cause it to be made known by handbills, the beating of drums, and other war sounds, that this or

---

* Here, and further on, he gives the fixed characters of the old Italian comedy.

VOL. II.   Q

that great comedian has arrived; then the woman goes after the drum dressed in man's clothes, girt about with a sword, and thus the people are invited in every place: 'Whoever would see a beautiful comedian, let him come to this or that place.' Thither come running all the curious people, and are admitted for three or four kreutzers into a yard, where they find a platform erected, and regular scenes. First there begins splendid music, just as if a troop of asses were all braying together; then comes a Prologus, making his appearance like a vagabond; afterwards come beautiful and ill-adorned persons, who make such a cackling that every one begins to find the time long, and if perchance any one laughs, it is more at the simplicity of the spectators than because he finds somewhat laughable. Then comes Magnificus, who is not worth three hellers; Zany, who truly does his best, but waddles like a goose walking through deep mud; a shameless Ruffiana, and also a lover, whom it would be disgusting to listen to long; a Spaniard who knows not how to say more than *mi vida*, or *mi corazon;* a pedant who jumbles all sorts of languages together; and Buratinus, who knows no other gesture than that of twirling his hat or his hood from one hand to the other. The best of them has so little capacity as to be unfit either to boil or roast, so that the bystanders all become weary, and laugh at themselves for having so long given heed to such insane tricks. And assuredly they must be idle folk or superlative fools to allow themselves to be caught there a second time; the incapacity of the players in the first comedy they perform, is so well known and cried down, that others of respectability are mistrusted on their account.

"There are now-a-days many genuine dramatic performances in vogue at almost all the market-places and fairs, namely the plays of Ceretani, of orvietan vendors, and other similar fellows. They are called Ceretani in Italy because it is presumed they have their origin and first commencement in a small spot called Cereto, near Spoleto in Umbria, and afterwards gradually attained such credit and consideration, that when they were to be heard there was as great a concourse of people assembled as were ever collected by the cleverest doctor of the liberal arts, nay even by the best preacher who ever entered a pulpit. For the common people run together in crowds, gaping with open mouth, listen to them the whole day, forget all their cares, and God knows how difficult it is,—even the peasants find it so,—to keep one's purse in such a throng.

" When one sees these cheats take a whole lump of arsenic, sublimate, or other poison, indiscriminately, that they may make proof by it of the excellence of their orvietan, it should be known that, in the summer-time before they came to the place, they have filled themselves with lettuce dressed with so much vinegar and oil that they might swim therein, and in winter they stuff themselves upon fat ox-brawn well boiled. And this they do that they may by means of the fat of the brawn and oiliness of the salad, with the coldness of their nature, obstruct the internal passage of the body, and thus weaken the sharpness or heat of the poison. They have besides this also a secure way of managing, namely, before they enter the place they go to the nearest apothecary, who generally in the towns is in or near the market ; there they ask for a box of arsenic, from which they select some small bits, and wrap them in paper, begging the apothecary to deliver the same to them when they send for it. Now when they have sufficiently extolled their wares, so that nothing more remains but to make proof of them, they send out one of the bystanders, in order that there may appear to be no fear of deceit, to the apothecary, that he may obtain some arsenic for the money which they give him. This said person runs forthwith, that there may be no hindrance in such useful work, and as he goes, considers that though he has been deceived a thousand times, he cannot be so this time, he will se well to that. Mean-

time he comes to the apothecary, demands the arsenic for his
money, receives it, and runs with joy to the orvietan vendor's
table to see the marvel ; this one holds meanwhile in his
hand little boxes, amongst them one wherein he puts the
aforesaid arsenic, he speaks and addresses the people for a
time before he takes it, for in a case of so much danger there
must be no haste ; meantime he changes the aforesaid little
box for another, wherein are small pieces of paste made of
sugar, meat, and saffron that they may appear like the former.
These he then eats with singular gestures as if he were much
afraid, and the peasants stand by open mouthed to see whether he will not soon burst asunder ; but he binds himself up
firmly that this may not happen, although he knows that
there is no occasion for it ; he afterwards takes a piece as large
as a chestnut of his orvietan or stuff, and all the swelling dis-
appears as if there had been no poison in question.   ' This,
dear gentlemen, will be a precious orvietan to you.'   Whereupon the peasants undraw their purse strings, and thank God
that they have such a dear good man, and can obtain in their
village such costly wares for so little money.

"But who would venture to describe all the cunning
practices whereby these strollers contrive to make and collect
money ?   For my own part I fear I should never get to the
end of it.   Yet I cannot refrain from describing some of their
tricks.

"One rushes through the street, having with him a young
girl dressed in boy's clothes, who bounds about, jumping
through a hoop like a monkey.   Then he begins to tell, in
good Florentine, some remarkable jests or pranks, and meanwhile the little maiden sets to work in every kind of way,
throws herself on all-fours, reaches the ring from out of the
hoop, then bends herself backwards, and picks up a coin from
under the right or left foot, with such graceful agility that the
lads have pleasure in looking at her.   But finally he also can

do nothing further than to bring out his wares, and offer the same for sale as well as he can.

"But those who boast themselves of being of the race of St. Paul, make their appearance with much consequence, namely, with a great flying banner, on one side of which stands St. Paul with his sword, but on the other a heap of serpents, which are so painted that one fears to be bitten by them. Then one of the party begins to relate their genealogy, how St. Paul, in the island of Malta, was bitten by a viper without injury, and how the same virtue was accorded to his descendants; then they make divers trials, but always keep the upper hand, having a bond and seal thereupon. Finally they lay hold of the boxes which are standing on the table or bench, take out of one a salamander, two ells long and an arm in thickness, from another a great snake, from another a viper, and relate concerning each how they had caught it when the peasant was reaping his corn, who would have been in great danger therefrom, if they had not come to his relief. Thereupon the peasants become so frightened that they dare not return home till they have had a draught of the costly snake-powder, and bought still more to take home to their wives and children, that they may be preserved from the bite of snakes and other poisonous reptiles; and the game does not end herewith, for they have still more boxes at hand, which they open, and take out of one a rough viper, out of another a dead basilisk, out of another a young crocodile brought from Egypt, an Indian lizard, a tarantula from the Campagna, or somewhat of the like, whereby they frighten the peasants, that they may buy the favour of the Holy Paul, which is imparted to them by small written papers, for a consideration.

Meanwhile, because the people are still assembled together, another comes, spreads his mantle on the ground, places upon it a little dog which can sing *ut, re, mi, fa, so, la, si;* it makes also frolicksome somersaults, somewhat less than a monkey, barks at the command of its master, who is very ill clad, howls when the Turkish Emperor's name is mentioned, and makes a leap into the air when this or that sweetheart is named; and finally, for it is done to obtain hellers, his master hangs a little hat to his paw, and sends him round on his hind feet to the bystanders, for travelling expenses, as he has a great journey in prospect.

"The Parmesan also does not neglect the like opportunity with his goat, which he brings to the *Platz*; he makes there a palisade, within which it walks up and down, one foot behind the other, and sits up on a little platform of hardly a hand's breadth, and licks the salt under its feet. He makes it also go round upon its hind legs, with a long spear over its shoulder, making fools of all beholders, who present it with pence for food.

"Sometimes a bold rope-dancer is to be seen, who walks on the rope, till at last he breaks his leg, or falls headlong; or a daring Turkish juggler who lies on the ground, and allows himself to be struck on the chest by a great hammer, as if he were an anvil; or by a jerk, tears up a big pile which has been driven by force into the ground, whereby he obtains a good sum for his journey to Mecca.

"Sometimes a baptized Jew makes his appearance, who bawls and cries out, till at length he collects a few people, when he begins to preach about his conversion; whereby one comes to this conclusion, that he has become a crafty vagrant instead of a pious Christian.

"In short there is no market-place, either in village or town, where some of these fellows are not to be found, who either perform divers facetious juggling tricks, or sell various drugs.

"These are the tricks of charlatans, strollers, and jugglers, and other idle people, whereby they get on in the world."

Here ends the narrative of Garzoni. Numberless light-footed people also of the same class thronged into the German market towns.   But besides the old traders and jugglers, a new class of strollers had come into Germany, harmless people of far higher interest for these days, the wandering comedians.   The first players that made a profession of their performances came to Germany from England or the Netherlands, towards the end of the sixteenth century.   They were still accompanied with rope dancers, jumpers, fencers, and horsebreakers; they still continued to furnish the courts of princes and the market-places of great cities with clowns and the favourite figure of jack-puddings, and soon after, the French "Jean Posset," on bad boarded platforms still continued to excite the uproarious laughter of the easily amused multitude.   Shortly after, the popular masques of the Italian theatre became familiar in the south of Germany and on the Rhine.   At the same time that the regular circulation of newspapers commenced, the people received the rough beginnings of art; the representation of human character and the secret emotions of restless souls by the play of countenance, gestures, and the deceptive illusion of action.

It is remarkable also, that almost precisely at the same period, the first entertaining novels were written for the people.   And these spontaneously invented pictures of real life had reference to the strolling people; for the adventures of vagrants, disbanded soldiers, and in short all those who had travelled in foreign countries, and had seen there an abundance of marvels, and undergone the most terrible dangers with almost invulnerable bodies, were the heroes of these imperfect creations of art.   Shortly after the war, Christoph von Grimmelshausen wrote 'Simplicissimus,' 'Springinsfeld,' 'Landstörzerin Courage,' and the 'Wonderful Vogelnest,' the heroes of which are gathered from strollers; these were followed by a flood of novels describing the lives of rogues and of adventurers.

Faust have been gathered and formed into the old popular tale. After Luther's death, it is evident that they penetrated into the courts of the German princes. It was an adventurer of this kind, "Jerome Scotus," who, in 1593, at Coburg, estranged the unhappy Duchess Anna of Saxe Coburg from her husband, and brought her into his own power by villainous means. Vain were the endeavours of the Duke to obtain the extradition of Scotus from Hamburg, where he lived long in princely luxury. Five-and-thirty years before, the father of the Duke Johann Friedrich, the Middle-sized, was long deluded by an impudent impostor, who gave herself out to be Anne of Cleves (the wife who had been selected for Henry VIII. of England), and promised him a great treasure of gold and jewels if he chose to protect her. Another piece of credulity bore bitter fruits to the same prince, for the influence which Wilhelm of Grumbach, the haggard old wolf from the herd of the wild Albrecht of Brandenburg, gained over the Duke, rested on his foolish prophecies concerning the Electoral dignity and prodigious treasures. A poor weak-minded boy who was maintained by Grumbach, had intercourse with angels who dwelt in the air-hole of a cellar, and declared themselves ready to produce gold, and bring to light a mine for the Duke. It may be perceived from judicial records, that the little angels of the peasant child had a similarity, unfavourable to their credibility, to our little old dwarfs.

There was at Berlin, about the time of Scotus, one Leonhard Turneysser, a charlatan, more citizen-like in his occupation, who worked as gold maker and prepared horoscopes ; he escaped by flight the dismal fate, which almost always overtook his fellows of the same vocation who did not change their locality soon enough. The Emperor Rudolph also became a great adept, and amalgamated in the gold crucible both his political honour and his own Imperial throne. The princes of the seventeenth century at least show the intense interest of dilettanti. During the war the art of making gold became very desirable. At that period, therefore, the adepts thronged to the armies; the more needy the times, the more numerous and brilliant became the stories of alchemy. It was proposed by an enthusiastic worshipper of Gustavus Adolphus, to make gold out of lead; and in the presence of the Emperor Ferdinand III. many pounds of gold were to be made, by one grain of red powder, from quick-silver; a gigantic coin also was to be struck from the same metal. After the peace, the adepts resided at all the courts; there were few dwellings where the hearth and the retorts were not heated for secret operations. But every one had to beware how he trifled with the reigning powers, as the paws of the princely lions might be raised against him for his destruction. Those who could not make gold were confined in prison, and those who were under suspicion, yet could fabricate something, were equally put in close confinement. The Italian Count Cajetan was hanged in a gilded dress, on a gallows at Küstrin the beams of which were adorned with cut gold; the German Rector von Klettenberg was beheaded at Königstein, where fourteen years before, Böttiger was kept in strict cloistral confinement, because he had produced innocent porcelain instead of gold. There is no doubt that it was the case with the adepts and astrologers, as it ever has been with the leaders of a prevailing superstition, that they were themselves convinced of the truth of their art; but they had strong doubts of their own knowledge, and they deceived others as to their success, either because they were seeking the means to attain to greater results, or because they wished to appear, to the world, to understand what they considered of importance. These however were not the worst of the lot.

The most mischievous of all were, perhaps, the skilful impostors, who appeared in Germany, France, and England, with foreign titles of distinction, shining with the glimmer of secret art, sometimes the propagators of the most disgraceful vices, shadowy figures, who by their worldly wisdom and the limited intercourse of nations were enabled to bring themselves into notoriety. Their experience, their deceptions, their secret successes, for a long period overpoweringly excited the fancies of Germans. Even Goethe considered it worth his while to repair to the spot and set on foot serious investigations as to the origin of Cagliostro.

The changes in the moral diseases of that society, of which we are the representatives, can be gradually traced. After the war astrology and horoscopes fell into disuse. The princes sought for red powder, or the unknown tincture, whilst the people dug for money pots. Dilettante occupation with physical science introduced again to the people the ancient divining rod, by which springs, murders, thefts, and always concealed gold, were to be discovered. The superior classes again realized in their own minds the ancient belief in mysterious men, who by unknown proceedings, in unfathomable depths, had obtained the power of giving supernatural duration of life, and had confidential intercourse with the spirit world. Besides the honourable order of Freemasons, with their Humanitarian tendencies, there arose more secret unions, wherein the weak minded of the time were enticed to a refined sensuality and sickly mysticism, and an extensive apparatus of absurd secret teaching.

Since the end of the last century a vigorous dash of the waves of German popular strength has washed away these diseased fantasies. The old race of strollers too have diminished in number and influence. It is only rarely that Bajazzo, with his pointed felt cap, bewitches the village youth ; the meagre neck of the camel no longer stretches itself to the flowering trees of our village gardens, the black dog seldom rolls his fiery eyes at buried chests of silver. Even the impostors have learned to satisfy higher demands.

CHAPTER VIII.

ENGAGEMENT AND MARRIAGE AT COURT.
(1661.)

It has ever been part of the German character to maintain propriety of conduct in intercourse with others, to keep up a good appearance, to do homage to superiors, and to require a respectful demeanour and address from inferiors. The forms of intercourse were accurately defined, and the number of significant turns of speech was not small, which introduced every social arrangement, and like a boundary stone, preserved the pathway of life. But the groundwork of all this old precision was a sound self-respect, which gave to individuals a feeling of certainty as to what was to be conceded or received, and therefore civility was generally real. If there was any discord in his soul, the German did not usually conceal it; and then he became so thoroughly coarse, that he gained evil repute with all the western nations. It is true, princes were accosted with much devotedness, words of submission were used as now; but the prince and the citizen, the nobleman and the artisan, met together as men, and a strong word or a warm feeling often broke through the most courtly forms. This, however, changed after the war. The old feeling of decorum was lost, the egotism of the unbridled was harsh and wounding; the proper, but often narrow-minded pride of citizen and nobleman was broken, and the simple patriarchal relation between prince and subject was lost during thirty years of calamity and distrust. Men had become more prudent, but weaker, and for the most part worse.

But the beginning of a new state of society was visible. With all this ruin Providence had mercifully sent a remedy. By many a roundabout way, through French and Italian fashions, and after long wanderings in every foreign nationality, the German mind was to be renewed. It was a wonderful trial of durability, but it was necessary. Like Prince Tamino in the magic play, the poor German soul passed through French water and Italian fire; and from that period a weak flute-like tone sounds only occasionally in our ears, telling us that the German character has not yet sunk entirely under foreign phantasies.

It has been customary to consider the intellectual sway of Italy and France, from Opiz to Lessing, as a great calamity. It is true, it has given neither beauty nor strength to the German; but we are no longer in the position of the great man who for a century struggled against French taste. It was with him a duty to hate whatever caused a hindrance to the wakening popular vigour. But we should at the same time remember that this same foreign element protected the German from the extreme of barbarism. Our imitation was very clumsy, and there was little worth in the original; but it was to the countless bonds of international intercourse that the Germans then clung, that they might not be utterly lost.

The moral restraints upon the wilfulness of individuals had been broken, and the meagre externals gathered from abroad, of fashion, respect, gallantry, and a taste for foreign refinements were the first remedy. It was a new kind of discipline. Whoever wore a large wig, and later, even powder in the hair, was obliged to hold his head elegantly still, wild movements and violent running were impossible; if men were not prevented by their own delicacy of feeling from boldly approaching too near to women, a hoop and corset were a rampart for them; if the courtesy of the heart was less, the duty of being gallant in conversation was a benefit. In a circle where a coarse soldiers' song had been preferred, a polished song from Damon to Daphne was a great improvement, and even the fade cavalier, who cut his finger-nails in society with a gilded knife, and threw himself down with a French flourish, was by far more estimable in society than an unbridled drunkard, who in his intoxication did the most unseemly things, and could not open his mouth without an oath.

Those who assumed to be the élite in Germany soon fashioned their life after the foreign model. Even during the war many foreign customs had become naturalized; not only in court ceremonials and in the intercourse with ambassadors, but also in the dress and manners of the citizens. However great was the influence of France, that of Italy was not much less. The service of the *cicisbeato*, and the "State" ceremonials, had penetrated from Italy into France; the Roman court long remained the highest model, in all questions of etiquette, to the diplomats of Europe. Both countries took their share in holding sway over Germany. In the south, Italy ruled till the eighteenth century, indeed in Vienna it continued still longer to influence the aspect of the higher society; but in the north, especially in the Protestant courts, the French model prevailed, and this copy, like the other, was a clumsy one. But whilst at the great courts, for example Vienna, the cavalier assumed at least something of the impulsive versatility of the Italian; in the smaller towns social intercourse was slow and prolix, carried on in endless phrases, which appeared the more grotesque in proportion as the men were coarse who endeavoured to set themselves off by the use of them.

Thus was the sunny path, along which men approached

the chosen of their hearts, charmingly strewn with the flowers of foreign manners. Whatever of indigenous was retained, was adorned with laborious gallantry, and became still more tedious. Before we attempt to give a specimen of honourable German love, it will be fitting to disclose to the sympathizing reader something of the style of courtly wooing and marriage. Therefore the following gives the course of wooing of a cavalier, about the year 1650 :—

" When a person of condition at Vienna wishes to marry some one, he begs of her parents to allow him to wait upon her, but he must already have made her acquaintance, and know that she is well inclined towards him. When this has been granted by her parents, the affair is already half agreed upon, and he gives his servant a new livery, and dresses himself in his best. Every day he must write to her early, and inquire what she is doing, what she has dreamt of, when she will drive out, and where she intends to dine. Besides this, he sends her a nosegay, for which sometimes a ducat must be paid. Then she returns him an answer, and he makes his appearance at her door at the right time, helps her into the carriage, and rides next it with head uncovered, on the side where his lady sits. When they arrive, he dismounts, opens the carriage door, and again hands her out. In Austria they generally offer themselves as guests to the houses of others. When he has learnt where his lady is to dine, he offers himself also as guest, and does this half an hour beforehand. When at table, he presents a finger-glass to his love alone, even though there may be more distinguished ladies there ; he offers, it is true, the water to others, but none accept ; his lady alone does not refuse. Then he places her chair, waits upon and converses with her ; when she desires to have something to drink, he hands it to her on a plate, which he holds under the glass whilst she is drinking ; he places fresh plates before her and takes the old away, and he always pledges her health to his left hand neighbour. After dinner he again hands her the finger-glass, for which reason he sits next her; he then removes her chair, fetches her gloves, fan, and veil which she had left, and presents them with a profound reverence. After the repast is over, the hostess takes his lady with her to her room. There also he begs for admittance, which is not refused him, and waits upon her in like manner. From thence they go to vespers, and then in summer to the Prater, or in winter in sledges with torches. This state of things continues for at least three months.

" Now when these three months are over, the betrothal is celebrated, and the marriage invitations are written. Then the bridegroom makes three presents. First a silver casket, wherein are some pairs of silk stockings, some pieces of silk stuffs, some pairs of gloves, handkerchiefs, twelve fans, ribands, and laces. The second present consists of silver ornaments; the third of jewels, bracelets, earrings, and pendants of precious stones, or pearls for the neck. He also presents a dress to his mistress's maid. Some send every day a new present. Then he gives his servant again a new livery, engages more servants for himself, and at least one page and two lackeys for his future wife. Court ladies of high distinction, who drive with six horses, do not bestow presents on their bridegroom, unless it be from overflowing liberality; but others present a night-dress to their beloved, their portrait in a small casket, and on the marriage day linen; six shirts, six collars, six pocket handkerchiefs, six pairs of ruffles, and to every servant a shirt. The bride pays the expenses of the eating and drinking at the marriage, and the bridegroom the cost of the music.

On the wedding-day the bridegroom drives, towards evening, in his own carriage, or that of an intimate friend, dressed entirely in silver brocade, just as the bride is dressed; he wears a wreath of diamonds which are put together from the jewels of friends, and afterwards returned. Behind him drive all the male wedding guests. He waits in the church till the bride comes. Her bridal train is three ells long, borne either by a boy of noble birth, or a young lady. The bridegroom goes to meet her, helps her out of the carriage and leads her in, and thus they are united together in matrimony. The wedding ring is generally of gold and silver mixed, and plaited in the form of a laurel wreath; it has a precious stone in it, in order to signify that their truth and love shall be endless. Then they betake themselves to the marriage house, where the feast is to be celebrated. After the meal the men take forthwith their swords and mantles, and room is made for the dance, and then come the two bridesmen. Each has a burning torch in his hand; they make a bow to the bridegroom and the bride, and ask them to dance. Then they both dance alone. The nearest relations are next asked, and so on all the rest in succession. These dances of honour are performed to the sound of trumpets and kettledrums. The cavaliers then lay aside their swords and mantles, and all dance together. After the dance the relations accompany the bride and bridegroom to their bedroom, there the mother commends the bride to her husband with impressive words. Then all go out."

Thus did the wealthy noble woo and wed at Vienna, which after the war rapidly filled with landed proprietors who thoroughly enjoyed life. New families were in possession of the confiscated properties, the Imperial generals and faithful councillors had abundantly taken care of themselves. A residence in the desolated country was wearisome, and many great proprietors had no old family interest in their property. Besides the Imperial nobles, sons of German princes and many of the old nobility of the Empire thronged to the Imperial city, to seek diversion, acquaintances, and fortune at court or in the army.

But in proportion as the devotion of the noble servant to

VOL. II.   R his mistress was great, the hope of a happy conjugal union was insecure. And the prospect was not more favourable in the families of the great princes of the Empire.

The rulers of Germany attained to a comfortable condition, after the peace, sooner than others. Whatever could be done by the people, seemed to be for their advantage. To the old taste for drinking, hunting, and not always very seemly intercourse with women, was now added the pleasure of having a body guard who were drawn up in uniform before their castles, and rode by their carriages along the roads. After the war every great prince maintained a standing army; the old feudal lords of the country had become Generals. It was in this century that the great princely families of Germany, the Wettiners, the Hohenzollerns, the Brunswickers, and the Wittelsbachers, gained their influential position in European politics. Three of them obtained royal thrones, those of Poland, Prussia, and England, and the head of the Wittelsbachers for many years wore the diadem of the Roman Empire. Each of these houses represents a great European dynasty. But however different their fortunes may have been, they have also met with a retributive fate. At the time of the Reformation, the Imperial throne with supreme dominion over Germany was offered to the house of Wettiner; the family, divided into two lines, did not listen to the high call. At the battle of Linien, in 1547, it lost the leadership. A hundred years later, the possibility of founding a powerful house was offered to the Wittelsbacher, by the union of the Palatinate with the old Bavarian province and Bohemia, which even the Hapsburgers have never attained to. But one son of the house killed the other at the Weissen Berge. Only the Hapsburgers and the Hohenzollerns have understood how to keep together.

The general misfortune of the German Princes was, that they found little in their oppressed subjects to excite awe or regard. For the soul of man is most easily fortified against encroaching passions when his worldly position makes a strong resistance possible for those who surround him. A firm feeling of duty is only formed under the pressure of strong law. Whoever overrides it will find it easier to do great things, but incomparably more difficult to do permanently what is right.

At an earlier period the life at courts was rough, often wild, now it had become frivolous and dissolute. The combination of refined luxury with coarse manners, and of strict etiquette with arbitrary will, makes many of the characters of that time especially hateful.

The sons of Princes were now better educated. Latin was still the language of diplomacy, to that was added Italian and French; and besides all knightly arts—in so far as they still existed—military drills, and above all, *politesse*, the new art which rendered men and women more agreeable and obliging in society. Some knowledge of state affairs was not rare, for there were still quarrels with neighbours to be brought before the supreme court of judicature and the Imperial Aulic Council, and solicitations to his Imperial Majesty, and complaints to the Diet, without end or measure. But the person who exercised most quiet power in the country was the lawyer, who was generally at the head of the administration; and occasionally a power-loving court preacher.

The ladies also of the princely houses had the advantage of some degree of instruction; many of them understood Latin, or at least were acquainted with Virgil (from a bad translation into German Alexandrines), and Boccaccio in the original. Quarrels about rank, ceremonials, dress, the love affairs of their husbands, and perhaps their own, formed the daily interest of their lives, together with trivial intrigues and gossiping: the stronger minded conversed with the clergy on cases of conscience, and sought for consolation in their

hymn book, and occasionally also in their cookery book.
But German literature was little adapted to ennoble the
feelings of women, and such as those times did produce, seldom
reached them in their elevated position; a tasteless court
poem, an Italian strophe, and sometimes a thick historical or
theological quarto sent by a submissive author in hopes
of receiving a present of money. The marriage of a princess
was concluded upon reasons of state, and it frequently happened that she was burdened from the very first day with
a dissolute husband. Undoubtedly not a few of them were
consigned to their royal vaults with most choice and solemn
pomp, on whom the sunshine of a deep heartfelt affection
had never shone during life: the care of their own household, and even that sweetest of all cares, the education of
their children, was taken from them by the new court
arrangements. Undoubtedly in many marriages, a good
heart made up for the deficiency of the education of that
time; but scandalous occurrences were frequent in the
highest families at that period.

The domestic relations of these distinguished families
belong also to history, and much is very generally known of
them. A picture of one of these will here be made use of,
in order to show that our generation have no occasion to lose
heart in contemplating it.

When the Imperial party, after the year 1620, persecuted
the daughter of the King of England, Elizabeth, wife of the
Palatine, with satirical pictures, they painted the proud
princess, as going along the high road with three children
hanging on by her apron, or, as on the bare ground eating
pap from an earthenware platter. The second of these children obtained, through the Westphalian peace, the eighth
Electorate of the German Empire. After many vicissitudes
of fortune, after drinking the bitter cup of banishment, and
seeking in vain to recover his territory, the new Elector,

Karl Ludwig, looked down from the royal castle at Heidelberg on the beautiful country, of which only a portion returned into the possession of his line. His was not a nature which bore in itself the guarantee of peace and happiness : it is true that in his family he was considered jovial and good-humoured, but he was also irritable, hasty, and passionate, covetous and full of pretension, easily influenced, and without energy, inclined to venture rashly on deeds of violence, and yet not firm enough to effect anything great. It appears that he had derived from the blood of the Stuarts, besides a high feeling of his own rank, much of the obstinacy of his ill-fated uncle Charles. In the year 1650, he had married Charlotte, Princess of Hesse, the daughter of that strong-minded woman, who, as Regent of her country, had shown more energy than most men, and whose powerful matronly countenance we still contemplate with pleasure, in the portrait by Engelhard Schäffler. The mother described her own daughter to the Elector as difficult to rule ; the Electress was indeed passionate and without moderation, and must often have disturbed domestic peace by her frowardness and jealousy. A young lady of her court, Marie Susanne Loysa von Degenfeld, daughter of one of the partisans of the Thirty years' war, a person according to all accounts of great loveliness and much gentleness, mixed with firmness, excited a passion in the Elector which made him regardless of all considerations. After many angry quarrels he divorced his wife and at once married his love, on whom the title of " Raugräfin " was bestowed by the Imperial Court. The cast-off Electress turned in vain to the Emperor Leopold, to effect a reconciliation with her husband. This petition is here given according to Lünig, from the rolls of the German Empire, 1714.*

* Some tedious passages are shortened, and it is necessary in one place to soften the angry expressions for the reader of this book.

"We, by the grace of God, Charlotta, Electress, Countess Palatine of the Rhine, born Landgravine of Hesse, offer to the most august Prince and Sovereign of Sovereigns, Leopold, by the grace of God, father of the fatherland, our most dutiful, obedient, and submissive greeting and service.

"Although the manifold and weighty business of the Empire with which your Imperial Majesty is troubled at this time, might well frighten us from disquieting you with our private affairs, yet we presume with profound humility to set before your Imperial Majesty our most pressing distress, and the mighty injuries inflicted upon us at this time without any fault on our part, because it is well known to us that your Imperial Majesty is at all times assiduous in helping most graciously the injured to their rights.

"It is not, I hope, unknown to your Imperial Majesty that we have, for nearly eleven years, been united in matrimony with his Most Serene Highness Prince Karl Ludwig, Count Palatine of the Rhine, Elector of the Holy Empire. At that time his Princely Highness, in frequent discourse, both before and after marriage, promised us by the highest oaths, an ever-enduring faith and conjugal love ; and we on our part did the like. Being then animated by such reciprocal love, we have served his Highness in all conjugal obedience to the best of our power, so far as our womanly weakness permitted. We have also, by the grace of God, reared two young princes and a daughter in all love, so that his Princely Highness ought in justice to have abstained from divorcing himself from us.

"We submissively beg your Imperial Majesty to understand that, after three very severe confinements, we clearly traced by many tokens, no slight alienation in the feelings of our lord and husband, which would justly have given rise to suspicion in our minds, if our confiding spirit had not attributed what was good and laudable to his Princely Highness.

For when we once, according to princely custom, presented
his Princely Highness with a beautiful Neapolitan dapple-
gray colt with all its appurtenances, he said to us : 'My
treasure, we henceforth desire no such presents, which diminish our treasury ;' and the very same day he presented the
horse to one of the lowest of his nobles.   This insult did so
grieve us that, with weeping eyes, we lamented it to our gen-
tlewoman, Maria Susanna von Degenfeld, of whose secret
doings we had not at that time the slightest idea.   She thereupon made answer, ' That if at any time she should meet with
the like behaviour from her future consort, she would refuse
all cohabitation with him.'   By these words she intended
nothing else than to incense us against our lord and master.
Not long after, a ring was purloined from us by the said von
Degenfeld out of our drawers.   This must without doubt
have been a concerted plan, for our lord and husband had
required this ring of us, and when we could not find it, his
Princely Highness was greatly irritated against us, and thus
broke out : ' You make me think strange things of you as
concerns this ring ; I had thought you would have taken
better care of it.'   Whereupon we answered, ' Ah ! my treasure, foster no evil suspicions against me ; it has been purloined by some faithless person.'   But his Princely Highness
continued : ' Who may this faithless person be ?   Perhaps
some young cavalier, on whose finger you may yourself have
placed it.'   This caused us so much pain, that we were led
to speak somewhat severely to his Princely Highness, and
said, ' No honest Prince would thus calumniate me.'   Whereupon he replied, ' Who gave you the right to upbraid me as
a dishonest Prince ?   If I hear aught further of this kind
from you, you shall be rewarded with a box on the ear !'
Thereupon we did not answer a word, but wept bitterly.   But
this von Degenfeld comforted us deceitfully, and spoke thus :
' Make yourself happy, Electoral Highness, and be not so

much afflicted, it will soon be found again.' By these words
she then tranquillized us. But not long afterwards a very
noteworthy Latin epistle was put into our hand by a trusty
servant, which he had found accidentally in the chamber of
our lord and husband, the contents of which I cannot forbear
enclosing. It is to this effect—

" ' To the Most Serene Highness the Elector Palatine Karl
Ludwig, Duke of Bavaria, *dilecto meo.*

" ' I can no longer oppose your Electoral Highness, nor
any longer deceive you as to my inclinations. *Vicisti jamque
tua sum,* I unhappy one,

" ' MARIA SUSANNA, BARONISSA A DEGENFELD.'

" When, by God's Providence, we got this letter, we forthwith perused the same with great consternation ; but as we
are not much versed in the Latin tongue, we despatched the
aforesaid trusty servant to the Most Noble Lord, Johann Jacob
Graf von Eberstein, our dear lord and cousin, who was accidentally stopping at Heidelberg, bidding him come to us, and
beseeching him as a friend and cousin to lend us his aid in
the interpretation of the said note. This he honestly rendered us. It cannot be told what great sorrow took possession of our hearts, when it became evident in how unjustifiable
and unprincely a way we had been dealt with. So distracted,
therefore, were we in mind, that we ventured so far as to
break open the coffer of the afore-mentioned Degenfeld, who
was not then present, and after earnest search found three
abominable letters of his Electoral Highness, likewise written
in Latin, in which he equally assures the Degenfeld of his
love.

" Then we could sufficiently see that our lord and husband
was minded to renounce all truth and love towards us. This
we wished at a fitting opportunity to forestal, and give his
Princely Highness to understand it in a covert way.

"It then came to pass accidentally, that a week after, his Serene Highness Friedrich, Lord Margrave of Baden, our dearly loved brother-in-law and brother, together with his loving lady and wife, our especially beloved cousin and sister, came from Durlach to Heidelberg to visit us. Now once when we were sitting at table, his Princely Highness the Lord Margrave, thus spoke to us: 'Wherefore, my lady sister, wherefore so sorrowful?' To which we answered thus: 'My dear lord and brother, perhaps there is truly reason for our sorrow.' Whereupon our lord and husband turning quite red said, 'There is nothing new in my lady and wife being angry without any cause.' We could not then, for our honour's sake, leave such a speech unanswered, but replied, 'It is those that prefer waiting women to wives who make me angry,' &c. Thereupon our lord and husband was quite taken aback, turned pale with anger, and gave us, in the presence of the said princely personages, such a severe box on the ear, that on account of the vexatious nose-bleeding, brought on by this, we were obliged to leave the table. But his Princely Highness the Lord Margrave was mightily indignant thereat, and said to our lord and master: '*Signore Electore, troppo è questo!*' Whereto our lord and husband answered: '*Mio fratello, Signore Marchese, ma cosi ha voluto.*' But his Princely Highness the Lord Margrave spoke strongly to our lord and husband, and said that if he could have supposed his inconsiderate speech would have occasioned such discord, he would a thousand times rather have been silent; and if our lord and husband did not become reconciled to us before sunset, his Princely Highness was firmly determined to leave Heidelberg at an early hour on the morrow, without bidding him farewell. This worked so with my lord and husband that he promised his Princely Highness to pay us a visit, in company with him and his wife. This took place after the lapse of two hours, when our husband thus addressed us in our chamber: 'Is my treasure still angry with me?' We answered: 'I assure you, my treasure, that what happened at table gave me sufficient reason to be angry; but on account of the presence of my beloved lord and brother, and my lady and sister, to whom our discord is displeasing, I will forgive it with all my heart.' Thereupon our lord and master gave us his hand, and said, with a loving kiss, 'This shall wipe out my past delinquency,' after which they departed from our chamber. That night, however, we did not appear at supper, but sent our bedchamber woman and lord steward to make our excuses, as by reason of the necessary preparation of certain writings we could not appear. But as our husband feared we might disclose to our lord and brother what had before passed betwixt us, he came at ten o'clock in the evening, accompanied by two pages, to my chamber, and did there knock at the door. Now when we came to the door and found his Princely Highness, we were not a little amazed at this unhoped-for visit, and said: 'Why does my treasure visit us so late?' Thereupon his Princely Highness answered kindly, and sent back both the pages. But as at that moment those unseemly letters recurred to our memory, and as the consideration that we were of such high princely parentage, made it impossible to bear silently with such impropriety, we said: 'My lord and husband, I am quite resolved to abide alone till your Princely Highness resolves to deliver up a certain person into my hands, with full powers to punish the same for her past wickedness.' Our lord and husband answered: 'I should be glad at last to know who this person is; but I imagine the offence is not so great as your Princely Highness interprets it.' But we answered further: 'The offence is so great that the person can only atone for it with their blood.' 'Nay, my treasure,' said our husband, 'that verdict is too severe.' But we were minded to reveal fully to his Princely Highness the cause of our long affliction; we therefore took out of our pocket the letter which our servant had brought, and began to read it in an audible voice. Hereupon our lord and husband laughed and said: 'All a mere jest; my treasure knows right well that the Fräulein von Degenfeld has from her youth been assiduous in studying the Latin tongue, therefore I wished to try whether she was sufficiently versed in it, to answer in the aforesaid language a note prepared by me for the purpose. This she executed in the like jesting way; and we are determined to support her on account of her innocence.' We did not choose to wrangle with his Princely Highness, but said: 'We have long known how to distinguish between jest and earnest. If it please my treasure to furnish me with full proof that it was a jest I will gladly be content.' Hereupon our lord and husband answered: 'Why is so much proof required? Your Princely Highness is a woman, and has better means of examining the innocence of Degenfeld than I, in whom it would not be quite seemly. But I see well that innocent lady has lost all grace and favour with you. As, however, it is already very late, I wish my treasure to inform me whether it please her to be reconciled with me here?' We answered to this: 'I feel myself bound by virtue of my once given troth not to gainsay you in this.' But our lord and husband, with a hearty embrace, protested by all that was noble and holy, that, with the exception of this note, he had not trespassed against us, and promised yet once more, never henceforth to misbehave towards us, if we, on the other hand, would again render due obedience to his Princely Highness. All this we promised, hoping henceforth to live in peaceful wedlock, which perhaps might have come to pass if the devil had not sown his tares.

"For, three days after, when his Serene Highness the Lord Margrave of Baden had departed, a patent came to Heidelberg from your Imperial Majesty's illustrious Lord Father,

Ferdinand of ever-blessed memory, whereby our lord and husband was summoned to the Imperial Diet at Ratisbon, whereto we with our lord and husband betook ourselves at the appointed time.

"We deem it unnecessary to relate what great contumely we there suffered from our lord and husband, as your Imperial Majesty beheld it for the most part with your own eyes. This caused us to tarry yet a long time at Ratisbon after the departure of his Princely Highness. But when, after the lapse of a few weeks, we returned again to Heidelberg, we signified in a friendly way through one of the nobles to our lord and husband, that we were minded to greet his Princely Highness. But our lord and husband said with great displeasure to the said nobleman : ' Tell the bold Landgravine,' thus it pleased his Princely Highness to call us, ' I will have nothing to do with any one so pernicious to the country.'

"Now when this was notified to us we did not venture to accost his Princely Highness, but straightway went through the adjoining saloon to our chamber. But scarcely had we entered therein, when forty of the Swiss guard had already established themselves in our antechamber, who were commanded to keep guard over us, and not let us go out till they received further orders from his Princely Highness.

"Then did we learn with great anguish of heart that we, a freeborn princess, had been made a prisoner. We knew not what to do, for we could not write to our lord brother the Landgrave of Hesse Cassel, because we had no confidential person left to us whom we could despatch. We had thus no opportunity of effecting anything, for whenever our servants came to or went from us, they were always searched by the guard. On this account we resolved to write ourselves to our lord and husband, and to entreat his Princely Highness to release us from this most intolerable durance. We drew up therefore the following petition to his Princely Highness, and sent the same by a noble youth to his Princely Highness while at table.

" ' MOST SERENE HIGHNESS, AND DEAR LORD.

" ' How great annoyance I have suffered during the time which it has pleased your Princely Highness to place a prodigious garrison before my chamber, is not to be described. It moves me to remind your Princely Highness, that if you so behave to me, a poor princess, you will have to answer for it before God and the whole world.   It would be well moreover to bethink you, whether it is praiseworthy to keep guard over one single weak woman, with forty well-armed halberdiers, which might be sufficiently accomplished by two or three.   I cannot imagine what offence I have committed to deserve such harsh procedure.   I therefore entreat your Princely Highness, for God's sake to set me at liberty.   For during this time I have not been able to sleep three hours by reason of the noisy blustering and clatter of these indiscreet Swiss.

" ' Your Princely Highness's faithful unto death,

" ' CHARLOTTA PALATINE OF THE RHINE.'

" After our husband had read this writing, he commanded that all the Swiss saving four should be withdrawn, which was done forthwith, to our great content.   But his Princely Highness sent us a letter to the following tenour.

" ' To Charlotta, born Landgravine of Hesse.

" ' It surprises me much that you should venture to ask why I have put you under surveillance.   You cannot deny that on my return from Ratisbon to Heidelberg, I urgently commanded you to follow me without fail the next day.   But you did not do so till some weeks later, and during this period you spent so much money, that our subjects, who were sufficiently ruined without this, will for a long time have much to

endure.   You also know well how you disgraced me at Ratisbon by your hunting parties, and how—because I in my just
indignation, on account of your past frivolity of conduct and
wanton indecorum of dress in the presence of the assembled
Diet, have put you only under slight restraint—you have for
the past half-year refused to live with me as a wife.   This
culpable conduct has entirely released me from all bonds of
wedlock; and I am fully resolved to separate myself completely from you by a public act.   This, my purpose, has
moved me to assure myself of your person, that you may not
as a fugitive, by exasperating your brother and other friends,
bring evil on my country.   Finally, if you will keep quiet and
retired, and will consent to the divorce, I promise you on my
Electoral faith, that I will not only entirely free you from
restraint, but will assign you an income which will enable you
to maintain yourself right royally.   Thus saying, and expecting a decisive declaration from you,

" ' I remain your loving cousin,

" ' The Elector.'

" When this writing was put into our hands, we were in
such great affliction we did not know how to decide.   At last
we sent a noble bedchamber woman to our lord and husband,
commanding her to signify to his Princely Highness that we
were disposed to consent willingly to all his desires, except as
concerning the divorce.   For this, being an affair of conscience,
must be well considered.   I begged him therefore for a little
time for deliberation.   Undoubtedly if his Princely Highness
should please to accomplish a divorce by his own power, we
were much too weak to hinder him.   But we thought we had
never given his Princely Highness any sufficient reason for
repudiating us.

" The bedchamber woman delivered this in the best way
she could.   But our lord and husband thus answered : ' Fair

lady, tell your mistress we are now minded to give her henceforth more freedom, and to withdraw the four Swiss entirely
from her apartment.   It shall also be permitted to her to
walk below in the garden if agreeable to her; and she may
rest assured that I will find means to content her, but she
must not think of writing to her lord brother concerning our
purposes.   She must also agree to the divorce, for I am
minded to marry another.'

"The noble maiden had scarcely given us this answer,
when the four Swiss were with all speed withdrawn from our
apartment, and we went the same evening to breathe the
fresh air in the garden.   The day following our lord and
husband journeyed to the castle at Ladenburg.   In the evening, about five o'clock, the noble Count von Eberstein, our
loving lord and cousin, came to us.   He told us that the von
Degenfeld had been sojourning already three months at the
Castle of Ladenburg, and that our lord and husband had
betaken himself thither every week during our absence; nay
he had caused a special road to be made that he might the
sooner reach it.   Then we first discovered what had been the
aim of our lord and husband, and we lamented our misfortune
with many tears.

"A week after, our lord and husband sent us a note, the
contents of which ran literally thus:—

"'MOST SERENE HIGHNESS,

"'I wish to inform your Highness in a few words, that
in consequence of our afore-mentioned divorce, I have again
engaged myself in marriage with the noble Lady, Marie
Susanna von Degenfeld.   I therefore hope that your High-
ness will be therewith content, as it cannot now be altered.
For I have already sent for our dear and trusty Samuel
Heyland, preacher of the Lutheran community of our city of
Heidelberg, to unite us in Christian wedlock.   But as I know

well that your Highness has begotten me three royal children, it becomes me to furnish your Highness with a princely allowance for the rest of your life.   Therefore we grant unto your Highness the power to make use at your good pleasure of the half of the castle of Heidelberg, and you may receive from our lord treasurer sufficient money for your maintenance ; only you must reconcile yourself to my present wife, and inflict no injury upon her, that I may not have occasion to withdraw my favour from your Highness.

"'I remain your Highness's graciously until death,

"'YOUR HIGHNESS'S ELECTOR.

"'Ladenburg, April 15, 1652.'

"My answer was as follows :—

"'MOST AUGUST PRINCE AND HIGH-BORN LORD,

"'From your Princely Highness's letter I have learnt with the greatest consternation that your Princely Highness is minded now to cast me off entirely, and never more to recognize me as your wife. I will commend my cause, woeful as it is, to God, the righteous judge. I will henceforth consider myself as a widow ; whose husband still lives, led astray by a wanton worthless person, and drawn away from his lawful wife.

"'For the ample maintenance which your Princely Highness has ordered for me, I render you hearty thanks.   I will also be careful so to behave myself to your Princely Highness's concubine that she shall have no cause to complain.   Further, a nobleman from Stuttgart is here, who reports than in ten days his Serene Highness Prince Eberhard von Würtemberg, our dearly beloved lord cousin and brother, together with the lady his wife, are coming to visit us at Heidelberg.   So your Princely Highness will undoubtedly come here, and arrange that they shall have right princely accommodation.

" 'Datum Heidelberg, the 16th of April, 1657.

" Your Princely Highness's until death, but now deeply afflicted, lawful ELECTRESS OF THE RHINE.'

" After three days our lord and husband returned, bringing with him the von Degenfeld, under the escort of a hundred newly enlisted dragoons. Then indeed were we cut to the heart when we saw our former waiting-woman usurping our place and presented to every one as Electress, yet could not venture to say the least word against her. We kept a separate table, and had our own servants, and a body-guard of twenty cuirassiers appointed for our own selves.

" At last we bethought us we would once more endeavour to mollify our lord and husband. We sent for the two Princes our sons, and the Princess our daughter, dressed ourselves and the children in our best, and waited near the hall-door till our lord and husband rose from dinner and came out. Then we, together with our beloved children, prostrated ourselves before his Princely Highness, hoping thereby to mollify him. For if his Princely Highness would not recognize us as his lawful wife, our dearly beloved children after his death might be considered as bastards.

" Our children wept aloud, as did also the whole surrounding court, for it would have melted a heart of stone. Our lord and husband let us thus kneel, and stood in deep thought, not knowing at the moment what to say. His Princely Highness's eyes were filled with tears. Meanwhile the mistress von Degenfeld came from within, saw us thus kneeling, and spoke audaciously to our lord and husband. - ' *Signore Elettore, servate la parola di promessa.*' At these words our lord and husband clasped his hands over his head, and went away sighing. We however could no longer look over such iniquity, but ran into our chamber and seized a loaded pistol, determined to send a ball through the heart of this wanton, godless disturber of conjugal rights, this von Degenfeld. But when we came to her, and were on the point of discharging the pistol, it was taken away from us by the noble Count and Lord Wolf Julius von Hohenlohe, and discharged out of a window. But when our lord and husband heard this shot, he ran hastily out of his apartment, and asked who had fired. We said : ' Ah, dear treasure, I did it, with the intention of revenging your Princely Highness's honour on this monster.' But our lord and husband replied : ' Charlotta, Charlotta, cease these doings, if you would not be sent away forthwith from hence.' But we went off without making reply.

" Four days after a postilion came with a report that his Serene Highness of Wurtemberg would arrive within two hours. Thereupon our lord and husband sent to notify to us that his Princely Highness, with Mistress von Degenfeld, would go to meet the said Lord Duke. But we were to receive his Princely Highness at the castle. And thus it was. Three days were spent in all kinds of pastimes, in honour of the said Lord Duke, but we lived neglected, and were not once asked to dinner, notwithstanding the urgent entreaties of our much-loved lord and brother Duke Eberhard and his wife.

" At last we caused a repast to be prepared in our apartment, and invited thereto both these princely personages, as also our lord and husband, and our eldest son Prince Karolus. All these came except our lord and husband, who indeed at the intercession of the Duke would have been willing to come. But his Princely Highness was prevented by Mistress von Degenfeld, who, as we afterwards learnt, urged his Princely Highness with hard words, saying, she would no longer allow his Princely Highness to live with her, if he went to us.

"Our lord and husband said also to our Prince Karolus: 'Go thither and help your mother to entertain the guests, and tell her from me, that at this present I am prevented from visiting her by ill health, but by God's providence might be enabled to do so another time.'

"We discoursed during the repast with both the Princely personages on the best way of dealing with our affairs, but their Princely Highnesses advised us not to undertake anything against the life of this von Degenfeld, since we might thereby make our evil fate worse. Our lord brother, Duke Eberhard, took our hand, and promised that his Princely Highness would exert himself to the utmost to unite us again, but his Princely Highness would especially, immediately on his return home, write urgently to his vassal, Gustavus von Degenfeld, brother of the said Archmistress, to require the return of his sister home. If he did not do this, he would take his feoff from him, and bestow it on another. Meanwhile I was to supplicate your Imperial Majesty, most humbly, to move in this matter, and unite us again by your most gracious mediation.

"We cannot refrain also from adding that our lord and husband has not in any other way injured us by word or deed these three years, and we hope his Princely Highness will favourably receive such Imperial intercession, and again be gracious to us, a much oppressed and afflicted Princess, and not prostrate us entirely under this heavy cross.

"Therefore we most humbly submit ourselves, praying fervently to God Almighty that He may grant your Imperial Majesty continual health, long life, a happy reign, victory over your enemies, and all prosperity.

"Datum Heidelberg, July 26, 1661. Your Imperial Majesty's most humble and obedient servant, CHARLOTTA COUNTESS PALATINE OF THE RHINE, born LANDGRAVINE OF HESSE."

Here the letter closes. We can scarcely feel any warm sympathy with either of the contending parties. The husband appears thoroughly unworthy : we find vulgar threats, violence, and ill-usage, a perfidious attempt to deceive his wife, abject baseness in the evening visit, and intimidation by the clash of arms, and worse than all, was the manner of his divorce and re-marriage. The Church constitution of the Protestants remained an unfinished edifice, the rulers were but too much inclined to give themselves dispensations and licences as superior bishops. And of the Electress also ! What can we say ? How gladly would we sympathize with the deeply wounded wife and mother ; but she appears at best not very lovable ; she also was violent, insolent, strong in pouting, complaining, and weak at the moment when everything depended on her defence of her just rights. To say nothing of the remarkable scene at the Diet, her disobedience in remaining behind, gave the Elector, at all events according to the ideas of that time, a right to think of divorce. Not all that is most repugnant in this miserable history should be laid to the charge of the individuals ; much of what offends us was then usual. The respect for women was small, the familiar intercourse of the camp was a jealously guarded right of royal ladies, the evening visit of the husband, an honour which was not concealed from the court. But however much may be laid to the account of the manners of the times, there still remains so much individual imperfection as to leave a painful impression on the reader.

The Electress outlived both her husband and her rival. Soon after this letter, by the mediation of the Brandenburg court a contract of separation was concluded by the married couple, which assured to the Electress a yearly income of eight thousand thalers, with the right of spending it where she pleased. She resided afterwards at Cassel, and lived to see her rival give birth to fourteen children. Later she took the most benevolent interest in these children; and her own daughter, the celebrated Charlotte Elizabeth Duchess of Orleans, mother of the Regent of France, was bound by ties of the most intimate friendship with one of the young Raugravines. We may thank this female friendship for the beautiful letters of the Princess Charlotte Elizabeth, which are not only important for the history of that period, but also valuable, as showing how a prudent, intellectual and honourable German lady remained uncorrupted in the impure atmosphere of a Parisian court. The mother of the profligate Regent of France was all her life long a true German. She speaks with warm affection of her father, and with filial respect of her mother.

CHAPTER IX.

OF THE HOMES OF GERMAN CITIZENS.
(1675—1681—1683.)

WHILE foreign guests, courtesy and ceremonial were doing
their best to restrain the aftergrowth of a lawless time in the
upper classes, the German citizen was aided by the innate
character of his nation, its need of order and discipline, its
industry and feeling of duty. The marriage tie and family
life, his home and his employment were restored to him as of
old. The wooing still proceeded after the old German
fashion, the matrimonial agent still played his part, and the
betrothal presents of the bride and bridegroom were still
recorded with their accurate worth in money. Nay, the
wooing had become still more formal, even the mode of
expression was prescribed. The lover had to think over his
address to the maiden carefully; where his own inventive
powers were deficient, he was assisted by the indispensable
compliment book, the treasured morsel of the library. The
same style was adopted by the modest young lady; even
where the marriage had been settled for her, it was considered
desirable that she should not at once consent; nay, the
strictest decorum required that she should at first refuse, or
at least ask time for consideration. Then the lover made his
addresses a little more ardent, in rather a higher strain, and
then the interdict was withdrawn, and she was permitted to
say, Yes. But they were not pedants, they felt that long

speeches in these cases were pedantic, and that both parties who were contemplating matrimony, should express themselves in few words ; the lover had to introduce his proposal somewhat thus : " Mademoiselle ! Forgive me kindly, I pray you, for taking a liberty of which I myself am ashamed ; yet my confidence in your kindness emboldens me so much, that I cannot refrain from acquainting you with the resolution I have taken, of changing my present condition," &c. Then the well-conducted young lady had to answer after this fashion : " Monsieur ! I can hardly believe that what it has pleased you to propose to me is spoken in earnest, for I well know how little charm I possess to please so agreeable a person," &c. It had all been previously arranged by the matrimonial agent, they both knew what would be the result, but decorum required of the citizen, as courtesy did of the noble, that he should openly express his wishes by a proceeding which should make his resolution irrevocable. Of the agitation of the man, or the heart-beating of the maiden, we find nothing recorded ; we hope that both were happy, when they had gone through the trying scene, he without faltering, she without an outburst of tears.

In the year 1644, Friedrich Lucä, son of a professor at the Gymnasium, was born in the capital of the Silesian principality of Brieg. He studied as a Calvinist, first in Heidelberg, then in the Netherlands and Frankfort on the Oder, returned after many travels and adventures to his native city, became the court preacher at Brieg, and, after the death of the last Piasten Duke at Liegnitz, and the occupation of the country by the Austrians, was appointed pastor and court preacher at Cassel. He died after an active life, rich in honours, in 1708. As a copious historical writer, he was appreciated, but also severely criticised by his contemporaries. He corresponded with Leibnitz, and some interesting letters to him from that great man are still preserved to us. He

wrote also an autobiography, which has been piously preserved in his family for five generations, and was published by
one of his descendants.   ('The Chronicle of Friedrich Lucä.
A picture of the time, and its manners,' published by Dr.
Friedrich Lucä.   Frankfort a. M. Brönner, 1354.)   We will
here give Friedrich Lucä's account of his wooing.   This
event, so replete with excitement, took place the year he was
preacher at Liegnitz.

"Meanwhile, when my mind was least intent on thoughts
of matrimony, and the other proposals made to me had been
unheeded, a foreign lady, Elizabeth Mercer, whom I had
never seen or heard of all my life long, made known to me
her intention of receiving the holy sacrament from me privately, as she could not wait till it was again publicly given,
it having been so only a short time before.   The said lady
had come hither with the noble General Schlepusch and his
most dear wife, from Bremen, and resided at their noble
country mansion Klein-Polewitz, a mile and a half from
Liegnitz.

"On Sunday, the maiden presented herself at divine
service, and after the performance of the same, came from the
church to my house, and the holy communion being devoutly
concluded, I took occasion to discourse with her concerning
the condition of the Church at Bremen, as also to thank her
for two capons which she had sent me for my kitchen, and
then I dismissed her with the Lord's blessing.   In this my
first interview however with the maiden, I had not only perceived in her a refined and seemly demeanour towards me,
and discovered a beautiful conformity of mind with mine, but
I found in the effervescence of my feelings, and emotions of
my heart, an evident token that the spirit of love had been
somehow remarkably busy with me, for during my whole life
I had never experienced such an ardent affection for any
maiden.

"This my heartfelt but chaste love, I concealed firmly within my breast, and let no living soul know aught concerning it. The thought of this maiden accompanied me every evening to my rest, and rose up with me in the morning. Sometimes I spoke of her to my housekeeper, who was a well-bred and discreet woman, and she, without adverting to the motive of my discourse, extolled the maiden highly to me, and the like did also my sexton. I tormented myself now with secret love thoughts for a length of time, but at last spoke out my mind, thinking to myself: 'Why should thy soul afflict itself fruitlessly concerning a stranger maiden, who will again leave the country, and who will never fall to thy lot?'

"Half a year after, the good maiden Mercer had entirely passed from my remembrance, but the already forgotten maiden sent me an amiable greeting through the page of the Lord Baron Schlepusch, and signified to me that she was minded to communicate again. This message renewed the old wounds of my heart, and therefore I made inquiries of the page at some length concerning the maiden, with respect to one thing and another; but could learn little or nothing from him. I then sent an invitation to dinner on the Sunday through my sexton, to the Mistress Mercer, but this she did not accept, excusing herself by saying that she was accustomed to fast the whole of the day on which she communicated. Thus on Sunday, the maiden, all unconscious of my loving thoughts, came after church to my house. I gave her then, as before, the communion, and discoursed with her to the same effect on all kinds of subjects, to give her thereby some diversion. I would gladly in such discourse have learnt some particulars as to whether she were noble, and would like to remain in Silesia, but I could not ask such things this time. After a while the maiden rose to leave my house; and as she imagined I had a spouse, commended herself to her. I explained to her forthwith that I was a bachelor, having no wife.

During this discourse, my sexton as well as my housekeeper were present, and to them, as to myself, the demeanour of the maiden had always given the greatest contentment, yet they did not fathom my intent.

"Now did my trouble begin again. After maturely reflecting upon the matter, I could think of no means whereby I might learn the lineage and circumstances of the maiden, whom I always looked upon as a noble person, for I did not deem it expedient to open myself to any one. Meanwhile, I met one day, Herr Tobias Primer, the pastor at Nickelstadt, a pious, honourable, and upright man, although of the Lutheran confession. Now as I knew that the wife of General Schlegenack, whose husband had lately died and been buried with great pomp in the church at Liegnitz, went every Sunday, together with the maiden, to attend divine service in the Lutheran church at Nickelstadt, I begged of this Herr Primer, in a way that made it in no wise remarkable on my part, to inquire concerning the lineage and other circumstances of the Mistress Mercer. He undertook this, and promised me the following week a report thereupon. Herr Primer faithfully fulfilled his engagement, and at the end of the week reported to me in optima forma, what he had learnt from the *Frau Generalin*. Mistress Mercer was the daughter of Mr. Balthasar Mercer, formerly parliamentary assessor at Edinburgh, in Scotland, who had many times been sent to England by King Charles I. on weighty commissions, and once on a mission to Hamburg, where he was decorated with a golden medal of honour. Her mother, also called Elizabeth, was of noble lineage, born a Kennedy of Scotland. When in 1644 perilous troubles broke forth in England, her honoured father and also her brother, the court preacher Robert Mercer, as they had been favourites of the decapitated King, fled the kingdom with the whole family, from fear of Cromwell and his party; he went with all belonging to him to Bremen, where he lived on his own means, which were pretty considerable, till his happy end in 1650, leaving his widow, a pious, godly matron, with three sons and three daughters.   The sons had gone forth into the world, one to India, another to the Canary Islands ; of the daughters the eldest was married in London to a nephew of Cromwell, of the noble family of Cleipold, and the youngest to a merchant named Uckermann at Wanfried in Hess, the second was my love.   In the year 1660 her lady mother also died in Bremen, and was laid beside her honoured father in the church of St. Stephen, after which Mistress Eliza-beth had lived for a while with the widow of Herr Doctor Schnellen.   Meanwhile she became acquainted with the *Frau* Schlepusch, who lived at her property Schönbeck, near Bremen, and when soon after, the General Schlepusch and his wife departed for Silesia, they took her with them as a playfellow for their young daughter, to Klein-Polewitz, where she was always held in good esteem.

" This report and intelligence increased the ardour of my love for her, especially as I now knew that she was indeed of distinguished family, but not of noble extraction, and also because Herr Pirner had highly commended the maiden on account of her godly behaviour, piety, prudence, and many domestic qualities ; and the *Frau Generalin* had no hesita-tion in trusting her with the whole conduct of the household, during her many journeys to and fro.   Now my whole heart being filled to overflowing with a stream of chaste love, I poured it out for the first time to this honourable man, and revealed to his discretion what else I would not have dis-closed to any man in the whole world, namely, that if it were possible, and provided it were the will of God, I desired to make Mistress Mercer my wife, and I begged of him to lend me his faithful aid in this important affair, and help to promote my good purpose.

" The good man was willing to esteem it the greatest honour to perform this service for me ; he devoted his heart to the work, and gave expression to my intentions, first to the *Frau Generalin*.   Meanwhile I exchanged letters with him, and soon entertained good hopes.   *In summa*, the affair advanced in a short time in the most satisfactory manner, so that nothing remained but for me to visit her in person.   One Monday morning, having first sought aid of the Lord, I proceeded on horseback to Nickelstadt, called for the Herr Pirner there, and went with him to Klein-Polewitz, which lay about a quarter of a mile from thence.   The son-in-law of the *Frau Generalin*, Herr Heinrich von Poser, the royal receiver-general of taxes in the principality of Jauer and Schweidnitz, received us in the baronial mansion, conducted us with great politeness to the dining-room, where he entertained us with various discourse, like a highly-talented and well-educated cavalier.   Soon afterwards the *Frau Generalin* sent for me to her room, and welcomed me with much civility, receiving my compliments in return most favourably.   My proposals contented her right well, and she gave me good hope that my desires would meet with a happy issue.   In the mean time the table was spread, and the *Frau Generalin* with her maiden daughter, and Herr von Poser with his spouse, made their appearance, followed by good Mistress Mercer, who received me most courteously.   During dinner every variety of lively discourse was carried on, and my love was the true centre to which all were attracted. When dinner was ended, the whole company absented themselves, and left me and my love alone in the dining-room. On this occasion I opened my heart to her, and begged for her sympathy, hoping she might in some degree reciprocate my chaste love, and allow herself to be persuaded, under God's providence, to be united with me in wedlock.   Now as generally in love affairs a maiden's No is as good as Yes, so I considered my love's first uttered No as Yes, and was not thereby alarmed, but pursued my intent. Meanwhile, however, the *Frau Generalin* and the Herr von Poser passed to and fro, and teased us poor lovers with polite jests. At last our love could no longer hide itself under compliments, but burst forth like the moon from behind dark clouds, and we exclaimed, ' Yes, I am thine, and thou art mine !'   And now we called together the *Frau Generalin*, the Herr Poser, and he who was my rightful wooer, who then, as assistants and witnesses, confirmed our verbal Yes, by joining together our hands. As a pledge of my affection, I hereupon presented my love with a small Bible handsomely embossed with silver, and a ring with ten diamonds, which had been made for me at Breslau for fifty-three imperial thalers. But my treasure entered into a contest of love with me, presenting me with a ring with one diamond, which, on account of its size, was estimated at ninety imperial thalers. Now when the affair had in such wise come to an arrangement, we sat down again to table in the evening, and supped together with gladness of heart, till at nightfall I and Herr Pirner were conducted to two comfortable bedchambers. The following morning I expressed to *Frau Generalin* my thankfulness for all the honour she had shown me, took leave of my love and all present, and returned with Herr Pirner to Nickelstadt, and from thence back to Liegnitz. From there I corresponded weekly with my love, visited her every Sunday after the performance of divine service, at Polewitz ; treated her each time with a special present, and finally fixed with her upon St. Elizabeth's day, namely the 19th of November, 1675, for the conclusion of our nuptials.

" After this fashion did our courtship continue almost five weeks ; then as the appointed nuptial day was approaching, and everything necessary had been procured, and the wedding guests invited, and more especially as my former colleague at Brieg, Herr Dares, whom I had requested to unite us, had arrived at Klein-Polewitz, the *Frau Generalin* sent two coaches, the one with six, the other with four horses, to Liegnitz to fetch me and my guests; but as these coaches could not bring all, the Captain General, Herr von Schweinichen lent me one, item the Abbess of Non-nenklosters, item the city councillor, nay one with four horses, together with certain calèches, whereupon, by God's will, I with my guests repaired to Polewitz. After the marriage sermon, in which Herr Dares introduced the names Friedrich and Elizabeth very ingeniously and emblematically, the wedding took place by the light of burning torches, about six o'clock in the evening in the large dining-room, whereunto I was conducted by the Royal Councillors Herr Kurchen and Herr Caspar Braun, and my love by Herr von Poser and Herr von Eicke, brother to the *Frau Gene-ralin.* Before the wedding, Fraulein von Schlepusch had presented me with the wreath, and I had given her in return a beautiful gold ring. As soon as the marriage was com-pleted we sat down to supper, which had been provided by my love at our cost, and were all very blithe and merry. In such fashion did we entertain our guests for the space of three days with the greatest gaiety and contentment; and it all ended in confidential union and harmony. On the fourth day, accompanied by Herr Rath Knichen and his wife, I brought home my love to Liegnitz in the coach of the *Frau Generalin,* drawn by six horses."

Here we conclude the narrative of the happy husband; he had won by his wooing a most excellent housewife. In the midst of flowery expressions the reader will perhaps discern here the deep emotions of an honourable heart.

But the mode of expressing the feelings of the heart was altered. When a century before, Felix Platter related the beginning of his love for his maiden, he expresses his feeling in these simple words : " I began to love her much ;" Lucä, on the other hand, already expresses himself thus : " That the stream of chaste love filled his heart to overflowing." The bride of the Glauburger still decorously addressed her bridegroom in her letters as " Dearly beloved Junker ;" but now in a tender epistle from a wife to her husband, she accosts him as " Most beautiful angel."   In other European nations also, we find the same false refinement ; with them also the finest feelings were overloaded with ornament. Through the foreign and classical poets this style had been brought into Germany, partly a bad kind of renaissance, which had originated in an unskilful imitation of the ancients. But nevertheless it satisfied a real need of the heart ; men wished to raise themselves and those they loved, out of the common realities of life into a purer atmosphere : as angels, they placed them in the golden halo of the Christian heaven ; as goddesses, in the ancient Olympus ; as Chloe, in the sweet perfumed air of the Idylls.   In the same childish effort to make themselves honourable, dignified, and great, they wore peruques, introduced ridiculous titles, believed in the philosopher's stone, and entered into secret societies ; and whoever would write a history of the German mind might well call this a period of ardent aspirations.   These aspirations were not altogether estimable, by turns they became vague, childish, fanatical, stupid, sentimental, and at last dissolute ; but beneath might always be discovered the feeling that there was something wanting in German life.   Was it a higher morality ?   Was it gaiety ?   Perhaps it was the grace of God ?   The beautiful or the frivolous ?   Or perhaps that was wanting to the people, which the princes had long possessed, political life.   With the broken window-panes of the Thirty years' war, and the choice phrases of the young officers who banqueted in the tent of General Hatzfeld, this period of aspiration began ; it reached its highest point in the fine minds which gathered round Goethe, and in the brothers who embraced in the east, and it ended perhaps with the war of freedom, or amidst the alarms of 1848.

The home life of the respectable citizen of the seventeenth century was as strictly regulated as was his wooing, prudent and circumspect, even in the most minute particulars. His energies were occupied in strenuous labour from morning to evening, which afforded him a secret satisfaction. Thoughtful and meditative, the artisan sat over his work, and sought to derive pleasure from the labour of his hands. The workman was still full of anxiety, but the beautiful product of his hands was precious to him. Most of the great inventions of modern times were thought out in the workshops of German citizens, though they may indeed sometimes have been first brought into practical use in foreign countries. Scarcely was the war ended when the workshops were again in full activity, the hammer sounded, the weavers' shuttle flew, the joiner sought to collect beautiful veined woods, in order to inlay wardrobes and writing-tables with ornamental arabesques. Even the poor little scribe began again to enjoy the use of his pen ; he encircled his characters with beautiful flourishes, and looked with heartfelt pride on his far-famed Saxon *ductus*. The scholar also was occupied incessantly with thick quartos ; but the full bloom of German literature had not yet arrived. Everywhere, indeed, interest was aroused in collecting materials and details, and the industry and knowledge of individuals appears prodigious. But they knew not how to work out these details, it was pre-eminently a period of collection. Historical documents, the legal usages of nations, the old works of theologians, the lives of the saints, and stores of words of all languages were compiled in massive works, the inquiring mind lost itself in the insignificant, without comprehending how to give life to individual learning. It wrote upon antique ink-horns and shoes, it reckoned accurately the length and breadth of Noah's ark, and examined conscientiously the length of the spear of the old Landsknecht Goliah. Thus we find that industry did not obtain the full benefit of its labour; yet it assisted much in training the genius of our great astronomer Leibnitz; it also helped to give an ideal purpose to man, a spirit for which he might live.

The war had inflicted much injury on the artisan, and it was first in domestic life that he began to recover from the effects of it. The weaker minds withdrew entirely into their homes, for there was little satisfaction in public life, and their means of defence were diminished. There was now peace, and the old gates of the battered city walls grated on their hinges, but trivial quarrels distracted the council-table, and envious tittle-tattle and malignant calumny embittered every hour of the year to those stronger minds that exerted themselves for the public good. A morbid terror of publicity prevailed. When in the beginning of the eighteenth century the first weekly advertisers sprang up, and the Council of Frankfort-on-Main conceded to the undertakers of it, a weekly list of baptisms, marriages, and deaths, there was a general burst of displeasure; it was considered insupportable that such private concerns should be made public. So completely had the German become a private character.

There were few cities then in Germany on whose social life we can dwell with satisfaction. Hamburg is perhaps the best specimen that can be given. Even there war and its consequences had caused great devastation, but the fresh air that blew from the wide ocean through the streets of the honest citizens of a free town, soon invigorated their energies. Their self-government, and position as a small state in union with foreign powers, preserved their community from extreme narrow-mindedness, and it appears that in the period of laxity and weakness that followed the Thirty years' war, they became by their energetic conduct the principal gainers. Land traffic with the interior of Germany, as also nautical commerce across the North Sea and Atlantic Ocean, recovered their elasticity soon after the termination of the war.   Hamburg envoys and agents negotiated with the States-general, and at the court of Cromwell.   The Hamburgers possessed not only a merchant fleet, but also a small navy.   Their two frigates were, more than once, a terror to the pirates of the Mediterranean and of the German Ocean.   They convoyed, now Greenland and Archangel navigators, now great fleets of from forty to fifty merchantmen, to Oporto, Lisbon, Cadiz, Malta, and Leghorn, in short, wherever there were Hamburg settlements.

This commerce, inferior as it may be to that of the present day, was perhaps, in proportion to that of other German seaports of the seventeenth century, more important than now. The young Hamburgers went then to the seaports of the German and Atlantic Ocean, and of the Mediterranean, as they now do to America, and founded there commercial houses on their own account.   Thus was formed in Hamburg a cosmopolitanism which is still characteristic of that great city. But it was undoubtedly more difficult for that generation to conform themselves to foreign customs, than for the present. It was not devotion to the German empire, but an attachment to the customs of their daily life and family ties, which made the Hamburgers then, as now, rarely consider a foreign country as their fixed home.   When they had passed a course of years abroad, in profitable activity, they hastened home, in order to form a household with a German wife.   The warm patriotism and the prudent pliancy to foreign customs, which are peculiar to the citizens of small republics, were produced by this kind of life, and also the love of enterprise, and the enlarged views, which were seldom to be found then in the courts of Princes in the interior.   Thus the family of a Hamburg patrician of that period shows a number of interesting peculiarities which are well worth dwelling upon.

Such a family was that of the Burgomaster Johann Schulte, whose race still survives on the female side. Johann Schulte (who lived 1621-1697), was of ancient family, he had studied at Rostock, Strasburg, and Basle, had travelled, and married whilst secretary to the city council, and had then acted as envoy from Hamburg to Cromwell. He became burgomaster in 1668, was a worthy gentleman of great moderation of character, experienced in all worldly affairs as well as in the government of his good city, a happy husband and father. Some letters are preserved from him to his son, who in 1680 entered into partnership in a Lisbon house. These letters contain many instructive details. But most interesting, is the pleasing insight we get into the family life at that period; the terms the father was on with his children, the heartiness of the feeling on both sides; in the father the quiet dignity, and wisdom of the much experienced man, with a strong feeling of his distinguished position, and in all the members of the family a firm bond of union, which, in spite of all the inevitable disputes within the circle, formed an impenetrable barrier to all without.

A journey to Lisbon, and a separation of many years from the paternal house, was then a great affair. When the son, after his departure amid the tears and pious blessings and good wishes of parents and sisters, was detained by contrary winds at Cuxhaven, his father lost no time in sending him " a small prayer book; item, a book called ' The Merry Club,' and Gottfried Schulze's Chronicle, also a box of cream of tartar, and a blue stone pitcher with tamarinds, and preserved lemon-peel for sea-sickness." The son during his voyage, called to mind that he owed his brother three marks and six shillings, and anxiously entreated his mother to withdraw that sum for him from the eight thalers he had left in her

keeping.   The father liberally responded, that the eight
thalers should be kept for him undiminished, that his mother
would make no difficulty about three marks.   After the son
was established at Lisbon, regular supplies were sent of
Zerbster and Hamburg beer, butter, and smoked meats, as
also prescriptions for illnesses, and whatever else the care of
the mother could procure for the absent son ; he on the other
hand sent oranges back, and casks of wine.   The father
accurately reported the changes which had occurred in the
family, and among the citizens of the good city of Hamburg,
and zealously laboured to send his son, commissions from his
Hamburg friends.   Soon the son confessed to his parents
from that foreign land, that he loved a maiden at Hamburg ;
naturally one of the acquaintances of the family, and the
father sympathized in this love affair, but always treated it as
a matter of serious negotiation, which was to be cautiously
and tenderly dealt with.   It is clearly the object of the
father to put off the wooing and proposal till his son had been
some years abroad, and with diplomatic tact he meets his
son's wishes just far enough to retain his confidence.

What however is perhaps most characteristic of that period,
is the advice given by the father to the son as to the necessity
of adapting himself to the usages of foreign countries.   The
son is a pious zealous Protestant, whose conscience was much
disquieted at having to live among strict Roman Catholics,
and to join the practices so repugnant to him of Roman
Catholic countries.   What the father writes to him on this
subject, is here given from the first letters, with the slight
alterations necessary to make them intelligible.

" DEAR SON,

        " It is a week to-day since the last meeting of the
Council, under my government, for this year, and I sent in
the afternoon to the post-house to inquire whether the

Spanish letters had arrived, and received for answer, No. The following day, at noon on Saturday, Herr Brindts sent his servant with your letter of the 11/22 of this month.   As far as concerns your letter, we are in the first place all rejoiced that, thanks to God, you are in good health, which is a great mercy ; and then that you are well pleased with your partners, and on this account likewise you should thank the Lord, that you have met in a foreign country with such honourable and well-disposed men.   God grant that you may henceforth pass your time with all contentment, in peace and harmony, and also in a sound and prosperous condition till it pleases God to restore you to your country.   Nevertheless, in reading your letter I have remarked that your place of residence, Lisbon, and its inhabitants, both clerical and lay, are not altogether suited to you, and you do not find yourself quite right in your present position, owing to which I discover in you some traces of impatience.   It cannot be otherwise than that the change from Hamburg to Lisbon, the difference between the inhabitants of one and the other, their customs and behaviour, and many other things, should strike you with amazement, nay, even with consternation and anger ; but you must remember that there and in other places, you have had many predecessors in like case, with whom it has fared the same, and to whom the great change in everything, especially in religious matters, has appeared very surprising.

" According to the Latin adage, *post nubila Phœbus*, that is, bad weather is followed by brighter and more agreeable sunshine, which may the most benign God in his mercy fulfil to you, and grant that, as you met with and endured great dangers and bodily weakness by sea, the time which you may spend in Portugal may sweeten and brighten the former sour and bitter days, and that you may by degrees forget those bad days, and be comforted and rejoice in the good ones, which may the Almighty in his mercy constantly grant and bestow upon you.   Amen.

" Brother-in-law Gerdt Buermeister (who loves you as his child) told me to-day, that many things would indeed appear surprising to you on your first arrival at Lisbon, especially the seeing on all sides the forms of white, black, and gray monks and other persons ; but it would be only three or four months, before you would become accustomed to this and other things.   Now it is certainly true that one gets habituated in time to everything.   I was for four years constantly at Strasburg, and got so accustomed to it that it became alike to me whether I lived at Strasburg or Hamburg, and was never disturbed about anything.

" Believe me and others, you will find equally that a short time and a little patience will alter and improve all.   I trust in God, therefore, that I shall in the course of eight or ten weeks receive from you more satisfactory letters, especially as you gradually make progress in the language.   Brother-in-law Gerdt Buermeister says that he was twelve years old when he arrived at Lisbon, and he could not sufficiently describe his dissatisfaction ;   and whenever he descried the monks he thought they were devils ;   he would also have poured water on them from above, but would have got into difficulties thereby :   he says, that when he was obliged to go out he felt terrified, but he soon overcame his fears.   As regards religion, you must be judicious, and as much as possible avoid all hypocrisy, and never enter into discourse with your partner, nor with any one, on religious topics, but continue yourself at fitting times to read thereon, and also pray to God with devotion morning and evening, and put your firm trust in Him, that as He has so wonderfully called you to that place, He will also be, and ever remain your gracious Father and protector under all apparent crosses.

" You state that you have already once sinned from necessity, when the consecrated host was carried past—or as it is otherwise called the venerabile—and ask whether you have well done to pray for yourself, and whether the good God will hear and forgive you this sin. I cannot forbear relating to you on this occasion what befel me at Maintz : when, in 1641, I journeyed from Hamburg to Strasburg, and was obliged to remain quiet at Frankfort for a fortnight during the fair, I went to Maintz, which is four miles from thence. It so happened I was there a Sunday, on which a special feast was kept by the Roman Catholics ; so I ascertained in which church the Elector was to attend mass, betook myself there, and found in the church many devout people on their knees. Some had their *rosarium* or rosaries in their hands, and said the Ave Maria and Lord's prayer, others smote their breasts with their hands like the penitent publican, and repented of their sins. I thus in some sort inspected the people, and thought their devotion commendable, and wished also that such good devotion in outward demeanour in the church could be found among us Lutherans. Meanwhile the Elector came, and entered into the choir. I, as an inquisitive young man, pressed in together with him, and as I was well dressed, having round me a scarlet mantle, the halberdiers allowed me to pass, supposing me to be a young nobleman. In the mean time the Herr von Andlaw chanted the mass *in pontificalibus*, that is he had a bishop's hat or cap on his head, and a bishop's staff in his hand. I had good thoughts as I looked on all these ceremonies, and all was as yet well. But when the Herr von Andlaw raised the consecrated cup, then all knelt down who were standing by me, I did the same, and said a Paternoster. To this I was led by my curiosity, but you were led unavoidably, and I trust in God that He will forgive me and you this fault. Besides this once, I have been in the Roman Catholic church frequently in France, and especially at Orleans on a Sunday afternoon, and have heard good music, but have never found my limbs tremble as you write that you have experienced. One should not be like a timid hare, but maintain always a constant steadfast heart. You mention that in Lisbon there are many priests, and also many churches and monasteries. Well! let it be so, that is nothing to you ; however many priests there may be there they will not bite you, only take heed to yourself. No one can compel you to go to mass or into the church, and if at Easter you can obtain a ticket from an ecclesiastic, as if you had confessed and communicated, you have no further need to care about the priests. But if you see the priests at a distance coming towards you with the consecrated host, use all caution and turn into a byway, or go into a house.

"You write to me also, that many are already envious of you, and that Frick and Amsing are amongst the number. My son! who is without envious rivals ? The more a person prospers, the more there are who envy them. Therefore the Dutch say : *idt is beter, beniedt als beklaegt, als idt man onsen lieven Heer behaegt.* What think you of the many who envy me, but whereof I know only a few, most of them I know not. On that account one has to pray in the Litany : ' That it may please the Lord to forgive our enemies, perse- cutors, and slanderers, and turn their hearts.' I should have been glad to see that when Frick and Amsing invited you twice you had gone to them. You write that they would have cross-questioned you. But you are not such a child that they could have cross-questioned you, particularly as you could undoubtedly tell them what you chose, and what they ought to know. You write also that Frick did not take off his hat to you; now you are younger than Frick, and thus it behoved you to greet him first. You tell me also that Amsing gave good words with his mouth, while gall was in his heart ; to that I answer, that one must set a thief to catch a thief; give always good words to all, be they ecclesiastics or laymen, and keep to yourself your own thoughts, that is the way of the world.

"It is particularly satisfactory to us to find from your letter that you hope soon to make progress in the Portuguese language, which will cause you great contentment, and although on account of your deficiency in that language, you cannot yet give any special help and assistance in buying and selling, yet you can keep the books, and be assiduous in setting down and registering everything.

"Admonish your young Heinrich to fear God, and to that end to pray and read, and make him read to you in your room on the forenoon of Sunday from the *Molleri postilla*.

"Your mother has spoken to Gunther Andreas, and told him he must take heed, and when a vessel is noted up at the exchange to be laden for Lisbon, send a ton of beer by it. You have in your mother's hands not eight marks, ten shillings, but eight good rix-dollars, which I have before written to you. And if the eight rix-dollars are already gone, a ton of beer will not signify. You have always as much or more in hand. We will also, God willing, send you a present of fresh smoked Elbe salmon, for I have already had two salmon in the smoke three days, one of which we have destined for you. The salmon fishery promises fair, though as yet a pound costs one mark.

"Last Monday we held our Peter's, and yesterday our Matthias's collation, when I had a convenient opportunity to recommend you and your brother-partner to Herr Brümmel-man. The same reported to me that he had received letters from you, and the good honest man opened his mind to me thoroughly, and told me that he would answer you by this post, also that I need not doubt God would bless you and your brother-partner, and you would have no cause to complain. God grant you health, patience, and a constant cheerful spirit, also pleasure in and love for your business and work of superintendence.   A common proverb says : *ora et labora*, and let God be your councillor.   This do, and throw all your cares on the Lord, and it will be well with you.   Wherewith I conclude for this time, as I brought to a close yesterday my seventh year of administration, and by God's grace and favour have concluded it ; and together with the friendly greetings of all your dear belongings, I faithfully commend you to the secure protection of the great God, and remains always

"Your kindly affectionate father,

"Hamburg, Feb. 25, 1681.   "JOHANN SCHULTE, Lt.

"P.S. I have mentioned, in my letter of the 14th of January, if I am not mistaken, that the pleasant fellow Heinrich Mein served up to us and the ship's company a rarity, a dish of fish which had been cooked in Lisbon.   Now you might intend sending me a gift of the like in future, but do not do it, it would cost you trouble and money, and I care not much about it.   Vale.

"P.S. Your lady mother sends you most kindly greeting from herself, and is glad to find, *par curiosité*, that you here and there mention in your letters what kind of weather you have, and what vegetables and fruit you get in succession ; you may also touch lightly upon what meat and fish or vegetables you eat.   And you should look to it that you eat wholesome food, and above all not too much.   Here indeed the Elbe is open, and there is tolerably mild weather ; we have good Elbe and sea fish, only we have deep muddy roads, and a foggy thick atmosphere, whilst with you doubtless all is now green and gay and everything in blossom.

"P.S. As the price of letters to Spain and Portugal runs somewhat higher than to other places, I write, contrary to my usual habit and manner, somewhat small and *compresser*. Write small and light letters, but tolerably long ones, and *menagire* also herein.   Vale."

Thus far the cautious Burgomaster Johann Schulte.   He had the pleasure of seeing his son return safe from the land of monks, and united after many family negotiations to the maiden of his choice.

Labour undoubtedly makes men firm and enduring, and it more especially serves the egotistic interests of men of sound capacity ; but to any one whose vocation it is to be employed for the benefit of others, the service will be consecrated by a feeling of duty.   Every employment which is capable of maintaining life gives man also a position.   The journeyman is the official of his master, the housewife has the office of the keys, and every work develops even in the smallest circle a domain of moral duties.   The German has never been deficient in a feeling of the duties of home and of his trade.   There always have been citizens who were not only ready to die for their city, but who have sometimes passed a life of self-sacrifice for it.   The Reformation elevated the feeling of duty to a higher domain of earthly action and the self-denial and self-sacrifice of the pious shepherd of souls should always be highly esteemed ; but on closer observation, we perceive that the foundation of this more elevated feeling of duty was more especially of a religious nature.   It was the command of God which men sought to obey ; where the Scripture did not command with powerful voice, the feeling for the universal good was not so strongly developed, and the perception of the duties of their own position was uncertain.

It is instructive to notice that it was the armies brought together by the war which first raised the citizen's idea of the duties of his calling.   The soldier's feeling of honour not only developed itself in a noble esprit de corps, but became the source gradually of official honour in the citizen.   First of all it gave him honour in the eyes of others when he fulfilled his duty, but also it afforded himself internal satisfaction and a just pride.   Thus after the fidelity of the middle ages and the

piety of the Reformation there arose a new domain of moral
requirements.   There was more of feeling than of the result
of thought in it, but it was still an advance ; though at first
indeed only among the best.

Two years after the paternal admonitions of Herr Burgomaster Schulte to his son, at a little distance south of Lisbon,
the life of a Hamburger was put an end to by a fearful catastrophe.   The account of it is given in an old narrative.

Berend Jacob Carpfanger was one of the captains at
Hamburg.   He was born in that city in 1623 ; he got his
schooling, as was the custom, in the merchant service ; he
early became a member of the admiralty, and at last as
captain of convoys, commander of one of the vessels of war
which had to defend the merchantmen against pirates.   These
marine officers of the city, besides having to exercise the
highest official control in their fleet, had to perform diplomatic negotiations in the harbours, and sometimes were sent
for the same purpose to foreign courts.   It was necessary for
them to have some practice in business, and to know how to
associate with great lords, so as to maintain the honour and
fame of their city.   Carpfanger was considered in his city an
elegant, smart man, who knew better than most how to conduct himself.   He had an earnest countenance, almost melancholy, a high forehead, large eyes, and a chin and mouth of
great power.   His health appeared rather less strong than
was desirable in a seaman.   He had given proof that he
understood how to conduct a sea-fight, and had often been in
bloody actions.   For the Barbary pirates still continued their
depredations both on sea and land.   Not only in galleys, but
in large frigates did these birds of prey bear down upon the
swarm of commercial vessels.   It was just at that period that
the 'Hund' was the terror of European seas.   Far over the
channel, from Gibraltar onwards, on the great ocean, nay, on
the coasts of the Northern Sea, his swift vessels made their

appearance; dreadful were the harbour tales of their temerity, violence, and bloodthirstiness. In the year 1662, a squadron of eight Hamburg merchantmen had become the booty of these "barbarians."

In 1674, the burgomaster of the admiralty girded the silver sword on Captain Carpfanger, and handed to him the admiral's staff. Then the seaman swore before the senate, that he would manfully defend the fleet intrusted to him, and sacrifice everything, body and soul, rather than abandon his ship.

During the ten years that passed after that, up to his death, he made an annual voyage, starting with his fleet in the Spring and returning home in August. He had many severe struggles with storm and waves, and often complained how unfavourable the elements were to him.

Thus he went to Cadiz and Malaga, to the Northern frozen ocean, and to Lisbon. From an expedition to Greenland, his fleet of fifty vessels brought home a booty of five hundred and fifty whales. Once when returning home he was attacked at the north of the Elbe by five French privateers; in the course of a twelve hours' fight he sent two to the bottom by his shot, and they sank before his eyes with every man and mouse on board, the remainder escaped to the open sea. He was also engaged with the Brandenburg privateers. It happened that the admiral's red flag of Hamburg floated on the gaff of the Besan threateningly against the red eagle of Brandenburg; for in 1679 the great Elector was not favourably disposed towards the Hamburgers, and his little vessels of war had already captured many of theirs. The opponents met, but Carpfanger had strict instructions to keep on the defensive, therefore it came to a good issue. The large ship inspired the Brandenburgers with respect; they sent the long-boat with two officers to salute him, and "in order to inspect the arrangements of the ship." The Ham-

burger regaled them with wine in his cabin, and then they
politely took leave.   Their vessel fired a salute, which Carpfanger answered with equal courtesy, and then both sailed
away.

Again the captain on one of his voyages met with a fleet
of Spanish galleons in fight with Turkish pirates.   The
combat was taking an unfavourable turn for the Spaniards;
some heavy galleons had been cut out and overpowered by
the pirates.   Carpfanger attacked the pirates, and by a broad-
side freed the Spanish vessels.   He was on this account
invited to the court of Charles II., and presented by the king
with a golden chain of honour.

When in August he exchanged the winds and waves for
the narrow streets of the old city, even there little rest was
allowed him.   First there were disputes with the senate about
expenses, a writing of reports, the vindication of particular
arrangements which did not appear clear to the gentlemen of
the council table, or injured some private interest, and all the
vexations of the counting office which are so hateful to the
seaman.   For there is no lack of petty trading spirit in old
Hamburg.   In the winter of 1680, his dear wife died in the
prime of life.

Again and again he convoyed merchantmen to Cadiz and
Malaga: in 1683 he commanded the frigate 'The Arms of
Hamburg.'   The passage had been lengthened by a storm,
and a leaking vessel in the fleet, but it had already been made
known at the Hamburg Exchange that the captain was about
to return from Spain *viâ* the Isle of Wight.   Then there
came instead of him, sorrowful tidings.   These will be here
given; it is an example of the old method by which news was
rapidly spread.

"SORROWFUL TIDINGS FROM CADIZ IN SPAIN.

"From Cadiz 12/22 October.

"GOOD AND DEAR FRIEND,

"I could have wished that this my letter might have awakened joy rather than occasioned sorrow. But when we mortal men are in the highest tide of happiness, and think of nought but gladness, misfortune hovers over our heads.

"Such, alas! contrary to all expectation, has been the case with me and all who together with me came in the convoy-ship 'The Arms of Hamburg.'

"On October 10/20, I and our chief officers, as also the noble captain's son and his cousin, had the honour of taking supper with our noble captain. When it was about eight o'clock and we were on the point of rising from table, our cabin-watch brought the sad tidings that there was fire in the hold of our ship. Thereupon our noble captain and we all sprang up terrified from the table and hastened to the spot, where we found all the cordage in the hold already in full blaze. By the order of the captain, buckets and water-casks were speedily brought; much water was poured on it, and some holes opened because this place was not easily reached; all this in hopes of extinguishing the fire. Our people, especially the soldiers, who were valiantly urged on by their commander, worked assiduously, but all in vain, for no diminution could be perceived in the fire, but only increase. Divers guns were fired as signals of distress, in order to procure help, but fruitlessly, as the other vessels afterwards pretended they did not know what such firing signified.

"Thus the captain was obliged to send our lieutenant in the small cutter to the surrounding vessels, to acquaint them with our unhappy condition, to entreat the aid of their cutters and boats, and procure some pump-hose. They came, it is true, but stopped at a distance; for the fire was very near the place where the powder, which used to lie in the fore-part of the ship, was kept, and it was impossible, on account of the great heat, to bring it away ; so every one feared that the ship, and we all, one with another, should be blown up, if the flames were to reach it.   On this account many of the seamen gave up the work, and retreated into the boats and the large cutter behind the ship, or made away in foreign boats, however much we implored of these not to carry off our people.

" To those in our boat and great cutter, the captain called out from the cabin window, that they should remember the oath they had sworn to him and the magistracy, and not abandon him, but return on board, as at present there was no danger, and by God's help the fire might be extinguished.

" These certainly obeyed the command, and began to work again earnestly, but it all was of no avail for the fire increased more and more.   After working assiduously but fruitlessly for two hours, the lieutenant and shipmaster, as also the other officers, went to the captain, and informed him that, alas ! there was no more help, that it was impossible to save the good ship, and it was now high time to save themselves, if they did not intend to be burned in the ship or blown up with it.   For between the fire and the powder there was now only a plank of a finger-breadth remaining.   But the captain, who still thought to preserve the ship, and prized his honour more than life and everything in the world, answered that he would not leave the ship, but would live and die therein. His son fell on his knees before him, and besought him for God's sake to think better of it, and seek to preserve his life.   To whom he replied : ' Away with you, I know better what is intrusted to me.'

" Thereupon he commanded the quarter-master to place this his son, together with his cousin, in another vessel, which was then done.   He would not allow the least bit of his own property to be removed, that the men might not be disheartened thereby.

" Meanwhile it was suggested by some that it would be best to cut a hole in the ship and let her go to the bottom ; to this however the captain would not consent, but said he had still hopes of saving her.   Others advised to cut the cable and strand the ship.   This was at last agreed to, and the order given to cut the cable.   But just as this was about to be done, when the mizen and foremast were on the point of falling, and the people were still sitting on the fore-yard, the powder in the fore-part of the ship caught fire.   The force of it however being broken by the pouring in of a large body of water it only blew up with a whizz.   The fire burnt through the deck almost to the foremast, and as a stiff east wind blew above, and the vessel lay to the wind, it ran up the mast into the shrouds and sails, and in a moment over the whole ship.

" When the people who were still in the vessel saw this, they sought to fly with pitiful shrieks.   Some ran to the cabin, hoping to find safety there ; others to the gun-room. At the door of this last, the lieutenant, by order of the captain, had placed himself, together with a soldier with a loaded gun, to prevent any one from running through the room into the large cutter, which lay fastened just behind it.   The lieutenant was pressed through the door, and thus obliged to betake himself to the cutter, followed forthwith by a throng of people : many sprang into the boat.   As this however, was already pushed off, because the fire from behind burnt quite over, and as it appeared likely that the fire would reach the powder at the back of the ship, and all who were around and near it would be blown up, the poor men who were still in the ship, and did not wish to be burnt, determined to abandon themselves to the waves, and sprang into the water. It would have melted a heart of stone to have heard the cries and shrieks of these miserable men, driven about in shoals in the water, so that nothing but heads could be seen.   Now whilst

VOL. II.   U the fire was driven by the wind from the forepart to the stern with great power, its violence increasing with its duration, I stood in the cabin with divers persons round the captain; they moaned and wept before him, and at the same time exhorted him, saying there was no time now to remain any longer.

"I went from them to the window, to see whether there was yet a boat at hand, and found that the large cutter was still fastened to the ship. I took my resolution, and commending my life to God, sprang through the cabin window into the boat; which succeeded so well that I was saved therein without suffering any damage. As I turned my back to the captain, he, with the persons remaining by him, among whom were the commander and some soldiers and seamen, went out of the door. I thought they were seeking to save themselves, as indeed they were willing to do; for I perceived that they went to the great blaze with the intention of forcing the captain into a boat. But finding none, as the flames were already over their heads they left the captain and sprang overboard.

"As soon as I was in the large cutter, the lieutenant became visible; I asked him whether the captain was out of the ship, he answered that a Dutch captain had saved him. Now when we thought we were assured thereof, we loosened the cutter in all haste, for there were many people swimming about in the water, seeking to save themselves therein; and the cutter was almost dragged down by them, as many clung to its side. It was also to be feared that we should be blown up when the flames reached the powder.

"When we had gone about a cable's length from the ship, many pieces of it fell asunder by reason of the heat of the fire; and the grenades sprang one after another. The fire, at last, towards one o'clock, reached the powder in the powder room, and with one hollow clap the stern of the vessel blew up ; whereupon the remaining portion, with all that was still therein, went to the bottom, after the good ship had been burning about five hours.

"Meanwhile we came with our cutter to another ship lying in the bay, and put out the people who had been saved, with the exception of the necessary rowers ; with whom the lieutenant, during the remaining portion of the night, sought sorrowfully after the noble captain among all the vessels in the bay.   But in vain, as he was nowhere to be found.

"On the following day, about ten in.the forenoon, notice was given by the English cutter of Captain Thompson's ship, that the body of our captain, alas ! had been driven on to their boat's cable, and had been rescued by them.

"Thereupon, the now deceased good man was forthwith brought from the vessel of the said Captain Thompson, and as was fitting, was clothed in clean linen, for which Captain Thompson was paid with gratitude.

"Of all the men who lost their lives by this great misfortune (of seamen two-and-forty, of soldiers two-and-twenty), the deceased noble captain was the first that was found. Preparations were forthwith made for his funeral, and when everything needful was provided, on Saturday the 13th of this month, he was consigned to the grave according to Christian usages, here behind the Puntales, in the place where it is the custom to bury those of foreign nations.   Our *Domine* first preached a fine funeral discourse ; the body was convoyed by some twenty cutters, wherein were many distinguished captains and merchants ; in each the flags were half mast high, as a sign of mourning ; in like manner all the English, Dutch, and Hamburg ships lying here, testified their condolence by hoisting their flags and Jacks half-mast high, amid the firing of guns, whereof above three hundred were heard.

"Who caused this fearful fire and misfortune, or by what

negligence it originated, is unknown. The boatswain's son, who had been in the hold, and had to watch the lamp which usually burnt there, stated that he had gone from the hold upon deck, in order to speak to another youth, and on his return to the hold, found it in flames. God preserve other ships from a like misfortune, and comfort the widows and orphans of those who have been lost."

Here we conclude the news from Cadiz. According to another account the captain walked alone about his ship up to the last; others. declare that they saw him at an open port-hole, raising his clasped hands to heaven; and according to others, he last of all committed himself to the waves, either to be preserved or to sink as God willed it; and it is no wonder that the weakly old gentleman, after the mental and bodily exertions of the last hours, should have gone to the bottom. A great marvel had been observed by the sailors: three doves had for several hours hovered over the burning ship, to the time of its blowing up.* King Charles II. of Spain caused a monument to be erected on the grave of the Hamburg seaman; which, according to consular records, was only destroyed in the Spanish war, the beginning of this century.

We rejoice that the deceased kept his oath. The honour of his calling demanded his death, and he died. For it is better that once in a while, a brave, honest, and able man, though he were still able to save himself, should go down with his good ship, than that mariners should in the hour of danger want a model of enduring energy. He died as became a sailor, silent and collected; he laconically dismissed his own son; his whole soul was in his employment. May the German citizen never come to such a pass as to consider the deed of this man, strange and unheard of. In the inland

* They did not fail to make an engraving of the mysterious doves, which appeared shortly after with an interpretation.

provinces also, many hundreds of peaceable citizens since his time have died in the performance of their duty to the utmost of their power, and beyond it ; pastors in the midst of contagion, doctors in the lazar house, and helpful citizens in dangers from fire. And we hope that the reader will discern that this is the path of duty, and the general rule with us.

And still our hearts heave with the thought that in the same year in which Strasburg was so ignominiously lost, a fellow-countryman felt even as we should feel, namely, that there is not much cause for astonishment, and no occasion for crying and moaning, when any one dies in the performance of duty. And his memory should be honoured both by those who traverse the sea, and those who never hear its roar. The German had much degenerated after 1648, but he yet deserved a better life ; for he still understood how to die for an idea.

CHAPTER X.

GERMAN LIFE AT THE BATHS IN THE SEVENTEENTH CENTURY.

CIVILIZATION was undoubtedly, in spite of war and devastation, making continual progress, for it was not as in ancient times carried on by one people alone, but by large families of nations; and the blessing of this higher development in Germany first elevated the life of individuals. The century of the Reformation had increased the individual independence of men, and developed what was spontaneous and characteristic in various directions. After the war, the gap between the classes became greater; not only was there a difference in their dress, but in their social manners, their language and mode of life; each class endeavoured to close its ranks against that which was just beneath it. But this, however objectionable, was the first result of political progress. At one time the great classes of princes, nobles, citizens and peasants, lived in established relations to one another. The religious movement had created a social ferment, which was a bond of union between the cities and country aristocracy: now during the war all classes had been shaken together; a large portion of the nobility had been driven into the cities, and the impoverished landed proprietor sought a place in the service of the new state, or in the city community. Undoubtedly there lay within this the beginning of a higher life, but the old pretensions did not on that account immediately disappear; the less was the inward ground for social separation, the more carefully were outward distinctions preserved.

Servility towards persons of distinction became general; it extended from outward marks of courtesy, such as addressing them by their titles, to the actual sentiment. It was considered an honour by the citizen's daughter to receive compliments from a cavalier, and he expressed his bold addresses more smoothly, than her neighbour the poor pedantic *Magister*, or the awkward merchant's son.

The social intercourse also of the citizens amongst each other, was deteriorated by foreign manners. In the past century, the style of expression when at their ease, was not particularly delicate; but at that time it was considered thoroughly harmless, and had therefore not endangered the morality of the women. Now many honourable old words were proscribed, and in their place *double entendres* were prevalent; to be bold and skilful in words, not to speak out what was unseemly, but to signify it cleverly, became the fashion; and the women and maidens soon learnt to give a smart answer. The choice pleasantries, the attacks and repartees that we find in the small compendiums of civilities, which were for the use of the unassuming citizen, are so pitiable that they will not be given here.

But there was no want of hearty cheerfulness: the young people long continued to play the familiar games which are now confined to children; they journeyed to Jerusalem, and played at blindman's-buff, which, under the appearance of accident, gave fine opportunities of venturing on liberties; games of forfeits with witty fines appear not to have been usual yet, but sarcastic verses and riddles were in vogue; if at table there was liver served with the roast or fish, rhymes were made upon it by turns, no trifling affair, for it was necessary to produce something neat, and a dunderhead or a simpleton exposed himself dreadfully. Conversation was considered a serious matter, for which one should be well prepared; anecdotes and remarkable occurrences were with that view read beforehand, and he was highly esteemed who could introduce pertinently some pretty German verse.

After the war, dancing was frequent in family circles in the evening; and waltzing was the favourite dance with the citizens: before the lady was led to the dance she was greeted with a small speech, and if she were married or a bride, the bridegroom was so likewise: then the dancer had to lead her, so that her finger lay lightly on his. In the dance he was not to spring about, nor to oblige her to make unnecessary springs, which might toss her dress up to her girdle, nor was he to tear her dress with his spurs. After the dance there was another short speech and answer. Finally he was to take her home, and in doing so it was necessary to be on his guard that there was no rival lurking for him with a cudgel, as was often the case. When arrived at the dwelling, he had first to make his excuses to the parents for having, by escorting her, allowed his homage to be perceived, and then to the lady, whom he commended to the gracious protection of the Most High, and tenderly signified that he would wish to kiss her pillow.

It is not easy to form any true idea of the old society from the general literature, for the numerous writers of comedies and novels give us mostly caricatures; they find their account in bringing everything down to a low level. It is for this reason, therefore, that the unbiassed records of cotemporaries are so instructive.

In the olden time there were as now, baths to which all those resorted who wished for social amusement; and the bath life shows at least the forms of easy intercourse away from home; therefore a number of small pictures will be given here from the baths of Zurich, the most famous of all the German baths at the conclusion of the middle ages. The doings of the seventeenth and eighteenth centuries will be better explained by comparing with them, the former period of the fifteenth and sixteenth centuries.

Switzerland was by the peace of Westphalia entirely detached from the Empire; but the political separation had not led the German burgher life into foreign channels. The unity of mind remained, more than once have the literary men, the poets and artists of Switzerland, had an important share in the development of the German mind. Even now is this inward unity undiminished, and Germans and Swiss alike have reason to congratulate themselves on it. After the great war, the Swiss had honestly participated in the pleasures and sorrows of the German; they also had suffered by the war, and were in political troubles; a narrow-minded patrician government oppressed the country; there also, energy, public spirit and conscience, had been weakened.

The following narrative paints the state of things at Baden, and equally portrays the Bath life of Germans in the interior of the Empire.

BATH LIFE IN THE YEAR 1417.

The Florentine, Francis Poggio (1380-1459), one of the great Italians who spread the Humanitarian literature throughout their native country, then held the office of Papal secretary; in this capacity he was actively employed at the Council of Constance, and visited Baden from thence. He describes his impressions of travel in an elegant Latin letter to his friend, the learned Nicolo Nicoli; he himself was then an ecclesiastic. In order to understand thoroughly how much the reformation of the Church, which took place a century later, was brought about by the excited moral feeling of the people, we should pay attention to the cool, haughty freedom of tone of the following letter. Poggio was a great scholar and a prudent statesman; he was one of the most refined among the highly

cultivated Italians ; nay, more, he had a fierce, manly spirit,
and was always exhorting his literary friends to seriousness.
But with his classical literature he had also adopted the
spirit of a distinguished Roman of the time of Tiberius, and
it makes a disagreeable impression to find how mildly and
good-humouredly the secretary of the Pope, the priest, the
scholar, the offshoot of the civilization of his time, viewed the
profligacy of both ecclesiastics and laity.   His letter, which
follows here, is abbreviated in some places :—

"Baden itself affords the mind little or no diversion ; but
has in all other respects such extraordinary charm, that I
could often dream that Venus had come from Cypress, for
whatever the world contains of beauty has assembled here,
and so much do they uphold the customs of this goddess, so
fully do you find again her manners and dissoluteness, that
little as they may have read the speech of Heliogabalus, they
appear to be perfectly instructed by Nature herself.

"About a quarter of an hour's drive from the town, on the
other side of the river, there is a beautiful village, established
for the use of the baths ; in the middle of the village is a
large *platz*, surrounded by splendid inns, which contain a
multitude of people.   Each house has its own bath, which
can only be made use of by those who reside there.   The
number of public and private baths amounts altogether to full
thirty.   Two special places, open on all sides, are appointed
for the lowest classes of the people; and the common crowd,
men, women, boys, and unmarried maidens, and the dregs of
all that collect together here, make use of them.   In these
baths there is a partition wall, dividing the two sexes, but
this is only put up for the sake of peace ; and it is amusing
to see how, at the same time, decrepit old beldames and
young maidens descend into it naked, before all eyes, and
expose their charms to the gaze of the men.   More than
once I have laughed at this splendid spectacle ; it has brought

to my mind the games of Flora at Rome, and I have much admired their simplicity who do not in the least see or think anything wrong in it.

"The special baths at the inns are beautifully adorned, and common to both sexes. It is true they are divided by a wainscot, but divers open windows have been introduced therein, through which they can drink with, speak to, see, and touch each other, as frequently happens. Besides this, there are galleries above, where the men meet and chatter together, for every one is free to enter the bath of another, and to tarry there, in order to look about, and joke and enliven his spirits, by seeing beautiful women nude when they go in and come out. No guard watches the avenues here; no door, and, above all, no thought of impropriety hinders them. In many baths both sexes have access to the bath by the same entrance, and it not unfrequently comes to pass, that a man meets a naked woman, and the reverse. Nevertheless, the men bind a cloth round their loins, and the women have a linen dress on, but this is open either in the middle or on the side, so that neither neck, nor breast, nor shoulders are covered. The women eat frequently in the bath itself, of dishes contributed by all, which are placed on a table floating upon the water, whereto the men naturally resort. In the house where I bathed, I also was invited to such a feast; I gave my contribution, but went away, although they did urge me much to stay. And truly not from shyness, which we here consider as stupid and boorish, but because I did not understand the language; for it appeared to me absurd that an Italian, ignorant of German, should pass a whole day amongst lovely, fair ladies, in a bath, dumb and speechless, merely eating and drinking. Two of my friends however, who were present, ate, drank and toyed, spoke to the ladies through an interpreter, fanned them, and in short enjoyed themselves much. My friends were clothed in a linen dress, such as the men wear here when they are invited to a ladies' bath. I saw all from the gallery, their manners and customs, their good eating, and their free and easy intercourse. It is wonderful to see in what innocence they live, and with what frank confidence they regard the men; the liberties which foreigners presume to take with their ladies does not strike their attention; they interpret everything well. In Plato's Republic, according to whose rules everything was to be in common, they would have behaved themselves excellently, as they already, without knowing his teaching, are so inclined to belong to his sect.

"Many visit daily three or four of these baths, and pass there the greatest part of the day, in singing, drinking, nay in waltzing, and they play the lute if they are not seated deep in the water. But there can be nothing more charming than to see budding maidens, or those in full bloom, with pretty kindly faces, in figure and deportment like goddesses, strike the lute, then they throw their flowing dress a little back in the water, and each appears like a Venus. It is the custom of the women to beg for alms jestingly from the men who view them from above; one throws to them, especially to the pretty ones, small coins, which they catch with their hands or with the outspread linen dress, whilst one pushes away the other, and in this game all their charms were frequently unveiled. In like manner one threw them down twined wreaths of divers flowers, with which they adorned their heads while they sat in the bath.

"I bathed only twice a day, but attracted by the rich opportunity of such a spectacle and such fun, I spent the remaining time in visits to other baths, and threw coin and wreaths like the others.

"Then the playing of flutes, the tinkling on the guitar and singing resounded everywhere; there was no time either for reading or thinking; to have been here the only wise one

would have been the greatest folly, especially for one who will
be no self-tormentor, and to whom nothing human is strange.
I was deprived of the highest enjoyment, the main point,
the interchange of speech. So there remained nothing for
me but to feast my eyes on the fair ones, to follow them,
to conduct them to the games, and to escort them back again.
There was also such opportunity for near intercourse, and so
great freedom therein, that one needed not to trouble oneself
about regulating it.

"Besides this varied enjoyment, there was yet another
of not less charm. Behind the courtyards, near the river,
lies a large meadow shaded by many trees. Here every
one comes after dinner and diverts himself with singing,
dancing, and sundry games. The most part played at ball,
but not after our fashion, but the men and women throw to
one another, each to the one he likes best, a ball, wherein
are many bells. All run to catch it; whoever gets it, wins,
and throws it again to his love : all stretch out their hands
again to catch it, and whoever succeeds make pretence as if
they would throw it now to one person now to another.
Many other sports I pass over for brevity's sake. I have
recounted this to you, in order to show how completely they
are the disciples of Epicurus.

" But the most striking thing is the countless multitude of
nobles and plebeians, who collect here from the most distant
parts, not so much for health as for pleasure. All lovers and
spendthrifts, all pleasure seekers, stream together here, for
the satisfaction of their desires. Many women feign bodily
ailments, whilst it is really their heart that is affected ; therefore one sees numberless pretty women, without husbands and
relations, with two maid-servants and a man, or with some old
beldame of the family who is more easily deceived than bribed.
All the women come attired to their utmost with smart dresses,
gold, silver, and precious stones, not as if for the baths, but as

though it were for the grandest wedding.   There are here also
virgins of Vesta, or rather of Flora ; besides, abbots, monks,
lay-brothers, and ecclesiastics, and these live more dissolutely
than the others, some of them also live with the women, adorn
their hair with wreaths, and forget all religion.   All have the
same object, to fly from melancholy and seek cheerfulness,
and to think of nothing but a merry life of enjoyment ; they
do not wish to take the property of others, but to impart their
own freely.   And it is remarkable that among the great
number, almost thousands of men of different manners and
such a drunken set, no discord arises, no tumults, no partisan-
ship, no conspiracies, and no swearing.   The men allow their
wives to be toyed with, and see them pairing off with entire
strangers, but it does not discompose or surprise them ; they
think it is all in an honest and housewifely way.

"How different are these manners from ours !   We put
the worst construction upon everything : we find a pleasure
in slander and calumny ; the slightest suspicion is sufficient
for us, and equivalent to a clear transgression.   I often envy
the composure of the people here, and curse our perversity,
always restlessly seeking, and restlessly desiring.   We compass heaven, earth, and ocean, to procure money, are contented with no gain, satisfied with no profit.   We are continually in fear of future disaster, and are cast down by
unceasing mischances and anxieties, and in order to preserve
ourselves from being unhappy, we never cease to be so.   But
here they live for the day, contented with a little ; every day is
a festival, they desire no great riches, which would be of no
use to them, but they enjoy what they have, and fear not the
future.   If they meet with misfortune they bear it with good
courage.   But enough, it is not my purpose to praise them
and blame ourselves.   I wish this letter to be lively in order
that you, my distant friend, may find in it some portion of the
amusement I have enjoyed at the baths."

Here we have the elegant representation of the Italian statesman. The fifteenth century was truly a time of luxury and refined enjoyment, but what the foreigner relates is not so bad as the way in which he relates it.

The Reformation came. It exercised an influence even on the frivolous people who visited the baths. Life became more earnest and thoughtful, and the superintendence exercised by the authorities and pastors more strict. The number of married persons became greater, for it was one of the favourite tenets of the Protestant opposition, to promote marriage and domestic discipline. Much fewer became the number of those prelates and their ladies, monks and roving women, who were not joined in lawful matrimony. Thus after the time of Luther and Zwinglius, towards the end of the sixteenth century, we have a very different description of the baths of Baden, written by an honest German, the doctor of medicine Pantaleon, a Basle man, rector of the high school and of the philosophical faculty. Here follow some characteristic fragments.

" Bath life, 1580.—The free bath, called also burgher bath, is under the open heaven. It is so long and broad, that above a hundred men can bathe therein at a time. It is bordered round about with stone pavement, and many seats are disposed therein. One corner, a fourth part of the bath, is closed in by a wooden lattice, arranged for the accommodation of the women. But as the women in general come there, some are wont to go to the larger bath. In this every one, stranger or native, may bathe gratis, and divert himself for as long or short a time as he likes. On Saturday, especially, the people from the city and country come in crowds, and husbands and wives desire to have their pastime, and to beautify themselves. But herein one is much surprised, that they in such wise misuse cupping ; for every one will be cupped, and they think for the most part that they have not bathed if they have not had as many lancets stuck in them as the bristles of a hedgehog. And yet it would be far more useful to them to obtain a little additional blood.

"Poor people come oft to the baths of St. Verena, especially in May, some hundreds together. But they must first look about for an inn, that they may have some sort of home and not lie about in the streets, and there are three or four inns near the baths. The poor are daily maintained by the alms of pious people. They place their bowls in a circle on the wall round the bath, and remain sitting in the bath, and no one may point out his bowl. Then money, bread, wine, soup, meat, or other things are put in the bowls, and no one knows to whom they belong. Great hoards are sometimes collected; the warder who has his little house near the bath, distributes the gifts in due order, and exhorts the poor to pray and be thankful. After that, each takes what is in his bowl, and goes out. But as also there are oft mixed up among the honest, many bad rogues and idlers who will not work, but take the bread out of the mouths of others who are in need, it would be useful, were each poor person who is desirous to obtain alms, to bring a certificate from his magistrate that he is in need of it, and that the alms will be well applied. Many bad rogues would then be ashamed. If the poor do aught that is contrary to order and discipline, they are punished by the warder, and placed in the lock-up that stands below, near the house called the Lock and Key. When their month's stay at the bath is ended, they receive a dismissal from the warder; nay he desires them, according to the nature of their illness, to go away, to make room for others. They must attend to him also, under pain of severe punishment.

"The 'Stadthof' is a large cheerful inn, adorned with many beautiful rooms, saloons, and chambers. There are two large kitchens, one of which belongs to the landlord, who provides the guests with all kinds of meals, or with single dishes, according to every one's need. In the other, there is a special cook, for all those who buy their own food, and wish to have it cooked to their own fancy, for this is allowed to every one. In this house there are eight good baths, of which five are in common, the remaining three are let out to certain persons by the week for a fixed sum of money, with the chambers belonging thereto. The first is the gentlemen's bath, in which men, both noble and others, ecclesiastics and laymen, young and old, Catholic or Evangelical, come together without any disputes or quarrels, friendly and peaceably.

" This bath is almost the same height as the court, and whosoever sits therein, can look out through the doors into the court, and behold every one. Whoever wishes to use these baths, pays on entrance two *doppelvierer*,[*] or one *angster*,[†] and three *kreuzers*. Moreover the members of the bath community give breakfast at six o'clock every morning by turns, one much, another little, according as they wish to distinguish themselves. Although much eating and drinking is not good with the baths, yet it oft happens that many who sit three or four hours in the bath, need a little soup, and cannot go on without somewhat to drink. Yet it were well for some rule to be established, that each person should not have more than a quart of wine ; this would give the baths a better repute, and they could not then openly write and put in print, that here is a tippling bath wherein drunken matins are sung. For the members of the bath community can unite to settle these matters according to their pleasure. They pray before and after breakfast, and return thanks to the host in a pleasant song, hoping that he may live long in all honour, till he gives another breakfast. After that they

---

[*] A copper coin in the south of Germany.
[†] A Swiss farthing.

nominate him whose turn it is to be the next host, place a garland on him, and threaten him in a song that they will come to him the morrow with fifes and drums. But on Sundays and great festivals they discontinue their breakfasts and songs.

" At this bath a mayor is chosen by the majority of the bath community, likewise a governor, treasurer, chaplain, apparator, bailiff, and executioner, who after breakfast sit in judgment, in order to put an end to or punish any offences against order and discipline, which may have been committed in this or the other baths of the house. Each member of the bath community must also put his left hand on the mayor's staff, and swear to obey him. The fines which fall in, they give to the poor, or for wine, or they spend it amongst one another. Thus passes the morning in pastime. When any one has finished bathing, he takes a friendly leave, and gives an honourable farewell present.

" The second bath is the women's bath, in which divers honourable women and maidens meet together. In this the women also choose, every day, in turn a hostess, have a cheerful breakfast, thank the hostess, and with a wreath and pleasant song select another, as in the gentlemen's baths. They have also a special treasurer who keeps their money and presents in the treasury, which they spend in a friendly way together. But if anything unseemly or worthy of punishment takes place, they bring it before the mayor and court of the gentlemen, that some decision may be pronounced thereupon, according to old custom.

" In the third bath—the kettle—come all kinds of people, women and men, as many as fifty people together ; they are modest and friendly with one another, and eat what they can, and what pleases them. These also are subject to the court of the gentlemen's bath. Any one also, out of the gentlemen's or ladies' bath, may go into the kettle. On the other hand, those in the kettle bath, may not go into the others, unless they pay their share of the breakfasts. This bath has a very salutary effect, and the lame and paralytic are often brought here, who soon become vigorous and straight, and are able of themselves to go away, as in the year 1577, happened to a maiden from Waldshut, who did not over-eat herself, and bathed according to due order.

" The Margraves' bath was let out to special persons. The serene and right honourable Jörg Friedrich, Margrave of Brandenburg, who there bathed in person in 1575, was painted sitting therein on a horse. When I think of this bath, I cannot help laughing at a wonderful pleasantry that took place therein, and which is worth relating. In the aforesaid year a burgomaster and honourable councillor of the praiseworthy and far-famed city of Zurich, had sent a handsome bath present to the right honourable the Prince of Brandenburg, of wine and oats, and commanded Herr Heinrich Lochmann, the Banneret of Zurich, to present and deliver this. Now when he appeared with the present at Baden, it happened that the Prince was somewhat heated and weakened by the bath, so that for some days he could not appear at table, but kept quiet in his bedroom or in the bath. Meanwhile he commanded Duke Johann of Liegnitz and his councillors, to receive the foreign guests and provide them well. Now when they had made good cheer, and the Banneret was desirous to see the Prince, it was signified to him that the Prince received no one at present, but kept in his bedroom or the bath. Then the Banneret swore and vowed by his honour that he would be received by the Prince, and would on the morrow before he departed, if it could not be done otherwise, enter the bath with boots and spurs, and offer the Prince his hand, that he might tell his superiors he had seen the Prince. Now as I had sat at the table with him, and had been invited in the morning to bathe alone with the Prince, I respectfully signified to him what conversation had been carried on at supper, and what the Banneret threatened him with. I at the same time told the Prince of the great age of the Banneret, and his upright, valiant spirit, and begged of his Princely Grace, in case it should so happen, not to take it ungraciously. We sat thus together two hours, and spoke with one another of divers matters, when lo ! there comes my good Lochmann, who like an old simple associate, wished the Prince good day, waded in his boots and spurs through the water, and offered the Prince his hand. I remarked that the Prince changed colour. Thereupon the Banneret stepped back and begged the Prince to forgive him, as he had done it with good intent, that he might tell his superiors of the benignity and friendliness of the Prince. Then did thePrince, like a wise and eloquent gentleman, thank first the Banneret's superiors, and then also himself for the gift, and commended himself also to the favour of the men of Zurich. Thus he forgave him this boldness, which had proceeded from a good true-hearted spirit, and drank to his good friendship in a large goblet of wine. I received the goblet from the Prince and handed it to the Banneret, who pledged the Prince and drank to me from the goblet. He thereupon parted from the Prince quite humbly and joyfully."

Such is the narrative of the prudent Pantaleon. He is not like Poggio, a stranger who frankly, and in a spirit of curiosity, describes foreign manners, who perhaps had every wish to draw a friendly picture of the life at the baths, and who belonged to a nation which, as Poggio himself says, is surprised at nothing. But in the same degree as his character and conceptions differ from those of the Italian, so does the aspect of the baths appear altered in the century of the Reformation. A greater earnestness, prayer, and an organized self-police are not to be mistaken. The last, especially at that time, a general German idea, deserves attention. The

state authorities also had taken the bath life under their
supervision. Gifts were presented to the bath travellers in
the sixteenth century, as they still continued to make presents
on their departure to those who remained behind. As these
gifts fostered vanity and luxury to an extravagant excess, the
governments took serious steps to put a stop to them.

In the century of the Thirty years' war and of Louis XIV.
much of the self-control and political feeling of the men, and
piety of the women which had been perceptible at the baths,
as a consequence of the Reformation, was lost. Switzerland
suffered like Germany. The government was narrow-minded
and tyrannical, and among the subjects there was a deficiency
of self-respect, an aping of foreigners and of French manners.
Again did enjoyment at the baths become dissolute. But
even this is different from the frivolous, wanton behaviour of
the fifteenth century. The citizens thought it an honour to
court the adventurous cavalier from foreign parts, and to be
his parasite; the coquetry of the women also was more forward and common, and their almost unblushing connection
with the foreign bath visitors showed an empty heart, and too
often a great absence of modesty. There is a characteristic
account of these famous baths at this period also, by a frivolous Frenchman, De Merveilleux, preserved by a branch of
the German family Wunderlish. 'Amusements des Bains de
Bade,' &c., London, 1739.

LIFE AT THE BATHS AT THE END OF THE SEVENTEENTH CENTURY.

"Much had been told us of the splendid entrance of the
French Ambassador at Baden during the Swiss Diet.* We
hoped to find a princely court, but the present Ambassador in

* The Diet was then held at Baden, because the foreign diplomatist
could best be entertained there.

no respect resembles his predecessor.   He has no pages ; the
Count de Luc had six, as they tell me, as many secretaries,
and a like number of gentlemen of the bedchamber.   The
present man has a secretary, who they assure me has been a
servant, and no gentleman of the bedchamber.   His predecessor kept open table of fifty covers, with three courses, and
thus dined and supped every morning and evening, in order
to show honour to the Swiss.   The present one has his table
laid with a kind of *déjeûner à la fourchette*, soup, roast,
entremets, and dessert, but no variety ; every day the same, and
nothing good or hot.   Instead of one silver dish they would
give one, six of pewter.   The foreigners and the Swiss do not
seem content with this.

" But what does this signify to us ?   We live with our
Bernerins ; and have good living.   They would gladly get rid
of some of Bacchus's favourites from their town ; amongst
them the son of a delegate, we will endeavour to get him away
if we can.

" We go little into the city ; all people of distinction go to
the promenade, where there is pleasant intercourse.   As many
towns have Swiss fashions, which are not similar to the
French, such as the dress of the women of Basle, Lucerne,
Zurich, and other distant cantons, it gives one the impression
of a right gay masquerade, when all the visitors at the baths
are assembled for a dance.   The Swiss men and women are
much given to gallantry.   The ladies of Zurich have little
opportunity of amusing themselves, except at the bath season
at Baden, and they understand how to use this opportunity to
the utmost.   But if the French Ambassador is not at Baden
or does not keep open table, there is not very much amusement.   Every Swiss of any importance, is accustomed to have
good repasts at the Ambassador's yearly at Baden, so that
they are much dissatisfied with the comparison of the present
with the past.   The mothers tell their daughters of the plea-

sures they had in former times at the baths, and the young maidens are thereby incited to endeavour to procure some likewise. They labour to this end to the best of their powers, and the foreign cavaliers who know how to take advantage of the simplicity of these young city maidens, find themselves well off. For they are the daughters of magisterial persons, who have plenty of means to spend in Baden, and their marriages with the sons of their country are as good as settled, with such at least as speculate on places in the state, which are conferred principally by the fathers of these maidens ; and thus it comes to pass that these little flirtations at the baths, cause no disturbance in the arrangement which has been made concerning their marriage.

" We had the honour of an invitation from the minister, he invited us to a dinner with many ladies. Among others were two Mademoiselles S——, from Schaffhausen, daughters of good families. One of them has wounded more than one cavalier. There was much good entertainment that day ; nay, there was even some table plate won in a lottery. The ambassador found Mademoiselle S—— charming, and held her on his knee almost the whole evening of the ball, though he was suffering with his foot. The dance had one effect on the demoiselles which astonished us much. When they had danced very vigorously, and were very warm, lice made their appearance on the locks of their beautiful hair. That was rather unpleasant ; but the maidens had such beautiful skins that it became quite a pleasure to take off the vermin as soon as they became visible. The waters of Baden have the effect of producing these with young people ; therefore the Germans apply powder after powder but without combing themselves properly.

" These demoiselles were not the only beauties of this ball ; there were many pretty women there with their husbands and adorers. The Zurich ladies also would gladly have been there, but they were not allowed to visit the house of the French Ambassador, as their canton was averse to the renewal of the alliance with the King; nay, it was a transgression for a Zuricher even to enter the French hotel, therefore their wives and daughters only took a walk in the Ambassador's garden, who did not fail to betake himself there in an arm-chair on account of his bad foot. Every one on entering made him a reverence, and that procured him the pleasure of giving a kiss to each of these pretty city ladies, both mothers and daughters."

Here we conclude the narrative. These insipid and absurd proceedings ceased gradually towards the end of the last century. Even before the fever of the French revolution had seized the nations of Europe, the forms of social intercourse had changed, and still more so the feelings of men. The burgher life was still insipid, stiff, and *phillisträs ;* but the need of new ideas and deeper excitement had become general. Even the adventurers and cavaliers could no longer impose upon the credulity of their cotemporaries, by their old frivolity; it was necessary for them to be to some extent performers of prodigies, in order to get hold of the purses of others.

The Germans meanwhile, had found other places of amusement. The pleasure-seeking youths wandered to Spa and Pyrmont; hardly any now but the citizens of Switzerland assembled at the baths of Zurich. In conclusion, the society at Baden, as it was at the end of the last century, is thus shortly described.

LIFE AT THE BATHS AT THE END OF THE EIGHTEENTH
CENTURY.

" The magistracy stand in high esteem with the citizens, and endeavour to maintain this by the most formal behaviour. Owing to this adherence to forms, a journey to Baden was at

that period a great state transaction.   Farewell visits were
first made to relations and acquaintances.   The distinguished
people of Zurich ordered, as early as possible, the quarters
where they were to be accommodated in Hinterhof, that they
might not be mixed up with the common burgher class, who
then put up at the Stadthof.   The wealthy artisans whom
one met with there, were still greeted by the title of ' master,'
and generally in the second person ; and the patrician families kept exclusively together.   Immediately after an arrival
visits of ceremony were paid, each one made deep obeisance
to the other, and observed strictly the customary etiquette.
There was more solemnity than frivolity, and the freer proceedings of the young people were considered as deviations
from the rule.   They always showed themselves also at the
baths, dressed to the best of their power, according to their
condition in life, and even the négligé was carefully chosen,
and showed the quality of the person.   The gentlemen appeared in the morning in dressing-gowns of woollen damask,
out of the wide sleeves of which, ruffles of fine cambric fell
over the hands, and the *Badehren* (bath mantles) of both
sexes were trimmed with lace, and after the bath, in order to
be dried, were spread out ostentatiously as a show, on the
bars before the windows of the rooms.   In Zurich they
restricted the advance of expenditure by moral laws, prudent
considering the period, but frequently carried to exaggeration.
The material was accurately prescribed in which both sexes
were allowed to be dressed.   The women especially were kept
under strict observation, and they were forbidden to wear
blond, fringes, thread or silk lace, except on their caps ; all
openwork embroidery, all dresses of gauze, and all trimmings,
except of the same material as the dress.   The ordinance on
dress says further : ' Married women may be allowed to curl
their hair, but over the curls there must be nothing fastened
but a simple silk ribbon ; consequently the wearing of so

called tocquets, and of all feathers and other ornaments for the hair, were altogether forbidden ; further, the wearing of all enamel work and of portraits painted in miniature or other representations.' The men were forbidden not only all upper garments of silk or velvet, but even a lining of the like material ; further, all gold or silver stuffs and lacing, and all gallooned or embroidered horse covers and housings, except at the quarter musterings ; and to both sexes most especially all real or mock jewels on a penalty of fifty pounds. The tribunal, appointed by the government, which drew up these laws, and was charged to administer them, was called *Reformation.* Meanwhile the power of the *Reformation* did not extend beyond the frontier of the canton, although in one special article they endeavoured to stretch the mandate to those Zurichers who lived in other parts of the confederation, and especially in Baden. Here alone nothing was prescribed, and they indemnified themselves for restraint elsewhere, by adorning themselves with just those things which were forbidden at home. Many proud ladies and gentlemen, procured themselves objects of luxury for a visit to the baths of a few weeks, which were quite useless to them for the remainder of the year, and displayed themselves therein, in defiance of any reformers who chanced to be present. Gallooned dresses, which had once been worn in foreign parts, were here brought to light again out of the chests wherein they had been preserved, unused for years. The few jewels inherited from great-grandmothers were taken out of their cases to ornament the ears, neck, and stomacher ; and in delicately holding a cup of coffee, the little finger was stretched to the utmost, that the ring, brilliant with diamonds, rubies, or emeralds, might glitter before the eye. In great pomp, like the dressed-up altar figures, they passed along the dirty courts and alleys to admire and be admired ; but in order that their attire might not be injured, they seldom went further in this beautiful country than to

the meadows or to the play. It was a period of stiff buf-
foonery! That the young people of both sexes, often left
alone together till late in the night, danced more perhaps
than now-a-days; that the gentlemen sometimes sacrificed
largely to Bacchus; and that all, after their fashion, enjoyed
themselves right well, may easily be understood. People of
rank, some already smartly attired, others in choice morning
dresses, assembled usually before dinner in the Hinterhofe,
round a small stone table called the *Täfeli*, where they
usually returned again after the repast. Here they gossiped
good-humouredly on everything far and wide; no news was
left untouched, and many witty and delicate allegorical jests
were ventured upon and listened to. The return from Baden
took place generally in a very slow formal manner. After
manifold long, wordy and drawling compliments, and farewell formularies, packed at last in the lumbering coach, they
go; step by step, slowly, still making salutations right and
left from the coach door, up to the Halde."

Now Baden has become a respectable, modest, summer residence, little different from fifty other similar institutions.
Still however one may observe, not in Baden itself, but at
other baths in Switzerland, the ancient arrangement that
persons of the same sex may bathe together in a bath, amusing themselves without constraint; and not long ago at the
Leuker baths there were galleries round the baths, from which
many strangers might watch the bathers. But everywhere
the proceedings of men, even in these works of idleness, take
another form; and the garlanded maidens of Poggio, the
costly suppers of the time of Pantaleon, and the frivolous
patrician daughters, who, in defiance of father and bridegroom, went about from bath to bath with foreign cavaliers,
have vanished, and forgotten is the tedious ceremonial by
which particular classes were closed to one another.

CHAPTER XI.

JESUITS AND JEWS.
(ABOUT 1693.)

THE Churches in Germany, both Roman Catholic and Protestant, suffered from the weakness of the nation. Both had to pass through struggles and sufferings, which threatened destruction to every exclusive Church system ; they became too narrow to embrace the whole spiritual and intellectual life of men. Since the war, men had gradually felt the need of toleration. With the Protestants, Luther's principle again revived, that only inward conviction could bring men into the Church. It was later, that the old Church yielded a grumbling toleration. Science had discovered, amongst other things, that in spite of some passages of Holy Scripture, the sun does not turn round our earth, but our earth round the sun. Unwillingly did the Church receive this, after the discovery had occasioned her many a heart's pang.

The Protestant Church had fewer difficulties to overcome, but the aristocratic structure of the Roman Catholic Church, again so firmly united, and supported by great political interests, would naturally find it far more difficult to yield to necessity.

Whoever should wish to write a history of the religious conscience of Germans, would have to examine how it was, that after the war there arose in both confessions, precisely at the same time, a reaction of the heart against the ruling parties, which in spite of the difference of dogmas, shows a great similarity in the representations of this tendency. The need of elevation of soul, in a period which was poor in feeling, made the Protestant Spener, and the Catholic Spee and Scheffler into pietists, and mystics. It is true, the restraining power of the Protestant Church could no longer check the development of individuality. Through it the scientific man could easily satisfy himself, when he came, from the study of history, from observation of the heavens, from the secret of numbers, and through the weighing and measuring of the powers of the elements, to a new representation of the world of creation, and thereby to new views of the being of the Godhead. Thus the genius of the great Leibnitz was the growth of the Protestant Church. Any one also whose fancy took a wild flight, or to whom deep thought and meditation disclosed some peculiar aspect of the Deity, might easily release himself from Church-communion with his fellow-citizens, and unite himself perhaps with congenial spirits in some special community. Thus did Böhme, and the eccentric Kuhlmann, Zinzendorf, and Herrnhuter. This was incomparably more difficult in the Roman Catholic Church. Whoever attempted to go his own way, had to experience the anger of a strict mistress, and rarely did a powerful mind break loose from the restraint.

But the ruling majority of ecclesiastics had even in the old Church lost much of their energy. The warlike champion of the restored Church, the order of Jesuits, had itself suffered in its greatness; it had become powerful and rich, the connection between the provinces and Rome had been loosened, the independence of individual houses was greater, and the curse had fallen on it which pursues the prosperous. It became pre-eminently the representative of modern courtly splendour in church and school. Even in earlier times the order had not disdained brilliant displays, nor to enter into the feelings of the great world, but then it had been like the prophet Daniel, who only wore the Persian dress in order to serve his God among the heathen ; now Daniel had become a satrap. Through the Westphalian peace, the great mission work of the order was limited.   Still however, did it continue skilfully to draw within its circle the souls of individuals, whoever was rich or distinguished was firmly ensnared.   Its main object was not the salvation of souls, but the fame which would accrue to the order.   The greatest amount of work was done in the Emperor's territory.   Wherever heresy still flickered, the lay authorities assisted.   But one race, more stubborn and stiffnecked than the sons of the Hussites, or the Moravian brothers, incessantly excited the spirit of conversion in the order, it was the Jews.

Already in the time of the Romans, the Jews may have dwelt within the colonies on the Rhine, near the temple of Jupiter of golden Maintz, and the baths of the proud Agrippina ; they afterwards established themselves within the German cities.   In respect to German law they were as foreigners ; they were placed under the protection of the Emperor, who transferred his power over them to the Archbishop of Maintz, the Chancellor of the Empire.   As the Emperor's dear servitors, besides the other taxes, they had to pay him and the princes a penny offering, which was raised on Christmas-day.   This tax, one of the sources of the Emperor's revenue, should have been security for his protection, but it became an opportunity for the worst oppression ; and they were drawn upon for contributions on every occasion that money was wanted.   Their taxes reached to an exorbitant height.   On sudden money emergencies, or as an act of favour, the Emperor sold, or gave away his right of taxation to the Princes and cities ; and the year's rent of three, four, or even one hundred Jews, was a secure and important income.   Thus it was a source of gain to the

Princes and Sovereigns to possess many Jews, from whom they raised money to the utmost.

On the other hand it was an exclusive right of the Jews to lend out money on interest for notes of hand or mortgages, which was strictly forbidden to the Christians of the middle ages by the Pope and Emperor. Thus naturally the whole of the money dealing came into the hands of the Jews. And by the high interest which they received—especially on short loans—they must rapidly have acquired great wealth. But this boundless right was not secure against sudden attacks, both Pope and Emperor sometimes took the liberty of giving the creditor a dispensation from the payment of the interest, nay even of the capital.

Thus they became the financiers of the olden time in both great and little traffic, the richest persons in the country, in spite of monstrous imposts.

But this opulence stimulated still more the hate and covetousness of the multitude. In the early part of the middle ages they appear to have been seldom persecuted by Christian fanaticism. But after the Crusades, the declining Church and the populace of the towns vied with each other in seeking their lives and treasure. A tradition which continues up to the present day was brought forward against them. They were supposed to poison wells, to introduce the plague, to murder Christian children, use their blood at their Passover, and feed on their hearts; and to whip the consecrated host with rods, &c. Persecutions, plundering of houses, and extensive murders were almost periodical. Christianity was forced upon them by the sword, torments, and imprisonment, but usually in vain. No warlike people ever withstood brutal violence, with more heroic courage than this defenceless race. The most magnanimous examples of enduring heroism are mentioned by Christian writers themselves. Thus it went on during the whole of the middle ages, and still in the sixteenth century

we find the Sovereigns endeavouring to fill their empty coffers
from the money bags of the Jews, and the populace still
storming their houses, as in the wild Jewish outbreak at
Frankfort-on-Main in 1614. Some great scholars, physicians,
and natural philosophers among them, acquired a repute
which spread through all the countries of Europe, inspiring
even Christians with involuntary respect, but these were rare
exceptions.

Amidst all these adverse circumstances, the indestructible
vital energies of this people still continued, as we find them
among the Jews of the present day : privileged by the
Emperor, helpless before the law of the country, indispensable, yet deeply hated, desired, but cursed, in daily danger
of fire, robbery, and murder, yet the quiet masters of the
property and welfare of hundreds, in an unnatural adventurous position, and yet always steadily occupied, amidst
the densest mass of Christians, yet separated from them by
iron boundaries, they lived a twofold life ; in presence of
Christians they were cold, stubborn, patient, timid, cringing,
and servile, bowed down under the oppression of a thousand
years : yet all the pride of noble blood, great wealth, and
superior talent, the full glow of southern feeling, every kindly
emotion and every dark passion were to be found in that race.

After the Thirty years' war, the Jews obtained scarcely more
protection from the fury of the multitude, and their spiritual
trials became greater. If the Protestants, who were then
weak and embarrassed, vexed them more by repulsive arrogance than by their arts of proselytism, the old Church was
the more zealous. They were more prosperous in trade and
usury since the Westphalian peace, indeed a splendid prospect had opened for them. The diminution of international
wholesale business, the ruin of old commercial houses at
Nuremburg and Augsburg, the continued depreciation of the
coinage, the unceasing need of money, with the territorial

lords, small and great, was favourable to the multifarious activity of the Jewish business, which found skilful instruments throughout all Germany, and connections from Constantinople to Cadiz. The importance to German trade of the close cohesion of the Jews amongst themselves, at a period when bad roads, heavy tolls, and ignorant legislation, placed the greatest limits upon commerce, is not yet sufficiently appreciated. With unwearied energy, like ants, they everywhere bored their secret way through the worm-eaten wood of the German Empire : long before the letter post and system of goods carriers had spread a great network over the whole circuit of the country, they had quietly combined for these objects ; poor chafferers and travelling beggars, passed as trusty agents between Amsterdam and Frankfort, Prague and Warsaw, with money and jewels under their rags, nay concealed within their bodies. In the most dangerous times, in spite of prohibitions, the defenceless Jew stole secretly through armies, from one German territory into another ; and he carried Kremnitzer ducats of full weight to Frankfort, while he circulated light ones among the people. Here he bought laces and new church vestments for his opponents, the ecclesiastics ; there he smuggled through an enemy's territory, to some prince, arms and implements of war ; then he guided and accompanied a large transport of leather from the interior of Russia to the fair of Leipzig, he alone being capable by flattery, money, and brandy, of overmatching the covetousness of the Sclave nobles. Meanwhile, the most opulent sat in the well-grated rooms of their Jewish town, concealing securely, under lock and key, the bills of exchange, and mortgages of the highest lords ; they were great bankers, even according to our present standard.

The Jews of that period were probably richer in proportion to the Christians than now, and at all events, from the peculiarities of their traffic, more indispensable. They had

friendly protectors alike at the Imperial court, in the harem
of the Sultan, and in the secret chamber of the Pope; they
had an aristocracy of blood, which was still highly respected
by their fellow-believers, and at bridal feasts they wore with
pride, the jewels which some ancestor, long perhaps before
the days of Marco Polo, had brought from India, while
exposing his life to manifold dangers; or another had got by
bartering, from the great Moorish king at Granada.   But in
the streets the Jew still bore the degrading mark of the
unhonoured stranger; in the Empire, a yellow cockade on
his coat, and in Bohemia the stiff blue cravat; as in the
middle ages he had worn the yellow hat, and in Italy the red
mantle.   It is true he was the creditor and employer of
numerous Christians, but in most of the greater cities he still
lived closely confined to certain streets or portions of the city.

Few German Jewish communities were larger or more
opulent than that in Prague, and it was one of the oldest in
Germany.   Seldom does a traveller neglect to visit the
narrow streets of the Jewish quarter, where the small houses,
clustered together like the cells of a beehive, enclosed at once
the greatest riches and the greatest misery of the country,
and where the angel of death so long caused tears of gall to
trickle into the mouth of the believer, till every inch of earth
in the dismal churchyard became the ashes of men.   At the
end of the seventeenth century, near six thousand industrious
men dwelt there in a narrow space; the great money lenders,
as well as the poorest frippery dealers and porters, all closely
united in firm fellowship and common interests, indispensable
to the impoverished country, yet in continual warfare against
the customs, coarseness, and religious zeal of the newly
converted kingdom.

For the second generation were then living, of the new
Bohemia, which the Hapsburgers by scaffolds, expulsion, and
fearful dragooning, had won back after the battle of Weissen

Berge.   The old race of nobles was, for the most part, rooted
out ; a new Imperial nobility drove in gilded carriages through
the black Hussite city ; the old biblical learning had wandered
into foreign lands, or died away in the misery of the long
war ; in the place of the chalice priests and the Bohemian
preachers, were the holy fathers and begging monks ; where
once Huss defended the teaching of Wickliff, and Zisk rebuked
the lukewarmness of the citizens of the old town, the gilded
statue of the queen of heaven now rose triumphant.   Little
remained to the people of their past, except the dark stones of
Königsstadt, a rough populace, and a harsh piety.

There remains to us a little pamphlet of this time, for which
we are indebted to two of the Prague celebrities of the order
of Jesuits, the Fathers Eder and Christel, the first of whom
wrote it in Latin, and the second translated it into German ;
both writers are otherwise known, the second as a zealous
but insipid German poet.   From this writing the following
narrative is taken.

" Thus in a few years a hundred and seventy persons of
the Jewish persuasion, were purified in the saving waters of
baptism, by one single priest of our society, in the Academical
church of Our Saviour, of the college of the Society of Jesus.

" I will by the way, here shortly mention, the wonderful
bias of a Jewish child for the Christian faith.   A Jewess in
the Zinkower domain was in the habit of carrying her little
daughter in her arms ; one day she accidentally met a Catholic
priest, to whom she proposed to show her child, and taking
the veil off its little face, boasted what a finely-shaped child
she had brought into the world.   The priest took advantage
of this preposterous and unexpected confidence, to bless the
unveiled child with the sign of the holy cross, admonishing
the mother at the same time to bring up the said child in the
love and fear of God, but leaving all else in the hands of
Divine Providence.   And behold this little Jewess had hardly

begun to walk, when she forthwith considered herself a Christian, knelt with them when they knelt, sang with the singers, went out with them into the meadows and woods, made hay, plucked strawberries, and picked up wood with them ; besides this, she learnt of them the pater-noster and the angel's salutation, as also to say the belief; in short she made herself acquainted with Christian doctrine, and desired earnestly to be baptized.   The high born and Right Honorable Countess of Zinkow, in order to fulfil this maiden's desire, to her great delight took her in her carriage to Prague, that she might there, out of sight of her parents, more securely obtain the privilege of baptism.   But after the parents had discovered that their daughter, who had for so long a time carefully kept her designs secret, had become a Christian, they bitterly lamented it, and were very indignant with the priest who had blessed her in her mother's arms with the sign of the cross, for they ascribed to him all their daughter's inclination for Christianity.

" But by what intrigues the perfidious Jews endeavoured to frustrate every conversion, I have myself not long since had experience, when for the first time, a disciple in the faith of the Jewish race, Samuel Metzel, was placed under me for instruction.   The father, who had four children yet minors, was a true Israelite, out of the Egypt of the Jewish town, and had endeavoured, much and zealously, to bring them all, together with himself, out of bondage.   But, behold! Rosina Metzelin, his wife, who then had a great horror of the Christian faith, would not obey him ; and when she found that the four children were immediately withdrawn from her, this robbery of her children, was, like the loss of her young to a lioness, hard to bear.   She summoned her husband before the Episcopal consistory, where she sued for at least two of the four purloined children, which she had given birth to, with great labour, pain, and weariness, both

before, at, and after the time.   But the most wise tribunal of
the Archbishop, decided that all the children belonged to the
husband, who was shortly to be baptized.   Then did the wife
lament piteously, indeed more exceedingly than can be told
or believed ; and as she was afeard that her fifth offspring,
which was yet unborn, would be stolen from her after its
birth, she endeavoured earnestly to conceal from the Christians
the time of her delivery.   Therefore she determined first of
all to change her place of abode, as her present one was
known to her husband and children.   But there is no striving
against the Lord !   The father discovered it by means of his
innocent little daughter, who for some months had been constantly kept in a Christian lodging, and was unwarily
admitted by her mother into her concealed dwelling.   On
receiving this information, I sought out the Imperial Judge
of the *Altstadt* of Prague, who, without delay, despatched
his clerk to the house, to demand the new-born child from
the woman, and (in case she refused) from the Elder of the
Jewish people, as belonging to the now baptized father.   But
as these crafty Jews would not consent to deliver up the
child, a Christian midwife was ordered for the Jewish woman,
that the same might, by some womanly, pious contrivance,
carry off the child from the mother.   This midwife was
accompanied by certain prudent matrons.   The conductress
was to be Ludmilla, well known for her great godliness, wife
of Wenzeslaus Wymbrsky, who had gone through the baptism
of water and blood.   Her husband Wenzeslaus was, with this
his wife and five children, baptized in our church by his
Eminence the Cardinal and Archbishop of Prague in 1464.
It was above all displeasing to the furious Jews, to see
thirteen men of other families, following the example of
Wenzeslaus, abjuring Judaism the same year.   At last it
became insupportable to them that Wenzeslaus, by whose shop
many Jews had daily to pass to their frippery market, should

publicly set up in it the image of the crucified Saviour, and every Friday keep a burning lamp before it. Therefore he was greatly hated by the Jewish rabble, and often assailed with derision and scoffing. Now, once when he went, according to his daily custom, to the Teynkirche, an hour before day, three armed Jews fell on him, by whom he was mortally wounded with two poisoned pistol-balls, so that on the fifth day thereafter, he devoutly departed this life, without having been persuaded to name the murderers. The ringleader was caught later, and condemned to the wheel, but acting as his own executioner hanged himself with a rope. Now the widow of the deceased man, Ludmilla, could not slip in, with the little troop of pious women, unperceived, because the Hebrews with their sharp lynx-eyes watched narrowly. At that moment, many of them combined together and pushed their way into the room of the Jewish woman about to be confined. But Ludmilla did not take alarm at their presence, nor at the possible danger of death. She handed over the consecrated water she had brought with her, to the midwife, calling upon her in strong language, to deliver the woman and baptize the child. And so it took place, and the nurse took the child and baptized it. But the woman who had been confined sprang frantically from her bed, and with vehement cries, tore the child violently from the hands of the midwife. Forthwith, the city judge made his appearance with armed men, in order to separate the now little Christian son from the mother. But as she, like a frantic one, held the child so firmly clasped in her arms, that it was feared it would be stifled in extricating it from her, the judicious judge of the city contented himself with strictly forbidding the old Jews there assembled, to make the child a Jew. Thereupon it was commanded, by his Excellence, the Lord Count of the Empire, Von Sternberg, Chief Burgrave of the Kingdom of Bohemia, that this fifth child should be delivered over to the father.

Not long after, the mother also, who had so stubbornly adhered to Judaism, gave in, and was baptized.

" The father of the Jewish boy Simon Abeles, was Lazarus, and his grandsire Moses Abeles who for many years had been Chief Rabbi of the Jews. Whilst already of tender years, there had been discovered in this boy a special leaning of the spirit towards Christianity. Whenever he could, he separated himself from the Jewish youths, and associated with the Christian boys, played with them, and gave them sweets which he had collected from his father's table, in order to gain their good will. The Jewish cravat, stiffened with blue starch, which the Jews wear round the neck, thereby distinguishing themselves here in Bohemia from the Christians, was quite repugnant to Simon. As the light of his reason became brighter, he took every opportunity of learning the Christian mysteries. It happened that he was many times sent by his father, who was a glove dealer, on business to the house of Christopher Hoffman, a Christian glover. There he tarried in contemplation of the sacred, not the profane, pictures that hung on the walls, although the last were more precious and remarkable as specimens of artistic painting, and he inquired with curiosity of the Christian inmates, what was signified in these pictures. When in reply they told him, that one was a representation of Christ, another of the mother of Christ, the miracle-working mother of God, by Buntzel, and another, the holy Antonius of Padua, he exclaimed, from his heart, sighing : ' Oh, that I could be a Christian !' Moreover, a Jew called Rebbe Liebman bore witness, that the boy sometimes passed whole nights among Christians, and did not appear at his father's house.

" Now many maintained that this leaning to Christianity arose from a supernatural source, and was produced by the baptismal sign, which had been impressed upon him by a Christian, whilst he was in the cradle. When later this

report had been carefully investigated, it was certified that a
preceptor, Stephen Hiller, was once sent to Lazarus Abeles
to obtain payment of a debt, that he there found a child lying
alone in the cradle, and had, from deep impulse of heart,
baptized him with the elemental water which was at hand.
On being examined by the consistory of the Right Reverend
the Archbishop, this preceptor, who is now invested with a
chaplaincy, said that he did not know whether the child was
the little son of Lazarus ; nay, his supposition had been far
stronger, that it was the son of a Jewish tailor.   From such
evidence this weighty point remained doubtful.

After some years, the steadfast leaning of Simon's spirit to
Christianity, having so much increased that it began to be
clearly perceived at home, the astute boy, foreseeing well
that his parents and relations would spare no pains to put
impediments in his way, was minded to prevent this, by flying
from his father's house and Jewish friends, before the path
was closed against him.   Now while, on the 25th of July,
1693, Lazarus the father, kept the solemn day of rest in the
Jewish school, his son betook himself to a Christian house
near the Jewish town, which was inhabited by the newly
baptized Jew, Kawka, and that same evening summoned to
him Johannes Santa, a Jew who many years before had been
converted with his whole family, of whom he had already
heard a good repute, as a zealous man and assiduous guide.
For this man had, at the risk of his life, brought away Jews
who had a desire for the Christian faith, and their newly
baptized children from the Jewish town, had placed them
under instruction in our college of St. Clement, had provided
them with food, clothes, and lodging, and had for hours together read spiritual books, especially the Life of Christ, with
deep devotion to such as could not read, and whose greatest
pleasure it was to see them cleansed in holy baptism.   To
him Simon honestly opened his heart, and entreated that

Johannes would take him to the college of the Society of Jesus.

" There was no necessity for entreating, the man borrowed clothes of a Christian youth, covered Simon's head, which was shorn after the Jewish fashion, with a peruke, and conducted him across the Altstadter Platz to the college. In the middle of the said Platz, stands the large richly-gilded image of the holy mother of God, carved out of one stone. Johannes explained to his Christian scholar, that this richly-gilded image represented the Queen of heaven, the faithful mediator of believers with God. This Simon listened to with great eagerness, took off his hat without delay, bowed his whole body low, and commended himself with pious sighs, to the blessed mother of God, as her foster child. Hereupon he turned to his guide and thus addressed him : ' If my father saw this, he would straightway kill me.' Thus they reached our college between seven and eight o'clock in the evening. I was called to the door, and Simon imparted to me his desires with marvellous eloquence, and at the same time begged with such fervent zeal to be instructed in the Christian faith, that I was much amazed. I presented him the same evening to the Reverend Father Rector of the college. It almost seemed as if this twelve-year-old boy behaved himself, as afore time Jesus among the doctors, seeing that he answered various questions with an eloquence, acuteness, and judgment which far surpassed his age. When it was objected to him, that his late arrival excited a suspicion that he had committed some evil deed in the Jewish town, and sought a refuge in the ecclesiastical house, Simon answered with cheerful countenance : ' If there is a suspicion of any misdeed, let the truth be searched out by proclamation, as is usual in the Jew town. If I were conscious of any evil deed, I should have more hope of remaining unpunished among the Jews than among the Christians, for I am a grandson of Moses Abeles, their chief

Rabbi.' Then when it was suggested that he had come among the Christians in order to wear a peruke, a little sword, and fashionable dress, the boy made a face and said : ' I must confess that for a long time, I have not worn the Jewish collar.   Nevertheless, I do not desire to shine among Christians in any fashionable clothes, and will be content with my old rags.'   After he had given this earnest answer, he began to strip his hands of his gloves, to ungird his little sword, to tear the peruke from his head, and to unhook the clean little upper coat, determined were it necessary to follow the destitute Jesus, unclothed.

"By such unexpected answers and heroic resolution, he drew tears from the eyes of all present.   But when he was commanded to put his clothes on again, he soon dressed himself, and declared in strong words, which he oft repeated, that he withdrew from the Jews on account of their wicked course of life, and associated himself with Christians to secure his salvation, because he knew well it was impossible to be blessed without faith.   But when he was asked who had taught him, that faith was necessary to gain eternal life, he answered seven or eight times : ' God, God, God alone,' therewith he oft sighed and smote his breast with both hands. Then he went first to one priest, then to another, kissed their hands, fell on his knees to them, exclaiming : ' Fathers, abandon me not ; do not reject me, do not send me again among the Jews ; instruct me quickly, quickly and ' (as if he had a foreboding, and saw the impending evil floating before his eyes), ' baptize me quickly.'   Now when Simon received the assurance that he would be reckoned among the scholars in the Christian faith, he clapped his hands, and jumped for joy.   His whole discourse was as mature and discreet, as ready and free from hesitation, as if he had long beforehand reflected upon it in his mind, and learnt it by heart from his tablets, so that one of the four priests present turned with astonishment to another, and said in Latin : ' This boy has a miraculous understanding, which if not supernatural, is yet truly beyond his age.'

" Meanwhile, the darkness of night had come on.   But as there was not convenient sleeping room at present for this new little Nicodemus, he was with much inward striving of my spirit, left again in that Christian house from whence he had been brought hither, in order to spend the night in peace with the newly baptized Jew, George Kawka.   This one was called to the door of the college, and the boy was entrusted to him, with an express order to bring him again to the college at the earliest hour on the following morning, that they might provide him with a secure dwelling.

" In the interim, Lazarus became aware of the absence of his son.   Not finding him either with his friends nor among other Jews, and being a person of sound judgment, it occurred to him that his son must have gone over to the Christians. Early on Sunday Lazarus betook himself to the Christian house of the glove-maker Hoffmann, whom he did not find at home.   He concealed the loss of his son and his sorrow, and begged the glove-maker's wife Anna, instantly to call George Kawka there, because he had some weighty business to transact with him who was his debtor.   After a long Hebrew conversation with Lazarus, George Kawka came in all haste to the college, but to my great sorrow, unaccompanied by the Christian disciple.   He appeared painfully disquieted, but did not tell me a word of his conference with the father, but only said that Simon was not sufficiently secure in his dwelling, and that it was necessary to take good heed, or he would be entrapped by the crafty devices of the Jews.   After a sharp reproof for not bringing the boy with him when in such danger, according to my strict orders, I commanded him to go to the house forthwith and bring the boy hither.   This he promised but did not perform.   Now when George Kawka returned home, he pretended that he wished to go to church, and Simon prayed of him, as though he foreboded some impending treachery, with many words and tears, not to leave him behind, as the Jews would without fail lie in wait for him that day, and seize him in the house ; but that he would take him with him to church and so bring him to the college. Now when he with great sorrow of spirit perceived that George Kawka only answered with subterfuges, he withdrew himself again, after the departure of the same, into his hiding-place under the roof.

" Hardly had George crossed the threshold, when Katherina Kanderowa, a lodger, came from the country into her lodging-room, which was close to Simon's hiding-place, and saw the boy in his little Jewish coat, which he had again been obliged to put on. As therefore the said Katherina understood from the Jews who were standing round the house-door that they were seeking for the son of a Jew, who had fled from his father, and as she did not know that Simon was a disciple of the Christian faith, she drew him out of his corner, and dragged him down to the front part of the house. When the father saw his son, he presented to this woman thirty silver groschen, that she might thrust the boy, who was not strong enough to free himself from her hands, over the threshold. The boy called upon the Christians to support him against such violence, but in vain, for two robust Jews seized upon him each by an arm, and bore him along as if he floated through the air, to the Jew town and his father's house. But the father went craftily step by step slowly behind, in order to chat with the Christians, and make them believe that his son had only fled to the Christians, in order to escape lawful and deserved punishment. He easily persuaded the populace of this.

" But George Kawka betook himself after the end of this tragedy to me, and related the lamentable kidnapping of

Simon with many light worthless excuses. But I spoke
sharply to him, put clearly before his eyes, how evident it
was that he had played with the Jews under the rose, and
sternly charged him if he would not be made answerable
before the tribunal, for the treacherous betrayal of Simon, to
use all means without delay, and on the requisition of a
Christian judge to recover him from the hands of the Jews,
and deliver him up to the college. And truly it appeared as
if he obeyed the command faithfully and assiduously. He
searched the whole Jew town many days, and examined
almost all the houses, as was testified of him by the person
who accompanied and was associated with him. He thereby
turned almost all the suspicion of treachery from him; and
as Simon was nowhere to be found, he confirmed the report
that he had secretly been removed to Poland. At a later
period, George Kawka himself was driven by a bad conscience to take refuge in Poland, and has remained invisible
to this day.

But Simon was dragged with violence to his father's house,
and after that day, was never seen outside the threshold.
After their arrival at home, the father could no longer
control his anger, and beat his son with a stick so savagely,
that the Jews present began already to fear that he would
kill him. They therefore locked up Simon in a room in
which lived Sarah Bresin, afterwards a witness. But the
father endeavoured to break open the door of the room by
repeatedly running at it with violence, and at last angrily
left the house. When his anger was a little allayed, the
Jews gave up to him the severely-beaten boy, advising to
tame him by fasting. So Simon was locked up in another
room. There he passed seven painful months, in hunger
and imprisonment, daily loaded with curses and oft threatened
with death. But when the father saw that his son's spirit
was inflexible, and that on the Saturday before Shrove

Sunday, Simon again, before all the family, declared un-
dauntedly, that he would be baptized; he determined to go
to extremities.   And that affection might not restrain his
hand, he chose for assistant a Jew, Levi Kurtzhandl, a man of
savage spirit and in the vigour of youth, who had already before
advised him to poison the boy.   Levi Kurtzhandl invited the
boy into the room of his step-mother, and held converse with
him out of the Talmud, in order to convert him.   But when
Simon persevered in his intentions, he was knocked down by
Levi, and dragged by him and the father into the next room;
there both fell upon him furiously, broke his neck, and drove
his head violently against the corner of a wooden chest,
whereby the glorious soldier of Christ received a last blow on
the left side of the temple.

"Whilst this barbarity was going on, Lia, the step-
mother of Simon, together with the journeyman Rebbe Liebmann, were occupied in the next room making gloves.   On
hearing the moaning of the boy, and the noise of the murderers, she hastened into the room.   There she saw the dead
body on the floor, and both the murderers on their knees by
him.   Thereupon the woman was so frightened, that she
fainted, and had to be restored to her senses by Kurtzhandl
pouring vinegar over her.

"After the deed, Hennele, Lazarus's cook, came back, who
had been sent out of the house with the little children.
These, when supper-time was approaching, inquired where
Simon was.   They were obliged to take an oath to keep the
affair secret; whereupon, their father himself told them, that
he, with Levi Kurtzhandl, had deprived the boy of life as an
apostate from the law of Moses, after the example of the
patriarch Phineas.

"After that, Lazarus took counsel with Levi how to keep
the crime secret, not only from the Christians, but also from
the Jews, especially from the family of Burianer, who were

very hostile to all that belonged to the Abeles. Levi offered while it was yet night, to carry the body of Simon to his own house, and bury it himself in the cellar. But Lazarus feared lest some of the Burian adherents should discover it. They therefore decided on having the corpse buried in the public burial-ground of the Jews. And truly, the neck of the body was discoloured with blood, but otherwise there was no open wound to be seen, with the exception of a blow on the left temple of about the size of a ducat; so Lazarus called his household together, instructed and made them swear, that they would say unanimously that Simon had become insane, and in that state had fallen against the corner of the chest, whereby he had been mortally wounded on the left temple.

"On the following morning early, this glorious soldier of Christ was buried in great secrecy by two Jews, Jerochem and Hirsches Kesserlas, the coroners.

"After the burial of Simon, from his grave arose the first great summoner, the worm of conscience, which began to gnaw the heart of the godless Lazarus. Memory unceasingly persecuted his conscience, and the fear of worldly punishment ever hovered before his eyes. This fear was much increased by the journeyman glove-maker, Rebbe Liebmann. The same had after the deed, straight left Abele's house and made off, and had only again returned to his work after the burial. When Lazarus began to relate the particulars, Rebbe interrupted him, protesting that he did not desire to hear a word about the evil deed, as he had already heard the whole of yesterday's tragedy, related by the Jewish children in the public streets. This burst upon the astonished Lazarus like a thunder clap; without delay he collected and packed up all his light goods, sold his house in the Jew town, and resigned his hired shop in an aristocratic house, in order to settle himself in Poland. He was already prepared, on the following day, to take flight; but it was providentially ordained that the noble landlord of the house, who had leased the shop to him, was just then hindered by palsy in his hand from signing the release himself.

"Meanwhile, on the 23rd of February, one Johel, a Jew, not evil-disposed towards the Christians, went into the Jew town through the Sommer-thor, where he met some children playing, who were relating to one another, how Simon Abeles had three days before been fresh and healthy, and had early yesterday been buried without any funeral pomp. Johel betook himself without delay to the burial-ground, and found a freshly-raised grave; reflected upon all the other circumstances and reports, and came to the sensible conclusion that Lazarus was the murderer of his son. This he confided forthwith to a writer of the royal government in great secresy. After I had received intelligence thereof, and had earnestly admonished the Jewish informer to give a faithful report; he wrote down the following day all the lamentable particulars, in order to deliver them to the most noble government. They commanded the body of Simon to be disinterred, and to be closely examined by a doctor appointed for the purpose; and finally to take into custody those who were suspected of the deed, as also their accomplices. All this was set on foot cautiously and without delay. The body was disinterred under an armed guard; the Jews who had collected, and the Jewish doctor who was called in, declared that a bad blow on the head, and lastly a fit of insanity, had killed the boy. But the medical· gentlemen gave their opinion, that many indications, the broken neck and a small round wound on the temple, showed that the boy had died from a violent blow.

"Thereupon Lazarus Abeles was brought to see the body of his son. He turned pale and trembled, and was so confused that he remained silent, and for a good while could not say anything intelligible, nor answer anything distinctly.

At last as the Herr Commissary continued urging him to say
whether he knew the body of the boy, he answered with bent
head and weak voice that it was the body of his son Simon ;
and when it was further put to him what was the cause of
the wound on the left temple, he gave a confused and contra-
dictory answer.   He was therefore again taken to prison, but
the body of the boy was put into a Christian coffin, and
placed meanwhile in the cellar of the council house.   The
Herren commissaries were unwearied in cross-questioning
Christians and Jews.   But in spite of all indications,
Lazarus, and the women who were in special custody, Lia,
his wife, and Hennele, his cook, were almost unanimous in
their evidence : Simon had not taken flight from his father's
house to become a Christian, but for a long time had been
affected with a disease of the head, and therefore kept in the
house ; at last he had felt an extreme repugnance for food,
had become subject to violent fits of insanity, and thus had
met with his death.   All means of extracting the truth were
unavailing ; Lazarus Abeles and the two only witnesses then
known of, remained obstinate.

" One afternoon, the honourable Franz Maximilian Baron
von Klarstein, the official commissary, was reflecting on this
matter as he went home, and ascended the steps of his
house ; when it suddenly seemed to him that he received a
violent blow on the side, he turned round crossly, when
behold there appeared to him on the landing which divided
the steps from one another, a boy standing, who bowed his
head, and smiled sweetly with cheerful countenance, clothed
in a Jewish winding-sheet, wounded on the left temple, and
in size and age like Simon, as this gentleman had seen him
with his own eyes, on inspection of the body, when a lively
image of him had been impressed on his memory.   The
gentleman was amazed, and whilst he was sitting at table
with his wife and some guests, pondered in his mind what

this might signify.   Then he heard the tapping of a person's finger several times on the door of the dining-room.   The servant was sent out, and informed him that an unknown maiden desired instantly to be admitted.   Having entered, and being kindly accosted, the little maiden of fourteen answered that her name was Sarah Bresin, that she now dwelt among the Christians to be instructed in the Christian faith, and had shortly before lived as servant to the tenant in the house of Lazarus Abeles; there she had seen with her own eyes how cruelly Lazarus had attacked his son Simon, because he had fled to the Christians, in order to be baptized. Upon this and other evidence Sarah was confronted with Lazarus; before whom she declared freely, with much feeling and in forcible language, all that she knew.   But Lazarus roundly denied it all; and with frantic curses called down all the devils upon her head.   But when he returned to his prison, confusion and despair seized his soul; he perceived that his denials would no longer help him before the court, and determined by a last expedient to escape judicial proceedings.   Although both his legs and one hand were impeded by his fetters, yet he contrived to wind the girdle, called a *Tephilim,* wherewith the Jews bind their heads and arms during prayer, instead of a cord, round the iron window grating, and strangled himself thereby.   Thus on the following morning, he was found strangled.   For the Jews erroneously consider it allowable to throttle themselves, and oft-times do the like.   Judgment was passed on his dead body.

"After his death his wife Lia and the servant-maid Hennele being confronted with Sarah Bresin, made a public confession; the fugitive journeyman glover, Rebbe Liebmann, was also produced and confessed.   His Princely Grace the Archbishop decided that Simon should be buried in the Teynkirche, in the chapel of St. John the Baptist, by the baptismal font,

within a vault of polished marble, in a fine oak coffin covered
with red velvet, and guarded by a lock and three keys. Further, that the coffin was to be borne to the burial-place by
innocent and noble youths dressed in purple. The most
noble Frau Silvia, born Gräfin Kinskey, wife of his Excellency
the Lord Count of the Empire, Schlick, had a double costly
dress prepared for this day, an under dress of white satin and
an upper one of red, interwoven with gold, trimmed with gold
buttons and adorned with gold lace-work ; she provided also
stockings of the like material to cover the feet, and an exceedingly beautiful garland of gold and silver lilies and roses to
crown the head of the innocent martyr.

"Hardly had his most precious body been attired and laid
in the costly coffin, when the high nobility of both sexes
arrived, and pressed with godly impetuosity into the chapel,
where all were amazed, and praised the God of all marvels
when they saw that the holy pledge (the body of Simon) was
unchanged five weeks after his death, that no exhalation of
odour could be discovered or perceived, and that from his
death wounds there dropped continually fresh rose-coloured
blood. Wherefore persons even of the highest consideration
caught up this precious liquor with their pocket-handkerchiefs.
But others who were not provided with clean handkerchiefs,
or who could not get near enough for the great throng, made
their way to the old grave and tore away the bloody chippings
which lay therein. Afterwards the revered body was exposed
to view on this and the following day in the great hall of the
council house. But even there it was exceeding difficult to
approach it. At last on the 31st of March the funeral was
performed. An armed force in three ranks surrounded the
council house for two whole hours ; throughout the whole
city resounded the pealing bells of seventy churches. Meanwhile the synagogue and the whole body of Jews were ready
to swoon away with anguish, because they feared the ven-

geance of the Christian populace would fall upon them. It
was indeed almost a miracle that no deed of violence was
committed, for in the past year, the Christians had more than
once for the most trifling reasons, fallen upon and plundered
the frippery market and Jew town, and had also, as is well
known, attacked the Jews themselves, severely injuring and
even murdering some.

" When towards ten o'clock, the painters had finished a
double representation of the martyr Simon, the church ceremonies began.   After the coffin had been closed, the commissaries prepared to seal up the keyhole, but as the paper which
was to be sealed over the lock might be injured, they desired
to have a suitable silk ribbon, and when this became known
to the most noble persons present, they tore what they had of
such material from their heads, stomachers and arms.   His
Excellency the Reichsgraf von Martinez also unbound the
ribbon that was hanging from his sword-hilt.   But a ribbon
of red satin was chosen for this purpose, which the most noble
and right honourable the Countess Kolowrat had worn ; this
was cut in two and placed over the lock and sealed.   After
this the martyr's coffin was covered with a costly red velvet
pall prepared for the occasion ; in the middle of the funeral
bier was a fine picture of Our Lady, and on both sides angels
with palm branches.   Sixteen good youths of noble descent
bore the funeral bier on their innocent shoulders ; they wore
red mantles with gold lace glittering on them, and wreaths of
silvered roses wound with red silk.   Then the pealing of bells
sounded through all the three towns ; the clouds suddenly
cleared from off the heavens ; the multitude covered every
roof, and occupied every window ; they had flocked together,
not only from the three neighbouring vine-clad mountains, but
from distant places and cities.

" The city authorities led the host of the funeral train ;
after them followed the lately baptized young Jews, adorned

with red badges, before whom two church banners of like material were borne. Next a countless multitude of school-boys .from all the schools of the three towns, ranged under eight purple flags; thirdly all the young students from the under Latin schools. Fourthly above four hundred heads of the Latin brotherhood from the schools, before whom was carried cross and banner under a canopy with lighted wax tapers. They were followed by a fifth of the higher student brotherhood of Our Lady; among them many doctors, and assessors, and divers nobles of the Empire; before them also were borne the cross and banner with the canopy, and in their hands they carried burning wax tapers, and flaming white torches. Sixthly came the first set of choristers, then the clergy in their vestments, then the second set of choristers; after them the deacons, parish priests, and the very reverend the prebendaries with the officiating priests, and beside them went the city soldiers in long rows. Seventhly came the sixteen finely attired youths bearing the glorious corpse of the martyr Simon. On both sides of the coffin went twelve boys with burning. red torches, dressed in exquisitely beautiful purple linen. Eighthly following the coffin came the most noble the President and Governor of Königreichs, all holding red torches in their hands; they were followed by the most distinguished nobility of both sexes in great numbers, and lastly a countless multitude of God-fearing people.

" The accomplice of the murderer, Levi Hüsel Kurtzhandl, was the son of wealthy parents at Prague; he was tall, and twenty years of age, with a daring countenance, was passionate, had a bold eloquence and ready wit, and was perfectly acquainted with the Talmud, which he had studied eleven years. He had concealed himself with his Jewish bride nine miles from Prague. After diligent inquiries, armed men were despatched there who put him in irons, and brought him in a carriage to Prague on the 22nd of March. Although the commissaries, having formerly had similar cases, doubted whether the least atom of truth could be extracted from this flint, yet they confronted him with the witnesses. But notwithstanding the affidavits of three witnesses, he acknowledged nothing. He was threatened with the executioner and the rack, but that had no more effect upon him than threatening a crab with drowning. For he trusted he should be able to endure the rack, and so escape. Nay, he was hardy enough to say, that this trial was carried on contrary to all law and justice. Thus he was, according to law, condemned to the wheel on the evidence of three witnesses, though without his own confession.

"He however hindered the execution of the sentence for seven months, having by means of a Jewish relation brought the affair before his Imperial Majesty Leopold. The proceedings were now delayed by Jewish tricks, and so tardily carried on, that it might plainly be seen, that the culprit was only seeking a delay of some years in order to obtain a mitigation of punishment or to obviate it by a voluntary death. At last the tribunal obtained an order that the accused should deliver in his defence within fourteen days; his frivolous pleas were rejected, and the sentence of the tribunal confirmed by his Imperial Majesty. He however adhered to his declaration : 'I am innocent of the blood of the murdered boy.' This he oft repeated before Father Johannes Brandstedter of the Society of Jesus, an unwearied apostolical labourer, who met a blessed death four days after Kurtzhandl, from the virulent poison he had imbibed in the work of love by a sick bed. When he inquired of the condemned whether he could meet death with resignation, and exhorted him to the reception of the saving faith, Levi answered with a cheerful aspect and without embarrassment : 'I care as little for death as for this straw '—he held one in his hand, which he thereupon threw away—' but as concerns the faith, we will now argue out of the holy Scriptures which of us two holds the true faith. But the father must not think he has a common simple man before him, for I studied the Talmud for eleven years.'

" Thus began a controversy concerning the faith ; the priest attacked the Talmud with powerful theological evidence, and Levi apprehended everything by the strong capacity of his understanding.   At last he threw his Jewish bible away from him, impatiently saying : ' Let it be as it may, I abide by the faith in which I was born.'   As on the following day the obdurate youth began to harp upon the same string, the priest set about the matter again in another way ; he no longer spoke to him, but turned to his fellow-prisoners, and read to them divers evidence from the holy Scriptures, whereby he proved that the Messiah had already come.

" This, Levi listened to quietly and thoughtfully, and although he gave no indications of being inclined to the holy faith, yet it might be seen by his countenance that he was not as averse to the presence of the priest as yesterday.   On the third day Levi, hardened as he might be in other respects, yet desired that the father should return in the afternoon, as his presence was a special comfort to him in his miserable position. When the priest promised him this as an encouragement, the stony heart appeared softened. In the afternoon, the father in his holy simplicity placed such reliance on the Jew, that he removed all the others, and remaining alone with him, kindly and urgently begged of him to give both himself and him consolation, by relating at his pleasure, as the greatest secret, truly and faithfully, what he knew of the death of Simon.   At this unexpected address Levi was quite amazed ; he continued long silent ; but at last struck with the rare confidence shown by a Christian priest in a Jew, he conceived a high esteem for his uprightness, and persuaded by the father's promise of secrecy, confessed before him and one of his fellow-prisoners, with great signs of sorrow, with bent shoulders and head hanging down on the left side, that he had, at the instigation of the father Lazarus Abeles, laid violent hands on Simon, and caused his death from zeal for the law of Moses.

" Upon receiving this confession the priest was exceeding joyful, and strove with all his powers, by arguments and urgent entreaties, to persuade him to turn himself magnanimously to God.   But to this Levi would not return any satisfactory answer ; and when, as evening twilight was creeping on, the priest prepared to go home, Levi raised his eyes to heaven, and said with a deep sigh : 'Father, where shall I be at this time to-morrow ?'   Whereto the priest replied : 'My son, in heaven, if you embrace the Christian faith ; but if you die in Judaism, in hell as a hardened Jew.' Thereupon he in the most friendly way wished him a good night and a blessed end, and went away.

" On the following day the priest found the condemned man dressed in white linen for the impending tragedy, as if he had prepared himself to be baptized.   After a friendly greeting the father asked him in which faith he had at last resolved to die ?   Hereunto Levi returned this answer : 'I will die in the same faith in which Abraham, Isaac, and Jacob died. And as in the olden time Abraham offered up his son, so will I to-day sacrifice myself for my sins.'   When the priest made a further rejoinder, he said with a pleasant countenance and in a calm manner : 'I humbly beg of you, father, not to trouble me any more about baptism, for I will now pray from the Psalms and prepare myself for a happy death.'   Thereupon he began to repeat the Psalms, but without the girdle called a *Tephilim,* although the Jews usually consider prayer without binding the forehead and hands a sin.   But he prayed with such contrition of heart and such vehement beating of the breast, and penitential tears, that his fellow-prisoners and all present were greatly astonished at his remorse.

"After a prayer that had lasted more than two hours he gave himself up quickly into the hands of the executioner, and thus accosted him with a cheerful countenance : ' Do to me what God and my judges have commanded you.' He then turned to his fellow-prisoners, took a friendly leave of them, and humbly begged of them to forgive his past failings.

" After ten o'clock they took him, amidst the gaze of countless multitudes, from the prison, and bound him in a hide, whereat he showed no sign of impatience or displeasure. Only he sometimes raised his bound hands in prayer to heaven. Thus was he dragged by a horse to the field of action.. When he perceived that the accompanying priest in the middle of the Platz was in danger of being severely injured by a horse, he begged with sympathizing voice that he might go in front to avoid the danger."

Thus far the Jesuit's narrative. On the scaffold Levi made a manly confession of his deed before all the people, with a request that the witnesses who had only spoken the truth should no longer be kept in prison. The details of the execution were particularly horrible ; the experienced executioner could not—so the writer states—break the strong body of the criminal on the wheel. At last Levi called to the priest by his side and asked him in a clear voice what he would promise if he should consent to be baptized ? When the father promised him, besides forgiveness of all his sins, also a speedy death, Levi answered : ' I will be baptized.' The Church triumphant hastened to impart private baptism, much disposed to attribute this unheard of bodily strength and calm of the malefactor to a special miracle of Divine Providence. Levi repeated the prescribed formula with a strong voice, and received calmly the now effective stroke of death.

This is the sorrowful history of Simon Abeles. Whoever judges the Jesuit narrative impartially will discover in it

something which the narrator wishes to conceal; and whoever contemplates with horror the fanatical murder, will
nevertheless not spend much sympathy on the fanatical
priests.   They tear the scarcely born child out of the arms
of its mother; they consider it a pious contrivance to steal
the suckling secretly from her, by means of spies and tale-
bearers; by promises and threatenings, and excitement of the
imagination, they win hosts of proselytes in baptism to their
God, who is very unlike the God of the gospel; with the
skill of experienced managers, they make use of a miserable
murder, for the sake of bringing on the scene a real tragedy,
and of the dead body of a Jewish boy, in order by pomp and
glitter and enormous processions, and if possible by miracles,
to recommend their faith to both Christians and Jews.
Their fanaticism, in alliance with the burgher magistracy
and the compliant law, stands in comparison with that of a
despised, persecuted, and impulsive race; cunning, violence,
malice and a corrupt morality, are to be discovered on both
sides.

During yet two generations, the zeal of the Jesuits against
the Jews continued to work, the struggle of two foreign communities on German ground.   The one consisted of the sons
of the old dwellers in the wilderness, whose leader, the Lord
Jehovah, brought them forth with their flocks and herds,
going before them in the fiery pillar, and pouring his wrath
on all who fell away from him.   And opposed to these were
the followers of a Spanish nobleman, who had undertaken the
monstrous task of forming the souls of men like the wheels of
a machine, making all the highest intellectual powers serve
the one single object, of a priesthood to the one appointed
officer of the great head of the church militant, Jesus.

What were Loyola and his school to the ancient Abeles
and to Levi Kurtzhandl? How ancient was Loyola? Their
fathers had slaughtered the sacrificial victim three thousand

years before the first Jesuit had tortured a Jewish heart ;
their descendants, they were sure, would offer sacrifice three
thousand years later in the kingdom of Messiah, after the last
Jesuit had been collected to his mother Lilith.   The fearful
S. J. which shone in gold on the stones of the college, how
long would it last ?   In the time of their grandfathers it had
its origin, in the time of their grandchildren it would be
erased.   What was this new device to the seed of Abraham ?
An extravagance, a short plague of Egypt.   Proudly did the
Roman Catholic church look back on seventeen hundred years
of victory and conquest, but more proudly did the despised
Jew look upon his past, which stretches back to the dawn of
the world, for his faith was seventeen hundred years old
when Christ was baptized.   Both the judgment of the pious
fathers of the Church and the pious Jews was narrowed,
and their comprehension of the Highest disturbed by old
traditions.

When Jehovah spoke to Moses on the mountain, his law
became the groundwork of a higher moral law, to the hordes
in the desert ; when Jesus proclaimed to the apostles the gracious message of love, his teaching was a holy treasure for
the human race.   Since then, the Jews have continued unweariedly to solemnize their Passover ; still do they shun the
meat of the swine, and swing the young cocks on atonement
day ; but the foundation of their faith has long vanished, also
their pastoral state on the borders of the Syrian wilderness.
For many centuries also, the pious fathers of the Roman
Catholic church have offered their holy sacrifice daily ; but they
also, have already ceased to be the most pre-eminent of those
who live under the law of the new covenant.   The Bohemian
peasant, who benevolently raised up the sick Jew on the high
road, without tormenting the soul of the stranger with efforts
to convert him, was more Christian than they ; that man of
science, who risked his life under the anger of the Church,

that he might understand how the lightning was made by
God, and the earth caused to revolve, was more a proclaimer
of the Eternal, than they ; and that citizen who died for his
duty, in order to teach that the general weal is of more value
than that of individuals, was nearer the most perfect pattern,
than they.   Among them also, undoubtedly, were many good
highminded men ; the Jesuit, Friedrich Spee, met his death
in a pesthouse, like that sailor in the flames.   But those who
thus lived, are precious to us because they showed themselves
to be good men ; whether they were considered good priests
we know not.   When this same Spee protested so vehemently
against the burning of witches, which his Church so zealously
carried on, he published his writings, without his name, in a
Protestant place.

Since Moses, and since the first feast of Pentecost, the
Lord had never left himself without witnesses ; he had given
the nations of the earth a new culture, had led them to a
higher civilisation.   He had given them a new code of morals,
he had unlocked the other half of the earth, he had willed
that the new spirit in men should be contained in the narrow
space of one book, which might pass from hand to hand, from
one soul to another, from one century to every succeeding
one.   Restlessly and unceasingly did the Divine Spirit agitate
and stir the hearts of men ; ever more mighty and more
holy did these manifestations of the Eternal, appear to men of
powerful intellect ; it was a different manifestation to that of
the old writings, it was also another word of God, another
aspect of the Eternal, which was discovered.   Thus men now
sought the God of the human race, of the earth, of the uni-
verse, not only in the old faith but also in science.   Together
with the Jesuits and Jews there was Leibnitz.

This new culture has elevated the Jews ; their fanaticism
has vanished since the Christian zeal which persecuted them
has ceased, and the descendants of that wandering Asiatic

race have become our countrymen and fellow combatants. But the ecclesiastical community of the Society of Jesus, already once expelled, then revived again, remains to this day what it was at the beginning of its emigration into Germany—alien to the German life.

CHAPTER XII.

THE WASUNGER WAR.
(1747.)

The great century of enlightenment began with blood and the thunder of cannon. The Spanish war of succession raged on the western frontier, within the distracted realm. Bavaria and Cologne fought under the ban of the Empire, in alliance with Louis XIV. against the house of Hapsburg.

The constitution of the Empire had become weak. In the east the Hohenzollens already held a powerful position by the side of the Hapsburgers; from the beginning of the century they had become kings independent of the Empire, and the Electoral house of Saxony, had shortly before obtained the insecure possession of the Polish Electoral throne.

Condemned witches were still burnt on the funeral pile; the ecclesiastics of three persuasions still carried on a wearisome strife; the intolerance of the Church, the pressure of poverty, want of great political interests, and the pitifulness of the small sovereigns and their courts, still weighed upon the masses.

Ever wider became the separation of classes. Etiquette only permitted the princes to have intercourse with the citizens in particular cases, and under prescribed forms. It therefore occurred sometimes that a good paternal ruler disguised himself as a private man, withdrew into a chamber apart, put on his old dressing-gown, and took a pipe in his mouth, in order to be enabled to have direct intercourse with his citizens, and thus learn their wishes from themselves. During such hours his princely dignity was, to a certain degree, suspended, but instantly he quitted the room he was again within courtly interdict.

Yet it was just at this period that numerous mesalliances took place. Among many of the higher nobility, wild nature broke through the restraint of court usage, and more than once a city maiden had the doubtful advantage of becoming the persecuted wife of a Prince of old family. Seldom did the wife obtain from the Emperor the rights of equal birth; the marriages were generally morganatic, and the children refused the succession.

Among the German princes, the course of whose life was changed by a union of this kind, was Anthony Ulrich, Duke of Saxe Meiningen; born in 1687, the youngest of three brothers, he became, according to the custom of his house, joint ruler of the country, that is to say, the elder brother exercised the rights of sovereignty, but the younger ones received a portion of the revenues of the country. In his youth, this prince had travelled; in the war of succession he had served through some campaigns as an Imperial officer; and at the peace of Rastatt, he quitted the army with the rank of Major-general. A fiery youth, courteous and accomplished, affable as becomes young princes, not without an interest in intellectual pursuits, he had, following the prevailing fashion, zealously collected objects of art and natural curiosities; with a lively disposition and chivalrous demeanour, he was the favourite of the country which he only nominally ruled. Whatever entered into his head, he carried on wilfully and recklessly, with an iron perseverance which might have led him to great things. Then it became his lot to fall in love with Philippine Cesar, the daughter of a Hessian captain, lady of the bed-chamber to his sister, the Abbess of Gandersheim; he took her to Holland and married her.

For many years he did not avow his marriage. His life became unsettled; he kept his wife concealed in Amsterdam, and strictly commanded his servants to keep secret his place of residence; he received letters from home in roundabout ways, and was always moving to and fro in the land of his fathers. But when his wife became more precious to him, and sons were born, the stubbornness of his nature was brought forth, he revealed his marriage, and required of his family the recognition of it, and the right of succession for his children.

The displeasure of his proud house now broke out. The recognition was denied. Such a marriage was considered by the Court altogether monstrous, but it was always doubtful whether the decisions of feudal law were competent to declare this marriage invalid. Therefore the Dukes of Saxony met together in 1717, and decided that all unequal unions in their house were to be considered as only morganatic, and the children were never to be allowed the rights of succession.*

Anthony Ulrich remained firm. He solicited the Imperial court, and strove unweariedly against the council of the country, who took advantage of this quarrel to diminish the revenues of the Duke. But his nature was not easily bent. When in 1722, the last feudal tenant of Altenstein, one Hund von Wenckheim lay dying, and the commissaries of the government were standing by the death-bed to take possession of the vacant fief, Anthony Ulrich rode suddenly into the court of the castle, and in spite of the protest of the councillors, who were also his servants, entered the chamber

* It was particularly offensive to them, as an elder sister of Anton Ulrich's wife had just married the master of the Ducal Chapel, Schurmann, at Meiningen.

of the dying man, sang with him the evening song and the penitential hymn, and passed the night, armed with pistols and other weapons, in the castle. As soon as the vassal had closed his eyes, he entered the room, and according to the old usage took possession of the vacant fief, and seating himself in a red velvet arm-chair, said : " I hereby take possession of my third share, without prejudice to the two-thirds of my brothers." He then called in his attendants as witnesses, and according to the prescribed usage, struck his hand forcibly on the table, so that a jug upset, symbolical of the moveable property, and caused a chip to be cut out of the door of the chamber of death, and of the dining-room. After this he swore into his service all who had not fled ; he then rode out, cut splinters from the oak wood, and bits of turf from the meadows, as further tokens of having taken possession, and went back to Meiningen. But when he returned to the castle, he found the gates closed and guarded by grenadiers, and all his threats and protestations were of no avail.

He afterwards wished to take his wife and children to one of his own possessions, and lead a peaceable life at home. But such was not his happy lot. His brothers obtained a decision from the Imperial high court of judicature, according to which he was not to take his wife and children into the country of his fathers, and if he should venture to do so, he was never to usurp for them the title of princes. He now however went himself to Vienna and so worked there, with the help of large sums of money, and through the medium of his military acquaintances—the Spanish minister, the Marquis of Perlas was his supporter—that the Emperor Charles VI. raised his wife Philippine to the dignity of Princess of the holy Roman Empire, and her sons and daughters to be dukes and duchesses of Saxony, with all the privileges and rights, *i.e.* those of the succession.

Against this, the whole house of Saxony, and those of

Hohenzollen and Hesse, who were interested by the settlement of succession, rose in opposition. At first, however,
Anthony Ulrich was victor. His eldest brother died, and the
second was a weak man. So he became in 1729, the real
ruler of the country. Then he brought his wife and eldest
son under the ducal roof at Meiningen. For eleven years
the stubborn prince rejoiced in having established his own
will. But the struggle with his house had embittered him ;
and added to restlessness and violence, a litigious spirit had
come over him. Peevish and endless were the disputes about
the government, and the discord with his brothers and his
favourites ; the little country was divided into two parties ;
ministers and officials threw themselves on the one or the
other side, and sometimes the machine of government stood
still. The Duke lived generally with his wife and children
out of the country, at Vienna. The legal proceedings with
the agnates about the equality of birth, which still continued,
and vexatious quarrels with neighbours, gave him but a
gloomy satisfaction. He had gained no trifling knowledge of
the forms of public law, and conducted all his suits himself.
They seem to have taken up the greater part of his time.

But the victory was to be followed by a sad reverse. The
new Emperor of the house of Wittelsbacher, Charles VII., was
with very evident reference to Anthony Ulrich's affair, bound
on oath not to legitimatize any notorious mesalliances, and to
declare the right of inheritance of such children null and
void. Therefore the rank given to the Duchess of Meiningen
and her children was repealed. Anthony Ulrich had recourse
to the Diet. But in vain. This also declared that his
application must be refused, and the Emperor Francis I. of
Lorraine confirmed this decision.

It was a cruel stroke of destiny. The wife of the Duke
had the good fortune not to outlive the last Imperial decision ;
she died a few weeks previous to it ; whilst her husband was

fruitlessly setting heaven and earth in motion at Frankfort to ward off this fate. But the two parties quarrelled even over her coffin. The brother, and co-ruler with the Duke, refused to allow the corpse to be buried in the royal hereditary vault, nay even denied her the usual tolling of the bells for royal personages. Anthony Ulrich rushed furiously from Frankfort and commanded the tolling and the burial in the royal vault. Orders and counter orders crossed each other during several weeks ; now the tolling began and now it was stopped. As Anthony Ulrich, who had again hastened to Frankfort, had commanded that the coffin should not be deposited anywhere but in the royal burial place, it was kept in a room in the castle covered over with sand ; there it remained a year and a half, till in 1746, Anthony Ulrich's last brother died. Then the Duke in order to give satisfaction to his wife even in death, caused his brother's corpse after lying in state, to be placed in the same room next his wife's coffin and like hers to be covered over with sand. There the two coffins remained for a year, when they were both quietly deposited at the same time in the royal burial place.

Now Anthony Ulrich, once the youngest of his family, remained sole ruler and the eldest of his race, but Meiningen was a source of annoyance to him. He could not take his dear children home as Dukes, therefore he went to them at Frankfort. His agnates could scarcely conceal the impatience with which they awaited for his death in order to take possession of the inheritance of the last of the Meiningens. He had passed the greater part of his life in struggle with them ; now he would be revenged. Out of spite to them he married at the age of sixty-three a Princess of Hesse-Philippsthal. He had ten children by his first wife and eight by his second. He announced every fresh birth to the agnates on a sheet of the largest royal folio.

He died at Frankfort-on-the-Main in 1763. Even in his last

testament the stubborn determination breaks forth, of bringing the two sons of his first marriage into the country as co-heirs. All the children of the first marriage died unmarried.

His was an unprofitable life, but it well deserves the sympathy of a later 'generation. A strong passion disturbed his days up to his last hours. Mixed with a great love, a stream of gall penetrated into his heart, flowing unceasingly; his time, his money and all his talents were spent in the most sorrowful of all struggles—in family disputes. His brilliant youth gave great promise, yet how profitless to others, nay to himself, was his whole manhood. In his old age he dwelt in a foreign city, divided between his past and his new domestic life, to which he could never get thoroughly accustomed. His spirit, once so lively and active, and his unbending will, were so engrossed with his personal affairs, that when he became the real ruler of his country he no longer took an interest in doing his duty.

It was not unnatural that Anthony Ulrich should, from his own experience, entertain a repugnance to the pretensions of the lower nobility at court, and it was quite in accordance with his character, to display his hatred when opportunities offered. This he did shortly after the death of his first wife, to the bereaved court at Meiningen.

In the royal palace at Meiningen the *Frau Landjägermeisterin*, (wife of the Grand Master of the chase), Christiane Auguste von Gleichen held the highest rank. Among the other ladies who had a right to be there, was a Frau von Pfaffenrath, born Countess Solms, but yet only the wife of a councillor, who had only just been ennobled, and to whom she had been married in a not very regular way, for her husband had been tutor in her parents' house : she had eloped with him, and had after many troubles accomplished a reconciliation with her mother, and obtained a diploma of nobility for her husband. Now Duke Anthony Ulrich, who

1747.]   THE WASUNGER WAR.   357

was residing at Frankfort, protected her, because, as the court whispered, her sister had the advantage of being in the good graces of the old gentleman. Naturally, she ought only to have ranked according to the patent of her husband, but alas! she raised pretensions because she was of high nobility. When therefore in October 1746, the doors of the dining-room were to be opened, and the page was standing ready to repeat grace, the Master-of-the-Horse entered and said to the *Frau Landjägermeisterin :* " His most Serene Highness has commanded that the Frau von Pfaffenrath shall take rank before all other ladies. Frau von Gleichen answered that she would never consent to that, but the Frau von Pfaffenrath had placed herself favourably and took the precedence of the *Frau Landjägermeisterin* before she could prevent it. Yet this determined lady was far from submitting tamely. She hastened round the table to the Duke's cabinet minister, and declared to him, as became a lady of character after such an insult : " If *Frau von* Pfaffenrath again goes before me to table, I will pull her back even to the sacrifice of her hooped gown, and will say a few words which will be very disagreeable to her." The cabinet minister was in a great embarrassment, for he knew the resolute character of *Frau von* Gleichen. At last he advised her to rise from the table before grace, then she would at all events go out first and so get the precedence. Thus the *Landjägermeisterin* maintained her place, but she was much offended, and so was the whole court, which split into two parties. This quarrel of the ladies made a commotion in the whole of the holy Roman Empire, occasioned a campaign between Gotha and Meiningen, and was only ended by Frederick the Great, in a manner which reminds one of the fable of the lion which took the royal share for himself.

Frau von Gleichen appealed to the absent Duke for reparation. She only received a strong and ungracious answer.

Irritated at this, she made inquiries into the former life of her
enemy, and propagated an anonymous writing, in which the
love affairs of the Countess were described with more energy
than delicacy. The *Frau von* Pfaffenrath complained of this
lampoon to the sovereign at Frankfort, and afterwards began
a course of proceedings against the *Frau Landjägermeisterin*
which even then was considered harsh and cruel. She was
called upon to crave pardon of the *Frau von* Pfaffenrath, on her
knees entreating her most penitently for forgiveness ; and when
she refused with these words : " I would die first," she was
taken in arrest to the council-house and there guarded by two
musketeers ; her husband also was put in an unhealthy prison.
Unshaken by such great sufferings the *Frau Landjägermeisterin*, in a beautiful letter full of self-reliance and noble sentiments, petitioned the Duke for her husband's freedom, her own
dismission from the service of the court, and permission to in-
stitute a legal defence against the Pfaffenrath. All this was
denied her. She was on the contrary carried by two musketeers into the room of the Pfaffenrath in order to beg pardon,
and when she again refused, she was taken into the market-
place of Meiningen surrounded by a circle of soldiers, and the
sheriff read aloud a decree, in which it was proclaimed to the
people, that the lampoon was to be burnt before the eyes of the
Landjägermeisterin by the hangman, and every one was forbidden, on pain of six weeks' imprisonment and a fine of a
hundred thalers, ever to speak again on the subject. The
letter was burnt by the hangman and *Frau von* Gleichen again
taken back to prison.

But now the friends of the Gleichen brought a complaint
before the Imperial chamber. But the repeated mandates of
the Chamber to Duke Anthony Ulrich and his government, to
give freedom to the Gleichens and to proceed according to
law, were not obeyed. After that Duke Friedrich III. of
Gotha, received a commission from the same tribunal to defend

Frau von Gleichen and her husband from further violence, and to deliver them from imprisonment in Meiningen, yet keep them in honourable custody. Duke Friedrich demanded the delivery of the prisoners from Meiningen, but his commissioners were not admitted into the city, nor his letter accepted; but it was signified to him, that if Gotha should attempt to free them by force, there was plenty of powder and shot at Meiningen. Betwixt Meiningen and Gotha there were endless quarrels and great bitterness.

Thereupon Duke Friedrich of Gotha prepared himself for armed intervention. He was a warlike Prince, who maintained a subsidiary force of six thousand infantry and fifteen hundred horse in the Dutch and Imperial service. He had, besides a large number of guns, a strong corps of officers and several Generals. On the other hand the military strength of Meiningen was small; it consisted almost entirely of the old fortifications and unskilled militia. These were assembled, and Meiningen was fortified as well as was possible in such haste. But it was not destined that Meiningen itself should become the scene of action, for the fury of war raged only about the town of Wasungen. It was indeed a remarkable coincidence that this place should become the theatre of war, for scandal says that it was considered the shield or place of refuge of Meiningen; and in the country there is a lying story about its councillors and a large gourd. The councillors mistook the gourd for the egg of a foreign horse which was to be hatched for the good of the town by the united powers of the councillors.

The struggle which then took place in the centre of Germany, between the Thuringian states of Gotha and Meiningen, is known by the name of the Wasunger war. In a military point of view it is of no importance, but is characteristic of the period. All the misery in the German Empire, the decaying state of the burgher life, the coarse immorality of the politics of that time, the meannesses, pedantry, and helplessness of the Imperial army, are shown to such an extent, that they might be a source of amusement, if they did not give rise to a more serious and better feeling, bringing to light the helplessness of the German Empire.

The narrative is here given by Lieutenant Rauch of Gotha, who took part in the war. He speaks in his diary as follows : —

" Early on the 15th of February, precisely at one o'clock, our whole division broke up from Tambach, and marched with burning torches through the wood beyond the so-called Rosengarten, in order that we might enter at break of day the Hessian village Flohe ; we knew not whither we were going. We continued our march through the city of Smalkalden up to Middle Smalkalden.

" When the cavalry came to the Meiningen village Niederschmalkalden, a Lieutenant, with about four-and-twenty militia men, stood right across the road, and would not let us pass. Here all three corps were obliged to halt. Major von Benkendorf, together with the Lieutenant-Colonel, rode up to the Lieutenant who was commanding there ; and the Major asked him what he meant by not letting us pass, and whether this was not a public road ? The Lieutenant answered : ' Yes ! it was a high road, but he had orders not to let us pass. Major Benkendorf might say what he liked, the Lieutenant would not listen to him.' The Major then took a letter out of his pocket which he wished to show him ; but neither would he take that. Whereupon the Major said to the Lieutenant : if he would not let him pass with his people he would force his way.

" The Lieutenant answered shortly, that we might do so, as he had not sufficient force to prevent him. The Major rode immediately to the guards, drew his sword, and approached the Lieutenant to see whether he would consent to treat; but he would not stir from the spot.   The Major asked him once more, whether he would yield up the ground ? But he remained firm.   Thereupon the Major gave his orders to the guard : March ! March ! and broke through.

"While they were passing, it happened that one of the horses pushed against the Meiningen Lieutenant and threw him down.   But he soon recovered himself, seized his weapon, and shot the serjeant-major of the guards, Starke, and then took to flight.   A horseman however, whose name was Stähm, pursued him forthwith, and would have cut his head in two, but the Lieutenant held his weapon obliquely over his head, so that the horseman Stähm cut in half the powder sack on the barrel.   But my good old Lieutenant thought he would run further, and sprang over a ditch, where the horseman might not be able to follow him, and thought he was now safe.   But the grenadier Hellbich fired and shot my old Lieutenant Zimmermann behind the right ear as he ran, so that he fell suddenly to the ground, and not a muscle quivered. The militia still standing there looked on at the game ; but the grenadiers fired some grenades among them, and they then took to their heels and ran away.

"Meanwhile all the streets of the village had been barricaded with carts and wagons ; but the Mayor and the peasants seeing their old Lieutenant lying dead, whom they had at all times considered as their bulwark, and observing that some grenades had fallen into their gardens, were in great terror, and began to ring the alarm bells that all the peasants might speedily assemble.

"In a moment all the wagons and carts were moved out of the way so that we might march.   The militia had fled to the village of Schwallungen, through which also we had to pass, and where again there was an officer in command of thirty militia, to whom they reported what had taken place in the village of Niederschmalkalden.   So the officer, who was

a shoemaker by profession, when he heard this report from the
fugitives, took such of his men as would go with him and tore
off to Wasungen before he had even caught sight of us.

"When we came to the afore-mentioned village, we formed
ourselves in column, fixed our bayonets, and thought what
will now take place? We marched on, and when we came to
the gate the officer and all the troops had fled, and there was
not a single man to make resistance. We marched straight
through with fixed bayonets; then we saw the portion that
had remained of the runaway shoemaker-Ensign's troop in
their uniform, with their cartridge boxes, peeping out of the
windows.

"My good shoemaker-Ensign was off, and had posted himself and the men who thus went out with him at the gate of
Wasungen, where again a Lieutenant, who was a good barber
—as I knew by experience, having myself been shaved by
him—had posted himself, and was awaiting us. The gate
of Wasungen was firmly closed with strong double doors, but
a sentinel stood without; so Major von Benkendorf called to
him that the gate must be opened. But the sentinel excused
himself, saying he could not. The said Major asked him,
'Who is there besides?' He answered: 'The Lieutenant.'
The Major said he must call his Lieutenant; whereupon he
ran hastily and fetched him out. Then came up my good
barber Lieutenant; the man was already well nigh dead of
fright, and his face was whiter than his shirt. The Major
accosted him sharply, asking how it was that the gates were
fastened, and whether a public high road did not pass through
there? He answered, Yes! So Major von Benkendorf said
he must that instant open the gates, or we would do it ourselves. When he heard this, being half dead with fright, he
begged for pardon, saying it was not he that could open the
gates, but the councillors who had closed them. The answer
was, that he must forthwith produce the councillors. Good

gracious! was there ever any one more glad than the good barber, who ran as if his head was burning; but meanwhile there was nothing seen or heard of the shoemaker-Ensign.

" At last the councillors came.

" When I saw these men creeping out of the little gate, I thought, ' What the devil! are these councillors? they are a fine lot!' The councillors looked a little respectable, but the burghermaster was up to the knees in cow-dung, and must have been fetched from clearing away the dung in the stable. Hereupon, Major von Benkendorf asked whether they were the councillors? They answered: ' Yes, and what did we desire?' The Major asked whether this was not the high-road to Nuremberg? They said, ' Yes.' ' Why then were the gates closed and barricaded, and we not allowed to pass through?' Then the president of the council answered: ' They were commanded by their government not to let any troops pass through, therefore they must keep the gates closed; they must do what their master commanded them.' But Major von Benkendorf repeated his former words, and said to them: ' They must open to us, and that quickly, for that we must march further; and if they did not open, we would do it ourselves.' The president of the council answered this, and said: ' We might do as we liked, but he could not open the gates to us.' But the dung-bespattered burgher-master then began: ' Nay! if you wish to march further, you can do so by the back road.' I thought to myself, ' If thou couldst but kill that cursed dirty fellow!' The Major then forthwith called to me, and desired that all the carpenters of the whole division should be summoned; which was done in a moment. Hereupon he asked once more whether they would amicably open the gate? if not, he would have them immediately hewn open. They might now see that we ourselves would open the gates if they did not prefer preserving them whole.

"The Major thought they would resolve to open them, but they said they would not, and we might do what we liked. Hereupon the Major called out: 'Proceed carpenters! hew the gates down!' Thereupon the carpenters set to work. When the knocking and cracking began, it was well worth seeing how the councillors, among whom was the Burghermaster, and the frightened barber-Lieutenant, began to run, as if carried off by the devil. In a moment both gates were hewn down, and the whole detachment marched with trumpets, drums, and fifes, into the city.

"As we marched in through the gates, the good barber-Lieutenant, and the shoemaker-Ensign, with their men, presented arms, and saluted both the officers of our detachment.

"Here we stopped, just as we were; everyone was hungry and thirsty. We officers made the citizens fetch us something to drink, and stood looking at and questioning one another. The snow was lying on the ground, and our men began to be impatient. I went to the inn where the Lieutenant-Colonel was in consultation with his officers; they were deliberating, and I could not speak with them. The citizens were already beginning to kindle their lights, and it did not appear how the affair was to end.

"At last the Lieutenant-Colonel came and sent forthwith to the councillors, who were already assembled in their council-room, deliberating what report they should make to Meiningen concerning the hewing down of their gates. But the president of the council had got scent of it, so he kept apart, and left the others to themselves, for all men could see that we could not go any further, as it was night. Now as the president was away, no one would go to the Lieutenant-Colonel, and each kept calling upon the other to go. At last one consented, and said: 'Some one must go, let what will happen.' When therefore he came to the Lieutenant-Colonel,

it was represented to him that the town must provide us with
accommodation for the night, whether they liked or not.
The Lieutenant-Colonel also added, that we should march
very early on the morrow; that the citizens were not bound
to give the smallest thing to the soldiers, who had to live on
their pay; therefore he need not deliberate any more about
it. The councillor begged to be excused, but said he could
do nothing himself, he must lay the matter before his colleagues, and see what they were disposed to do.

"Hereupon I marched forth again with the good councillor
to the Schlundhouse, where the other councillors were sitting.
When I entered the room with the plenipotentiary, he
delivered the Lieutenant-Colonel's message to them, in his
own words: 'That the Commander desired to have night-
quarters for his men, and that on the morrow at sunrise, they
would again march; that he could not help the citizens; they
must do so whether they chose or not; if they would not
do it, they must tell Lieutenant Rauch; in which case, he
would quarter the soldiers in houses according to the custom
with troops; they would get what they wanted, for soldiers
must live on their pay. No citizen was bound to give them
anything but a warm room and a place of rest.'

"Now every one shall hear what passed amongst these
councillors. The first who began, said: 'I do not assent
to this. Who asked them to wait so long here? they might
long ere now have marched away, if they had chosen.'
Another said: 'You are right, cousin Kurtz; I would rather
tear myself in pieces than consent.' The third then said:
'So, ho! first they hew down our gates, and then, forsooth,
they cannot go further, and expect us to give them quarters:
most decidedly not!' The fourth now spoke: 'The honourable Commander seems to be an honest man, but let him say
what he will, there is no doubt that we must provide food for
them, for truly they bring nothing with them.' The fifth

then began : ' That is right, cousin Hopf : do you not remember how it fared with us when the Imperial cavalry
came ? they behaved in like manner ; and afterwards we
could not get rid of them, but were obliged to keep them
with a good grace.' The sixth said : ' This will never do ;
we cannot provide them with quarters till we have received
orders from our government, otherwise we shall be punished.'
The seventh spoke thus : ' Did I not tell you, gentlemen,
what would happen, by keeping these people so long outside ?
Truly the President, Herr Läufer, has made off, and slips his
head out of the noose, leaving us to bear the brunt. Take
heed ; they say they will be off to-morrow, but they have been
marching yesterday and to-day, and to-morrow they will
make a day of rest, as they will need repose. Rest assured
that I am right ; what think you, gentlemen ? suppose we
were to send a messenger on horseback to Meiningen ?'

"I had listened to all the discussions of the councillors,
and now I began, and said : ' Gentlemen, you come to no
conclusion ; I will inform my Commander of it, let it fare
with you as it may.' But he who had gone with me to the
Lieutenant-Colonel, begged me to wait but a little, and they
would just send to the treasurer and city clerk to confer with
them. Here the strife began again, none would go thither.
At last one of them allowed himself to be persuaded, but soon
returned again, saying they had both ridden off when we
hewed down the gates. Then I said, ' Now, gentlemen, do
what you like ; I will not wait a moment longer.'

" Thereupon the eighth and last began to speak, he who
had accompanied me to the Lieutenant : ' Gentlemen, what
shall we do ; here they are, and you have heard what the
Commander says : if we will allot them no quarters, he will
let his soldiers go into whatsoever houses they please ; if they
fill your houses it is no fault of mine. I go home to close
mine. As many as come to my share I will take ; the others

I will show to your houses. You have heard of to-day's
misfortunes. At Smalkalden, friend Böhler's brother-in-law,
Lieutenant Zimmermann, is dead ; our gates have been hewn
down ; below are the soldiers thundering out curses. Gentlemen, let us billet them. The soldiers in the market-place
say they only wish they had shot the peasants who were with
the Lieutenant. What a calamity that would have been !
They say also that more shall be shot ; that one shall not be
the last. Thus you see that the same misfortune might come
upon us also. Ah ! gentlemen, if we had but such a prince
as he of Gotha is ! but ours troubles himself not about us ; he
lives comfortably at Frankfort, and let what will come to us,
he cares not. And who knows wherefore this has begun ?
These soldiers assuredly have not come for a pastime. One
can learn nothing from them. And how soon one night will
pass, or even two ! They are our border neighbours too ;
why should we not give them a night's lodging ?'

"They all agreed to this and sought for their old rate of
tax ; whereupon I had to tell them the whole strength of our
division.

"After that, I received an order to enjoin upon the soldiers,
when they received their billets, that they were not to un-
dress themselves, but were each of them to place his weapon
by his bedside, and soon as a call was heard, every soldier
was instantly to join his commanding officer fully armed, and
if any one was found in a state of drunkenness, he was to be
punished by running the gauntlet of the whole division ;
therefore an order was to be given directly to the assistant
executioner, to cut this very evening six hundred rods.

"None of the officers undressed themselves ; for the most
part they remained in company together, in order to be alert
on the morrow. When morning approached, the citizens as
well as the officers were listening for the beating of the drum.
They also had probably passed an unquiet night ; wherefore ?

because they were badly provided with beds, and had given them up perhaps to the soldiers for a douceur. This one might conclude, as in all the houses lights were to be seen throughout the night. In the morning, instead of the call from the staff of the grenadier guards, the réveille was beaten. Now, every soldier knows well, that beating the réveille signifies remaining quiet, or a day of rest; so we put our heads together to guess what this might mean. The citizens, also, when they saw that the soldiers did not break up, and prepare to march, laid their heads together likewise, and there was a great amount of whispering among them. My host, himself a councillor, came and asked me what was the meaning of our not marching further? I could give him no information.

"Now the misery began; there was only food for him who had brought bread. The citizens quarrelled with the soldiers, and asked why they had not marched away yesterday or early to-day, and whither we had intended to go? They told them the truth. It was such an uproar as is impossible to describe. The poor citizens who possessed no goods or houses, fled, and their dwellings were broken open by the soldiers, and one excess was committed after another.

"Meanwhile, all the councillors and burgermasters were called to Meiningen, where they were charged by their government, on pain of punishment, to signify to the citizens that they were not to provide anything for the Saxe Gotha soldiers. The bakers were not to bake, nor the butchers to slaughter the beasts; the innkeepers were not to prepare any food, nor the brewers to brew. This the councillors actually proclaimed to the citizens. And truly I was not able to get even three-pennyworth of cheese. The citizens who were prudent people, begged of us not to take it amiss of them; as we must accept good words instead of what they would have given us. If I wanted bread I had to send to Smalkalden for it, and give more pay to the messenger than for the bread.

"Thus we remained there, expecting the Meiningens, who never came. Meanwhile we found provisions ; we got most of them from Smalkalden ; the beer was bought in the Hessian village of Tambach, and the Jews brought us meat. At last the Wasungers became disloyal, turned round on their magistrates and said : ' We have all the troubles, and the other states the enjoyment ; this does not suit us ; we have promised to obey our government, but then they should protect us. If they cannot rid us of these people, we will bake, brew, and cook.' And from that hour they began to do all. For many years the citizens had not brewed nor sold so much beer as after this ; every week three and four brews ; bakers began to bake, who had long shut up shop ; the butchers did the like. Then the wise councillors went off again to Meiningen and reported everything ; whereupon the citizens were again cited to the town house, on a penalty of twenty gulden. But they were refractory and would not go, but sent thither their barefooted children, and heeded no more commands. When these wise councillors found this, they themselves began to brew.

"On the 22nd of May, on Whit Monday, 1747, an order must probably have come from Major S—— of which we officers learnt nothing. Hereupon there was a running and scampering to the Privy Councillor Flörcke at the ' Bear,' which was quite astounding ; now they ran in and now out. I thought : ' What the devil is the matter ?' yet I thought, if something is passing, I shall hear of it. The citizens also began to inquire : ' Wherefore is all this running to the commander at the " Bear ?" ' But I could give no answer.

"Whilst all this running hither and thither was going on, I went with Ensign Köhler to inspect the sentinels, and when we arrived at the upper gate, Majors von S—— and von

B—— and Captain von W—— met us. Major von S——
came straight up to me and asked me secretly, whether I had
heard any news? I answered, No; whereupon he inquired
of me, whether I knew that the Meiningens meant to attack
us that night? I replied: 'Well and good; if they come
they must knock pretty loud, we will be ready for them.'
He then said, would I wish to send my wife away? 'No,'
said I, 'she only came on holy Whitsun eve, and will not go
away till the day following Whit Sunday.' 'Indeed,' he
continued; 'but if the Meiningens come?' 'I shall gird a
sword round her,' was my answer, 'and she may defend herself.'

"Then Major S—— continued, saying, 'I was to make
my dispositions here, and see that all the gates and posts
were defended.' This is truly being deceived with one's eyes
open; to make dispositions before the eyes of men and not to
keep them!

"When I came down I called out to the soldiers: 'Attention! cease that chattering.' Then I began to arrange the
right wing, but had hardly placed four or five files, when
Captain W—— came running, and asked me, whether I had
not heard that I was to come with him directly. Here came
out the first result of their council of war. I did not delay
long, but ran directly to the Major, and asked what commands he had to give me; whereunto he answered, that I
was to take thirty dragoons and march them to the 'Bear,'
and there report myself to the Privy Councillor Flörcke, in
order to bring him in safety to Schwallungen. I forthwith
replied: 'I beg your pardon, Major, but that is not befitting
me, and I shall not do it; there are other officers there who
may be ordered to do this, but not I.' Now, in short, I
heard that the Privy Councillor wished to have me. Who
would have dreamt of such a trick? As if I would have
escorted the Privy Councillor from Wasungen! I would sooner

have taken him into the Werra. But no remonstrances would serve; they said I must and should go. This was the first trick! Hereupon I replied to the Major: 'So I must consider it an honour, that the Privy Councillor places such confidence in me, when there are so many officers in the division;' hereupon I received an order, to tell the officer at the lower gate that he should give information as soon as I had passed through with the Privy Councillor; this was the second trick. Who could have imagined such a trick? I will not write what I think of it. When I found it out I wished that all the horses of the carriages had died, that I might not be taken away from Wasungen by such cunning.

"Now I went forth, taking with me a corporal named Görnlein, and nine-and-twenty dragoons, and marched to the 'Bear,' where I found a carriage at the door, but saw the servant sitting within in the doorway. I called to him to inform his master I was there; whereupon the Privy Councillor called out to me from the carriage, 'I am already here.' Whereupon, I detached the corporal with fourteen men to go behind the carriage, while I went in advance with the others.

"Now when I came to the lower gate, I called to the serjeant, and bade him tell the major that I and the privy councillor had passed out. Meanwhile the soldiers were in great confusion at the rendezvous; but when the corporal announced that I had passed out with the Privy Councillor, the major immediately gave orders that all the soldiers should pile their arms, and go to their quarters to fetch their baggage; when they had dispersed, he sent to the guard to desire them to go forthwith and assemble at his quarters, which was done. Thus all the outposts were forgotten. At last the noise and bawling was so great, it reached the ears of the outposts, who went off without orders. Now when the soldiers from the guards came to the market-place, they

saw some of the soldiers coming back from their quarters
with their baggage, so they piled their arms and went off
for theirs.

"But this was not enough. Either the time appeared to
him too long before the soldiers were again assembled, or the
fear of death had already come upon him, or he was incited
to it by his comrades; but in short, he determined at once to
leave, and going down to the soldiers he called out, 'Allons!
March!' although the men had not nearly all assembled.
Then Captain Brandis, who had not consented to this at
their council of war, asked what this meant? whereto the
Major von S—— answered, they were to march into the
district of Britungen. The good man who was standing in
front of the Meiningen gate, then ran quickly to his house,
collected his things together, and threw them into his
portmanteau. He had well nigh been left behind.

"Now when Captain Brandis, and the musketeer who had
packed up his things, returned to the place of rendezvous,
all were gone, and there were only a few weapons remaining
there. So he sent on his servant, and waited for the remainder of the men. Now every one should know, in the first
place, that Major von S——, had not waited till all the
soldiers were collected together, still less had he thought of
the artillery; he had thought of nothing but calling out
'March! march!' and the sick officers (Captain Rupert among
them), and sick soldiers were forgotten; besides this, he
never set the troops in order, but marched them out as a
shepherd drives his cattle through the gate; and such a
shameful sight was never seen, nor can it be described.

"Captain Brandis now came marching through the town
with the soldiers he had collected; whereupon the citizens
began to call out after him: 'There they run like vagabonds;
they entered in the daylight and run away at night, like
thieves and rogues; the good Major von S—— is up and

away.' Captain Brandis swallowed all this patiently, and continued marching slowly with his troops. When he had come to a height in front of the town, some Wasungers, who were lying in ambush, fired at him; and when he had marched a short distance further, he found our artillery lying in a defile, without a single man to guard it, and it lay now with the wheels, now with the wagons uppermost, and hardly a piece was standing; for as there was a deficiency of chains, the gunners had fastened the guns with tow to the powder wagons, and these were breaking every moment. Captain Brandis with his men, remained with the artillery.

"Now I had to make my arrangements carefully. When I arrived at Schwallungen, I stopped my soldiers and the carriage, and went up to the Privy Councillor to inquire where I should convey him; whereto he, half dead with fear, answered, 'To the upper Inn.' Where the devil that was I did not know, till I found a dragoon, who having been there formerly, conducted us to the place; for I knew nothing about the village, nor where the inn lay; it was dark as pitch, and rained as if the water was poured from heaven in buckets. When I arrived at the inn he had designated, I caused the gates to be opened, and the carriage to drive into the court; the Privy Councillor alighted with his clerk who accompanied him, and retired into an upper room, for he knew the place better than I. I put a sentry on each side of the carriage, because the chancery papers lay therein. I desired the rest of the soldiers to place their arms in the house that they might be safe from the rain, and placed a sentry to guard both the arms and the Privy Councillor. I did not care any more about the said Privy Councillor, for I had, according to the orders of Major von S——, brought him to a place of security; where he would probably be about as safe as a cake among rats, for it was a Meiningen village; and according to all accounts there were no worse rogues in the whole country, than the inhabitants of Schwallungen.

" Having therefore executed my orders, I sent my sergeant to Lieutenant Griesheim, who was stationed with forty or fifty dragoons in the said village, to inform him that I had brought the Privy Councillor hither, and that he should come and release me from my charge. A short time after, the Lieutenant made his appearance, and was much amazed that I, being adjutant, should have come hither with a detachment, and could not help remarking on it.

" I said, it appeared to me more serious. However, this was now nothing to the purpose. I begged of him to set to work, and send for his soldiers, that I might march back to Wasungen with my detachment; whereupon he took the trouble of going himself for them. When he had collected about fifteen men, I told him he must take charge of the posts, as I wished at once to resume my march; the which he did, and so released me. Now it was right to pay my respects to the Privy Councillor, and ask him whether he had any commands for Wasungen? whereupon the man addressed me as if I were a thrasher, and asked me whether I had no orders to remain here? but I was prepared and answered him with the most perfect indifference, ' No, the devil has given me no orders to remain here; and it was no part of my duty to bring you here.' That he said I might settle with Major von S——. Whereunto I replied, ' I will most certainly do so.' After that he inquired of me more kindly what I wished to do at Wasungen, as the whole division were on the march, and would speedily be here. Then I said, ' Is that the way the cards are shuffled? that is good, truly.' Now whilst I was still standing in the room with the Privy Councillor, I heard the tramping of horses; I rushed down stairs and asked who it was. I received for answer, ' We are all here.' Then I was so horrified that I almost lost my senses; there were the two majors, who forthwith dismounted, hastened up stairs into the councillor's room, and I after them.

"Now they were beginning to relate to each other how fortunately they had escaped from the besieged Wasungen, but I would not let Major von S—— say a word, but asked him: 'Herr Major, what manner of conduct is this, to send me so cunningly away from Wasungen, without telling me that you were going to march out, and I have left there my wife and child, and all my property? Is this the custom of war? I know not whether you have received money for acting thus, or what I am to think of it. Are these your secret projects which are brought to light to-day? In the devil's name, I am not so young, nor have only become a soldier to-day; perhaps I know as well or better than you, what is the way to do things.' I was in such a rage, I would have staked my life against him.

"Now my dear reader, you must observe, that up to this moment I had neither seen nor heard a single man of the whole division, and did not know how matters stood. Major von S—— tried to comfort me, saying I need not be unhappy about my things; he would be surety for them; but I answered him quickly: 'Herr Major, how can you answer for my things? Why did you not tell me the truth instead of sending me out of Wasungen by such deceit? that is not allowable.' Then the Privy Councillor would have his say, and truly to this effect, that the Major was right in sending me away; that was his opinion. But I replied: 'By —— I require no clerks to give me orders; if I were a commander, I would tell those who were under me, what was going to take place, and what they were to do; but to act in such a way as this, is not honourable.'

"Thereupon I left the room, and when I came to the guard in the court, one Pleissner, a citizen of Gotha, a tinman,

who had been at that time on a visit at Wasungen, entered
the court, and said to me of his own accord; ' God help us,
Herr Lieutenant, what a sight that was at Wasungen! it
filled me with sorrow and vexation when our people marched
out in that way, for I am a citizen of Gotha. When our
soldiers marched out through the lower gate, the militia of
the country entered in through the upper gate, and visited
every house ; and sent off to Meiningen, Christian, Ensign of
Captain Brandis's company, who had been forgotten on guard,
and was going to his quarters to fetch his baggage. The
devil is in the militia ; they visited every house, and said they
would carry off all to Meiningen.'

"I will ask anyone to think what kind of temper I was in
then; Captain Ruprecht and many soldiers had been left ill
at Wasungen ; my wife and child and my small chattels were
also there ; and now I heard that the musketeer Huthmann
had already been carried off to Meiningen, so everything wore
a black aspect. I asked the citizen where our soldiers were ?
' Ah,' said he, ' they lie without, all in troops under the trees,
and Captain Brandis is still at Wasungen ; the field-pieces
lie all on the road upside down ; they cannot get on, as they
have no chains to couple them together, but they have made
use of the tow for that purpose, which breaks every minute.
I remained near them some time, but the Wasungers began
to fire at us from behind ; it was the devil to pay, and as it
also rained heavily, I thought I would get under cover.
Our people are lying so dispersed about the roads, that it
would take two hours to collect them, and I saw no officer
but Captain Brandis : the soldiers were swearing enough to
bring down heaven upon them; I was frightened out of my
wits and hastened away.'

" After hearing this I stood there, not knowing what to do ;
there was not a man of the whole detachment to be heard or
seen, and it rained terribly. At last the old grenadier cor-

poral came into the village with about ten grenadiers, wading
through the mud; I knew his voice from afar, and his
soldiers were swearing astoundingly; so I called out to them,
'What is the use of swearing? it cannot be helped now.'
'Aye, zounds,' said the corporal, 'I have gone through two
campaigns, but never had such a business as this. Is this to
be allowed? There is our captain lying ill at Wasungen, and
our major, who ought to take charge of us, is gone with
Major S—— to the devil; we are poor forsaken soldiers, but,
the devil take me, I will march to Gotha with the few men I
have here.' I asked him where the other grenadiers were;
but he did not not know whether they were in advance or
behind. 'We have not an officer,' he said, 'and no one
took charge of us,' so each one went where he chose. He
did not know that the two majors were at the inn; but if the
old corporal was foul-mouthed, his grenadiers were still worse.

"I had enough to do to mollify the grenadiers, and thus
things went on; every quarter or half-hour a small troop
came in, and if the first had made a clamour, the others were
still worse; finally, the artillery came, though it is usual,
under whatever circumstances one may march, to place the
artillery either in front or in the middle, and guard them as
one would guard one's soul. It might plainly be seen that
this commander had never seen a corps or army marching
with artillery, which must, according to the usages of war,
always be protected.

"The soldiery became more and more disorderly, and I had
to admonish them to be on their good behaviour before the
peasants, who were looking at and listening to us from their
windows, and making their jests upon us.

"At last, thank God, the rain ceased; a dragoon had led us
to a meadow which lay hard by the road, along which I
stationed the right wing, and taking command, told the force
off into divisions and half-divisions. Whilst I was doing this

I heard some horses in the distance coming at a great pace, so I thought, here comes the enemy; I forthwith called out to the right wing to send out some men and challenge the new-comers; at the same time I ran up to one of the grenadiers, and taking his musket from his hand, as during the process of dividing the men I had given up mine, I placed myself with some grenadiers in the middle of the road, and called out, 'Who goes there?' I was answered by a well-known voice, which I immediately recognized as that of Major von Benkendorf, as he did mine likewise. When I challenged him, he called to me, 'Do you not know me?' 'Yes, thank God!' I knew him by his voice, but could not do so before he spoke, on account of the darkness. Thus did God send to the children of Israel in the wilderness; here was the word fulfilled : God forsakes none who trust in him always.

"The first words of the major were : 'Children, what are you doing here?' I answered, Herr Major, God only knows, not I; we have been brought away in such a fashion, that we hardly know how we have come here.' He asked further : 'Did you all march?' 'Yes, there is no longer any one there except the sick, and those they have taken prisoners.' ' Oh, mon Dieu !' exclaimed he, 'we must return thither, even were we to sit down before the gates; where are your majors ?' 'At the Schwallungen inn.' Then he called out, 'Allons, children ! march away;' and galloped in all haste to the inn, where he may have found them at a good bottle of wine, but what kind of greeting he gave them, or compliments, I have not heard."

Thus far we have the valiant Rauch. In the further part of his diary he relates how the Gotha troops regained courage, returned to Wasungen and there drove out the Meiningens, who were equally eager to run away, as they had done, and again established themselves there.

Immediately after the first capture of Wasungen, the government at Meiningen, in great consternation, had sent Frau
von Gleichen with her husband there in a carriage, attended
by Gotha troops.   But it was no great pleasure to them to
see that the cause of the quarrel was done away with ; so the
poor court dignitaries met with a cold reception ; the health
of both was broken by sorrow, vexation, and long imprisonment.   In 1748, Herr von Gleichen died, and his wife soon
after.   Meanwhile, flying-sheets and memorials, mandates of
the Imperial chamber, and ministerial missives concerning
this affair, flew all over Germany ; the Gotha troops kept
possession of Wasungen.   Anthony Ulrich obstinately refused
to acknowledge the claims of Gotha to indemnification, and
the voices of numerous princes were loud in condemning the
sentence of the Imperial chamber, and the execution of it by
Gotha, as a violation of the sovereign rights of a German
ruler.   Frederick the Great did so likewise.

Just then, when the Duke of Saxe-Gotha was in a desperate
position, a new prospect and a new subject of quarrel presented themselves to him.   The Duke of Weimar had died,
and had settled that his cousin of Gotha was to be guardian
to his only son during his minority.   The Duke of Gotha
speedily entered upon the guardianship, and caused homage
to be sworn to him : upon this, a violent altercation again
sprang up between him, and the Duke of Coburg and Anthony
Ulrich, who both contested the right of the Gotha prince to
the guardianship.   Then Frederick II. of Prussia offered his
services to the Duke of Gotha, who was reduced to great
extremities, on condition that he should obligingly offer him
the small gift of two hundred picked men from the guards of
Weimar.   This was done ; thus the Duke of Gotha purchased the administration of this country, and the settlement
of the Wasunger strife, with two hundred men of the Weimar
guards.   Two hundred children of the soil of Weimar, to

whom the quarrel mattered not in the least, were arbitrarily given away like a herd of sheep.   Contrary to all justice, they were chaffered away by a foreign prince.

The two hundred followed King Frederick in the seven years' war.

CONCLUSION.

THIS work ends with the name of the great king. The social condition of the country in his time, although very different from the present, is well known to us; and even minute particulars, have become, through its history and literature, the common property of the people. Frederick became the hero of the nation. The Germans have exalted him even more than Gustavus Adolphus. He ruled the minds of men far beyond the boundaries of his limited dominions. In the distant Alpine valleys, among men speaking another tongue, and holding another faith, he was reverenced as a saint both in pictures and writings. He was a powerful ruler, a genial commander, and what was more valued by the Germans, a great man in the highest of earthly positions. It was his personal appearance and manners which made foreigners and even enemies admire him. He inspired the people again with enthusiasm for German greatness, zeal for the highest earthly interests, and sympathy in a German state. In the course of three centuries, he was the third man round whom the national love and veneration had entwined itself; the second to whom it was granted to elevate and improve the character of the nation. For the Germans became better, richer, and happier, when they were carried beyond the narrow interests of their private life, and beyond their petty literary quarrels, by the appearance of a great character daringly aspiring to the highest objects, struggling, suffering, persevering, and

firm. He was of their own blood, and in spite of his passion
for what was French, he was a thorough child of Germany,
reared in a hard time, and belonging to them. Under him,
the grandsons of those citizens who had passed through the
great war, began for the first time after a century to feel their
own powers. We delight to see, how the poor poet sings the
praises of him, who would so little appreciate the odes of the
German Sappho, or the outpouring of elevated poetry; still
more do we rejoice in seeing the whole people, even in Austria,
contending on his behalf, his image penetrating into every
family, and his name exciting everywhere party spirit, new
interests, and political passions. This has been the greatest
blessing of his whole life. He forced the private individual
to take part in political life; he created a state for the
German, which whether loved or hated, must become a continual object of care and watchfulness.

But though enthusiasm for a hero perhaps gives a capacity for the development of powers, it does not give stability.
The Germans had yet to go through severe trials after the
death of the great king. He had bequeathed to them the
first beginning of a German State, but the ruins of the
Empire of the middle ages lay defenceless against the western
enemy. The curse which since the time of Charles V. had
rested on the German Empire had not yet changed into a
blessing. Once more was Germany overrun by a great army,
once more did a league of German princes unite with a foreign
conqueror, even the state of the great Frederick was shattered,
the last hope seemed to have vanished, the German people
were crushed.

But in the rooms of the German peasants, the picture of
the old king, in his three-cornered hat and small pigtail, did
not turn his earnest look in vain on the life he had revived;
nor in vain had the mothers of the present generation run to
the churches to pray for a blessing on his arms. Now it was

that the full blessing of his energetic life truly manifested itself. The spirit of that great man lived again in the German people. Fifty years after the return of the king from the seven years' war, three hundred years after Luther strove earnestly to find his God, the German nation roused itself for the greatest struggle it had ever yet successfully carried on. The fathers now sent out their sons, and the wives their husbands to the war ; the Germans encountered death with a song on their lips, to seek a body for the German soul, a state for the fatherland.

In the year 1813, we find the conclusion of that great struggle which began in 1517. From the time of the contest of the Wittenburger Augustine against indulgences, to the march of the German volunteers against Napoleon, the German spirit carried on a great defensive war against a foreign influence, which issuing from Rome well nigh overwhelmed those who had once been the conquerors of the Roman Empire.

From this life-and-death struggle of three hundred years, Germany passed from the bondage of the middle ages into freedom. But though the spirit of the people became free, the reality of a German state was lost to them. The nation was almost annihilated by this unnatural condition. After a deathlike exhaustion it recovered itself slowly ; the resuscitated spirit was helpless, its form weak and sickly ; it was seeking unity of government. By a powerful development of strength, the foundation of it was laid in the beginning of this century.

Henceforth German Protestantism became a living, sound, and manly acquisition, a great national principle, the expression of the German popular mind, the peculiar German characteristic in every domain of ideal and practical life.

We all still feel how deficient and unfinished is the development of this, the highest principle of life in the German nation. But it is this feeling which gives us courage and leads us to struggle onwards.

What are here given from the old records are narratives of individuals of past generations. They are some of them unimportant passages from the lives of insignificant persons. But, as the outward appearance of any stranger we meet, his mode of greeting, and his first words, give us an impression of his individuality, an imperfect, an unfinished impression, but still a whole; so, if we are not mistaken, does each record, in which the impulses of individuals and their peculiar working are portrayed, give us with rapid distinctness a vivid picture of the life of the people; a very imperfect and unfinished picture, but yet, also a whole, round which a large portion of our knowledge and intuitive perceptions rapidly concentrate, like the radii round the centre of a crystal.

If every such picture gives us an impression, that in the soul of each man a miniature picture may be found of the characteristics of his nation; something will be learnt from a succession of these narratives, arranged according to their periods, however much there may be in them that is incidental and arbitrary. We shall discover the stirring and gradual development of a higher intellectual unity, which likewise meets us here in the shape of a distinct individuality; and therefore, these little sketches will perhaps help us to a more lively comprehension, of what we call the life of a nation.

Everywhere man appears to us, by his customs and laws, by language and the whole genial tendencies of his nature, as a small portion of a greater whole. It is true also that this greater whole, appears to us as an intellectual unity, which like an individual, is earthly and perishable, a thing which accomplishes its earthly existence in a century, as a man does his in a certain number of years. Like an individual, a people developes its intellectual capacities in the course of time, but more powerfully and on a grander scale. And further, a people consists of millions of individuals the tide of human life flows in millions of souls, but the conscious and unconscious working together of these millions, produces an intellectual whole, in which the share of individuals often vanishes from our eyes, so that the soul of a whole people seems to us, a self-creative living unity. Who was the man who created languages ? who devised the most ancient law of nations ? who first thought of giving poetical expression to an elevated tone of mind ? It was not individuals who invented these for practical purposes, but a universal intellectual life, which burst forth among thousands who lived together. All the great productions of national power, law, customs, and the constitution of states, are not the work of individual men, but organic creations of a higher life, which in every period shine forth in individuals, yet in all periods seem to unite the intellectual capacities of individuals, in one mighty whole. Each man bears and cultivates within his soul, part of the intellect of the nation ; each one possesses its language, a certain amount of knowledge, and a sense of justice and propriety ; but in each, this general nationality is coloured, concentrated, and limited by his individuality. Individuals do not represent the language or the moral feelings of the whole ; they only are, as it were, the single notes, which joined together produce a harmonious chord as part of the collective nation. One may therefore fairly, and without mysticism, speak of a national soul.

And if one examines more narrowly, one perceives with astonishment, that this law of development of a higher intellectual unity, differs remarkably from that which binds or makes an individual free. A man chooses freely for himself, between what will injure or be beneficial to him and his interests ; judiciously does he shape his life, and prudently does he judge the conceptions which reach his soul from the great world. But less conscious, less full of purpose and judgment than the determination of man's will, is the working of the life of the nation. In history, man represents freedom and judgment, but national energy, works incessantly with the mysterious instinctive impulse of a primitive power, and its intellectual conceptions correspond sometimes in a remarkable way, with the process of formation of the silently productive powers of nature, which bring forth from the seed, the stalk, leaves, and flowers of the plant.

From this point of view, the life of a nation passes in unceasing alternations from the whole body to the individual, and from the man to the whole body. The life of each man, even the most insignificant, gives a portion of its substance to the nation, and a portion of the collective powers of the nation lives in each man ; he transmits soul and body from one generation to another ; he adds to the language, and preserves the consciousness of right ; all the results of his labours are beneficial to the nation as well as to himself. The course of life of millions runs smoothly and imperceptibly along with the stream. But important personalities develop themselves from the multitude in all directions, gaining a great influence on the whole body. Sometimes a powerful character arises, which in some wide field of action, long rules the spiritual life of the people, and stamps the impress of its individual mind on the age. Then the life of the whole nation, which also flows through our heads and hearts, becomes as familiar to us as is possible for the soul of any individual man ; then the whole powers of the people seem for some years working for the one individual, and obeying him as a master. These are the great periods in the formation of a people. Such was Luther to the Germans.

But no nation develops its life independent of others. As the life of one individual works on that of another, so does it happen with nations. Each nation communicates some of its intellectuality to another. Even the practical forms of national existence, its state and its Church, are either advanced, or checked and destroyed by foreign powers. Close is the union of the minds of the nations of Europe, though manifold the contradiction of their interests. How constantly does one nationality derive strength, or experience trouble and disturbance from another ! Sometimes the energetic development of some particular national characteristic, exercises for centuries a preponderating influence on another. Thus once did the Jews, the Greeks, and the Romans. The German nation has experienced this foreign influence, both for good and for evil. From the ancient world came the holy faith of the Crucified One, to the wild sons of our forefather Tuisco : at the same time this warlike race received countless traditions from the Roman Empire, transforming their whole life. Through the whole of the middle ages, the nation was earnestly endeavouring to make these new acquisitions their own. Again, at the end of this period, after a thousand years had passed, began a new influence of the ancient world. From it came the ideal of the Humanitarians, the forerunners of Luther, and the ideal of the German poets, the forerunners of the war of freedom. On the other hand, from the Romish world, came upon Germany, with the highest claims, the pressure of the despotism of Gregory VII., and Innocent III., the devotion of the restored Church, and the lust of conquest of France. Then did Germany become depopulated, and the national life was endangered ; but the foreigners who had penetrated into it with such overpowering force, aided its recovery. All that Italians, French, and English had attained to in science and arts, was introduced into Germany, and to these foreign acquisitions did German culture cling, from the Thirty years' war up to the time of Lessing.

It is the task of science to investigate the productive life of nations. To her the souls of nations are the highest fields of investigation that man is capable of knowing. Searching out every individuality, tracing every received impression, observing even the broken splinters, uniting all discernible knowledge, more guessing at truths and pointing out the way, than apprehending them, she seeks, as her highest aim, to prove the intellectual unity of the whole human race upon earth.   Whilst pious faith with undoubting certainty places before man the idea of a personal God, the man of science reverently seeks to discover the Divine, in the great conceptions, which however they may surpass the understanding of the individual, yet are all attached to the life of the world. But however little he may consider their importance, in comparison with that which is incomprehensible in time and eternity, yet in his limited circle lies all the greatness that we are capable of understanding, all the beautiful which we ever enjoy, and all the good which has ennobled our life.   But in those spheres which we do not yet know, and are anxiously investigating, there remains a boundless work.   And this work is to seek the development of the Divine power in history.

THE END.

LONDON: PRINTED BY WILLIAM CLOWES AND SONS, STAMFORD STREET.

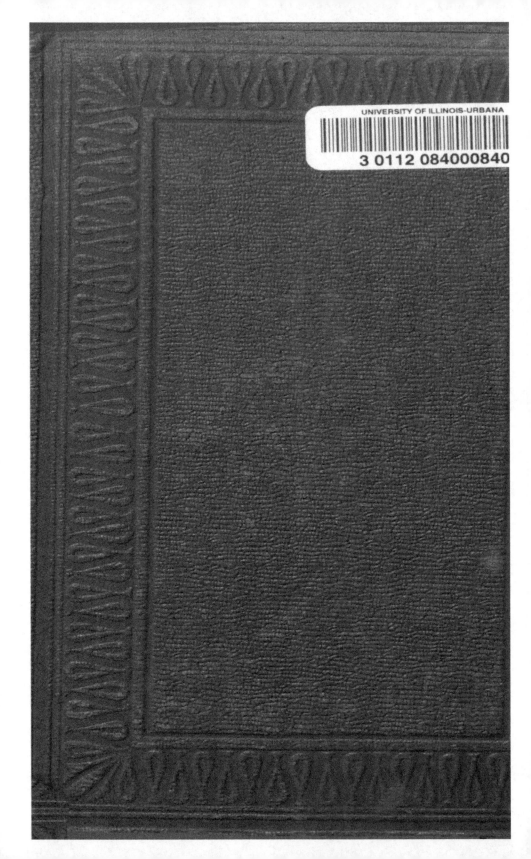

CPSIA information can be obtained
at www.ICGtesting.com
Printed in the USA
BVHW070813120819
555626BV00011B/2268/P